When the Colts Belonged to Baltimore

When the Colts Belonged to Baltimore

A Father and a Son, a Team and a Time

William Gildea

TICKNOR & FIELDS • NEW YORK

Library of Congress Cataloging-in-Publication Data

Gildea, William.
When the Colts belonged to Baltimore : a father and a son, a team and a time / William Gildea.
p. cm.
ISBN 0-395-62145-3
1. Baltimore Colts (Football team) — History.
2. Gildea, William. 3. Football fans — United States — Biography. I. Title.
GV956.B3G45 1994 94-16499
796.332′64′097526 — dc20 CIP

Printed in the United States of America

Book design by Robert Overholtzer

BP 10 9 8 7 6 5 4 3 2

Portions of this book first appeared in different form, in the *Washington Post* and *Reader's Digest*.

To Mary Fran

Many people helped me with this book.
I am especially grateful for guidance
from Faith Hamlin, Paul Hendrickson,
John Herman, Tony Kornheiser,
Paul Richard, Jeff Smith,
Jane von Mehren, and
Gail Winston.

◆

Part One

WHEN I WAS GROWING UP in Baltimore, my father took me to the Colts games. We went to almost all of them. Pop drove down a sidewalk once to get to a game on time.

I remember him saying emphatically, one day in November 1950 after the Colts had lost nineteen straight, "This Sunday they're going to win." We had to be there, even if my grandfather — my father's father — lay on his deathbed.

That Sunday we got up early and drove out into the country to see him. He was weak, his white hair mussed. To raise himself to a sitting position, he'd pull on the sash of his bathrobe, which he had tied to one of the bedposts at his feet. He was probably suffering from dementia; the family called it hardening of the arteries.

When he was young and lived on the north New Jersey coast, my grandfather would dig for clams evenings after work as a laborer until he'd filled a bushel basket. He'd place the basket over his shoulder and trudge home from the shoreline with his load, food for his family and his neighbors. He was tall and rugged and caring.

He may not have known that Pop and I left him that day, talking as he was about a nonexistent cemetery across the street when my father was trying to tell him about a Notre Dame game the day before. We slipped away because the

Colts were playing Green Bay, at the time the only team nearly as bad. When would the Colts win if not that day?

This is not to say that Pop took his father's imminent death lightly. When the expected happened two weeks later, he came home from the Read's Drug Store where he worked as a pharmacist at about one in the afternoon, which I'd never known him to do. He sat down at the gray Formica kitchen table, lowered his head, and cried. My mother put her hand on his shoulder.

For a moment I thought he was kidding, but when I realized he wasn't I went to another room. I understood his feelings at the wake in my grandparents' living room, flushed with heat and the scent of flowers. A distant cousin of mine named Bridey, who'd come down from New York on the train, took me for a walk around the block to get me some air. I thought that she or her wool coat smelled like mothballs as we walked slowly in the bitter night. She asked me if I missed my grandfather and I felt like saying I didn't know, he'd just died, but I said yes while trying to bear the image of the corpse by thinking about the Colts. They'd beaten Green Bay, 41–21. It was their only victory that year.

◆

The first game I remember my father taking me to was the first one ever played by the Baltimore Colts. It was September 7, 1947. I was eight years old. All I recall were the splintery benches of Baltimore's old wooden Municipal Stadium, long ago demolished, and the yellow jerseys of the visiting Brooklyn Dodgers. The final score, too: 16–7, Colts.

But the original Colts proved to be one of the worst teams in professional sports. Only a few weeks passed before Pop broke that news to me. Indeed, I recall them as mud-splattered and dull-looking in their green jerseys, which Pop said made them look smaller than their opponents. They belonged to a short-lived, never-celebrated league in the late forties, the All-America Football Conference. They lost by scores of 56–0, 42–0, and 35–7.

Yet, seated at Pop's side each Sunday, I regarded this hapless team as the center of our cosmos. When the Colts arrived from Miami, where in 1946 they had been known as the Seahawks, Baltimore was trying to live down a reputation as little more than a traffic jam between Washington and New York. Motorists forced to drive through the narrow streets before the harbor tunnels were built failed to see the romance of Route 40 while inching along in traffic or idling behind double-parkers carrying out crabs from Gordon's seafood house.

Bumbling or not, the Colts were Baltimore's first major-league team, and to many Baltimoreans they bestowed big-league status on the city. Players were coopted by civic pride, made to feel as if they had come home, were part of a family. The town-team symbiosis would endure; in 1973, defensive tackle Joe Ehrmann arrived from Syracuse University and observed, "You can't go to New York or L.A. and play for those teams and end up in somebody's living room like you can in Baltimore."

Pop loved the Colts from the start, and soon I did, too, and our love for each other grew as we kept on going to the games. Sunday was a ritual we shared. We'd go to Mass early and then drive together across the city to the stadium. The rides were quiet times spent discussing the team or contemplating its prospects that day and would end with one of Pop's traffic-dodging approaches down side streets and, invariably, into a miraculously available parking space.

What I didn't learn about the Colts from my father I gleaned from the old *Baltimore News-Post*. On his way home from work Pop would buy the fresh-off-the-press ten-star edition, with the latest sports news. Most evenings I'd be waiting at the door. I'd kiss him on the cheek, and he would affectionately sweep the paper into my midsection, like a quarterback handing off. I remember the winter nights best: Pop's cold face, the cold paper.

One night late in 1949 I waited anxiously. The All-America Football Conference was disbanding, and only three teams would be absorbed into the National Football League. The powerful Cleveland Browns and colorful San Francisco 49ers were shoo-ins. Baltimore and Buffalo were vying for the third spot.

"Did we make it?" I asked Pop the instant he stepped in the door. He showed me the huge front-page headline: COLTS IN 13-TEAM LEAGUE.

I let out a whoop. He grinned, but then asked quietly, "How do you think all the boys in Buffalo feel tonight?"

I didn't care one bit. But on January 18, 1951, I understood what he had meant. After an inglorious 1–11 season, the Colts went out of business. The owner sold all the players to the league for a total of fifty thousand dollars.

Bereft of our football team in 1951 and 1952, Pop and I stuck together by rooting for baseball's Orioles, then a minor-league team in the International League. Doubleheaders on Friday nights and Sunday afternoons were the best times. Driving home after games, Pop and I would replay the victories and, more often, try to make sense of the defeats. The defeats didn't seem as bad to me after a talk with Pop.

In 1953 a new Baltimore Colts team began play in the NFL. The franchise was shifted from Dallas, where attendance had been so poor that midway through the '52 season the Texans had become a traveling road team. Pop and I were there for the new Colts' first game on September 27, 1953 — at the still-under-construction, concrete-and-brick Memorial Stadium that replaced the wooden stadium on the same Thirty-third Street site. In sparkling royal-blue-and-white uniforms, these Colts, unlike their green-shirted predecessors, actually looked like a team. They beat the rugged Chicago Bears that day, too. At his side, I could feel my father's excitement. By then I was coming of age. My interests, the topics of conversation among my friends were beginning to change — to rock 'n' roll, to girls. But I never outgrew Colts games with Pop. Sundays remained solemnly reserved for us.

In 1956 the Colts signed quarterback Johnny Unitas. The Pittsburgh Steelers had cut him the year before without giving him a chance. Unitas threw a football with a daring we'd never seen and used surprise as a weapon we'd never imagined. If we thought he'd call the obvious play, he'd do the unexpected; if we anticipated the unexpected, he'd try the obvious.

His stature was not imposing — he was tall enough at six feet one and heavy enough at 195 pounds, but his shoulders were rounded and his legs thin. He was set apart by his skills, a coal-country toughness, and his bristle-brush haircut and black high-top shoes. His appearance, his ethnic roots, and his determination helped define him as an American hero, preferred for being enduring and silent, a person solitary, usually competing against some odds, often in pain.

Like golf's Arnold Palmer, Unitas catapulted his sport into a new age. Palmer took essentially a country-club activity and made it a sport. He was the first major golfer who *looked* like an athlete — his rolling shoulders gave him the appearance of a middleweight boxer. His gifts and his gait conscripted the army behind him. Unitas also stirred like an animal, almost every piece of his body moving distinctly when he played. As he approached the line of scrimmage, his arms jangled. He loped like a cat, his shoulders dropping one at a time as he turned slightly each way to survey a defensive alignment. He faded to pass sideways, with quick, mincing steps, and his indelible overhand passing motion became Baltimore's unsculpted monument.

He'd cock his arm high above his ear at the start of his signature throw, sometimes fake one way and pass another, releasing the ball near the top of a hammer-down thrust, spiral it out of his palm with bullet-speed or the touch of an angel. He combined a gambler's instinct and an artist's precision.

On the penultimate play when the Colts beat the New York Giants at Yankee Stadium on December 28, 1958, to win pro football's championship in the first sudden-death overtime game, Unitas put the ball in the air when he didn't have to. From the Giants' eight-yard line, he threw toward the right sideline to Jim Mutscheller, who was knocked out of bounds at the one. It was a pass to the open field that could have been intercepted and returned the length of the field for a *Giants'* victory. Shocked by his quarterback's audacity, Weeb Ewbank, the Colts' coach, asked Unitas why he'd taken the risk. Unitas told him there'd been no risk. "I'd have thrown it out of bounds if I had to," he said, leaving Ewbank to shake his head.

The Colts won most of the time during Unitas's career in Baltimore, 1956 through 1972, without undue celebration, a tone Unitas set. A certain photograph shows Alan "The Horse" Ameche plunged across the goal line with the winning points against the Giants in 1958, but more intriguing than the pileup is the figure in the corner of the frame. As if shrugging at history and high drama, Unitas already has turned away and is stepping, head down in the dusk, toward the locker room. Just another workday.

That game wed pro football to television; it was a masterpiece in black and white seen by fifty million viewers. Ike watched from his presidential retreat in Gettysburg.

Sports Illustrated called it the "best game ever played," and it came to be known as the *greatest* one ever played. It may not have been, but it was good enough and Pop took me to it. We spent Saturday night at my Greataunt Bea's apartment in Upper Manhattan, and the next morning, after one of her massive breakfasts of oatmeal and bacon and eggs and toast piled high, took the subway up to the Bronx. In my mind the day is like a grainy film. The afternoon was gray and, seated high in the middle deck behind an end zone, I recall the field and players as distant and small. But my feelings of satisfaction were huge: Our long-downtrodden team had conquered New York, and satisfaction warmed Pop and me even before we'd reached the steamy dining car on the Pennsy home that night.

Immediately after that performance Unitas was invited to be on "The Ed Sullivan Show," the picture window on American culture. Elvis Presley, the Beatles . . . almost anybody who was somebody appeared on "Ed Sullivan," performing onstage or taking a bow from the audience. But Johnny U. turned it down. He wanted to be with the team when it went home back to Baltimore.

Unitas took the Colts to another championship in 1959 and was still around in January 1971 to have a hand in the Colts' Super Bowl V victory. During eighteen seasons, the last with San Diego, he passed for more than 42,000 yards and for 290 touchdowns, and over a stretch of five seasons threw at least one touchdown pass in forty-seven straight games, a feat sometimes said to be football's equivalent of Joe DiMaggio's fifty-six-game hitting streak.

He had a brilliant supporting cast. Raymond Berry caught twelve passes for 178 yards that day against the Giants, making victory possible. From 1955 through 1967, Berry's accomplishments, despite physical limitations, gave testament to the American work ethic. He lacked strength and speed, and his legs of uneven length caused him to hobble. Yet he'd consistently come free on one of his circuitous pass routes in perilous moments to make an acrobatic catch of Unitas's throw. Often when he gathered in a pass, Berry was standing on tippytoe at the sideline, tilting out of bounds like Pisa's Leaning Tower.

The Colts used to practice behind an armory in Pikesville. Long after five o'clock darkness had descended and the team had gone in, one could hear from the sideline the scuffling of feet, the sound of a ball hitting a receiver's hands. Two figures in white uniforms could barely be seen. Unitas and Berry. They practiced together so much that during games Unitas never had to look for Berry when he was running a pass pattern. Then, almost magically, Berry and the ball would converge at the prearranged spot.

Lenny Moore was the team's breakaway runner. Opponents feared his shiftiness. Like Unitas, he wore high-top shoes but they were disguised. Moore's were made of soft leather and weighed almost nothing, and he taped them so that it looked as if he had on spats. His feet a blur, he ran around end with his shoulder dipped and arm extended to fend off tacklers, a blend of slipperiness and balance.

Towering, intimidating figures prowled the defensive line: Gino Marchetti, who seemed about to snort flames as he threw aside blockers to get to opposing quarterbacks; Big

Daddy Lipscomb, who politely helped up quarterbacks after he had leveled them; Art Donovan, a mountain no opponent could hope to conquer often.

During the fifties and sixties, Memorial Stadium was sold out every Sunday, and Ogden Nash, the team's unofficial poet laureate, penned zany paeans about his favorite players that appeared in such magazines as *Life* and *Holiday. Life* twice put the Colts on its cover. Nash wrote:

> The lucky city of Baltimore
> Is famed for its medicos galore.
> It's simply teeming with fine physicians,
> With surgeons, oculists, obstetricians,
> All dedicated men in white,
> All at your service day and night
> Except — and here's the fly in the ointment —
> When with Colts they have an appointment,
> And the vast Memorial Stadium rocks
> With the cheers of fifty thousand docs.
> They've caught the disease fate holds in store
> For the population of Baltimore —
> A disease more virulent than rabies,
> Felling men and women and even babies.
> The cynic becomes a true believer
> When caught in the grip of that old Colt fever.

Bobby Russell sang a song about the Colts:

> He's the 1432 Franklin Pike Circle Hero;
> And you can see him every weekend with a car
> full of kids and snow cones;
> During Christmas took the kids down to see
> the floats,
> When he wanted to stay home and watch the
> Baltimore Colts . . .

He makes it sound like the Baltimore "Coats." In the best cockney-cracker Baltimore accents, that's how it's pronounced — Coats.

As games began to sell out, Pop showed me how to find tickets without fail. We would split up in the stadium's west parking lot and position ourselves at the doors of out-of-town buses just as they rolled in. Someone always was unable to make it, especially on the buses from a distance, like York, Pennsylvania, or Harrisburg; people would send their tickets to be disposed of — and at face value. In a matter of minutes Pop and I would be back together and showing the other the location of the seats obtained. If Pop and I each bought two tickets, which happened occasionally, we'd quickly sell the extra pair. Then we'd be headed for the turnstiles, united in our resourcefulness, his arm around my shoulder. I could feel his elation. Climbing Memorial Stadium's steep ramps, we'd eagerly anticipate yet another fresh vantage point. We got to know every cranny of the stadium.

At two o'clock the roar would swallow the introductions: Marchetti, Donovan, Lipscomb . . . one after the other. To say nothing of Unitas. The rest of life was easily eclipsed when Johnny U. stepped into the sunlight on a Sunday afternoon.

Pop never missed a thing that happened on the field and wanted to share it all with me. He had a knack for sensing big plays as they unfolded. Most times he could even anticipate Unitas's play-calling. He'd poke me with his elbow or simply lean his forearm against my forearm, just in time for me to see a receiver materializing under a deep pass or a runner breaking free for a big gain.

For me, nothing matched the feeling of coming down the

stadium's concrete ramps with Pop amid a happy throng after the Colts had earned a hard victory. The last two minutes were all Unitas needed to call a game his own and set our hearts aglow like the late sun that by 4:45 hung just above the church steeples and identical little chimneys along the rows of brick houses.

◆

I'm reminded of the Colts each time I see my neighbor Jim Castiglia. Usually that's in church. A thickset, gray-haired man, he limps into the vestibule and takes his regular place in the last pew, left side at Little Flower in Bethesda, Maryland. He's in his seventies and played on the first Colts team in 1947 — materialized out of nowhere to score the first touchdown in the team's history on a wonderfully weird play that I find myself smiling about each time I see him. It's as if I'm nourished by his obscure feat that's virtually my own secret.

I can't imagine my mother letting me go that day because she was always worrying that I'd catch cold and thunderstorms were forecast. Jim told me that the second period was played in torrential rain, but I don't remember getting wet. My father must have done something at the roofless stadium to keep me dry, knowing he'd have to face my mother. I do remember the stadium's slanted dirt parking lot as a sea of yellow mud, which flowed like lava.

A few Sundays later, a glorious October day, we rode in Pop's black '46 Ford across the city to the stadium for another Colts game. "I can't wait to see Frankie Sinkwich," Pop said excitedly to his pharmacist friend Al Aaronson in the front seat. I was in back. Pop was leaning intently over the steering wheel, and his foot must have been hard on the accelerator because the 100 horsepower V-8 — his joy — was speeding down a long block near Johns Hopkins University. He had to be there for the kickoff. I recall this clearly because just then a car entered the intersection we were rapidly approaching. We screeched to a narrow miss, sliding sideways. "You can't beat a Ford's brakes," Pop said proudly. As I climbed back onto the big wool seat, I noticed Al's ashen face even as he was agreeing with my father — "You're right, Bill, you're right, Bill" — about the brakes and the handling beauty of a postwar Ford. At that moment I decided I could depend on Pop to steer us through any crisis. And I wondered aloud, "Who's Frankie Sinkwich?"

The Colts cut Castiglia to make room for Sinkwich, and every two weeks after that, Jim picked up a paycheck at the team's office. He'd signed a guaranteed contract for a fabulous eighteen thousand dollars for playing, as it turned out, just two games. That was three thousand dollars more than Sammy Baugh made the entire 1947 season over in Washington. "Can you imagine that?" said Castiglia, still amazed by his windwall but disgusted by such inept management. "What a lightheaded organization the Colts were."

One hundred and thirty-five players appeared at one time or another in the Colts' 1947 training camp in Hershey, Pennsylvania. None arrived less auspiciously than a first favorite of mine, "Little Doc" Mobley, five feet seven, 150 pounds. One day in Hershey a station wagon was dispatched to the bus depot to pick up some high school boys hired as locker-room attendants. The boys loaded their luggage into the back and piled in with it. A few blocks later, the driver stopped. "Darn it," he said, "we'll have to go back. I was supposed to pick up Mobley, too." Came a voice from among the boys and the bags in the rear: "You don't have to, mister, I'm back here."

Though Castiglia's Colt career was brief, he was around long enough to help introduce the sport to the city in a play apropos of this team and reminiscent of Roy Riegels's wrong-way run in the 1929 Rose Bowl. A Brooklyn Dodgers player returned the opening kickoff but fumbled. A teammate — Harry Buffington — scooped up the ball and lumbered the wrong way into his own end zone. Realizing his error, he then tried to pass, but the Colts' Augie Lio batted it and Castiglia fell on it.

"What the hell did you do?" asked Lio, on the ground, looking over at Castiglia.

"We just scored a touchdown," Castiglia said.

What the papers reported happening to Buffington the next night back in Brooklyn sounded apocryphal, but it was written as fact that he was stopped by police and ticketed for driving the wrong way on a one-way street.

Maybe because Brooklyn had a left-footed kicker, I began kicking a football with my left foot. Even when no one was around to play with, I played football by myself in the big yard next to the apartment house we lived in at 4412 Maine Avenue. I'd pass the ball and run under it to catch it, and I'd run around end and tackle myself by crossing one ankle in front of the other. Imagining I was a Colt, I'd fall forward for a first down or a touchdown.

One Sunday the Colts surprised us by taking a 10–0 lead over the Los Angeles Dons. I happily forecast victory, but Pop cautioned, "You can't count anything that's only half done." I remember the words because the Dons went on to score thirty-eight straight points. Final: 38–10.

Ben Agajanian played for the Dons, and I was pleased to have seen him by the time *Life* included him in an article called "The Place-Kickers." He had only one toe on his right foot, the result of an accident in college, and wore a sawed-off, square-toed football shoe, all of which I knew from Pop. I was surprised *Life* left out Lou Groza because Pop said he was the best. Back then, Lou "The Toe" used a little measuring tape so he could line up at the exact spot before kicking a point after touchdown or a field goal. My memory of him bending and measuring one Sunday in December 1947 remains as indelible as a photograph, probably because he did it so often; the Browns overwhelmed the Colts, 42–0.

Still, the Colts belonged to Baltimore. They had a marching band that practiced behind the reptile house at the zoo in Druid Hill Park. And they had a fight song: ". . . *So drive on you Baltimore Colts/Go in and strike like lightning bolts . . .*" They had majorettes and cheerleaders. A trumpeter married a majorette.

◆

I often think about the old Colts, and when I do I think of the apartment house in Baltimore where I grew up. It's where I came to know a world war was going on and where I fell in love with a football team from conversations with my father.

I have a small black-and-white photo of the three-story brown-shingle on Maine Avenue. My Irish-immigrant grandparents and I are posed out front on the sidewalk. I'm four or five years old, wearing short pants and holding an Easter basket. My grandfather John Gildea, who once gave me a tiny penknife and, putting a finger to his lips, instructed me not to tell my parents, has on a dark suit and vest and seems pleased about something, with his head cocked proudly. Annie Moran Gildea, wide-bodied and large-bosomed in her flowery dress, looks stern, the family granite. The neigh-

Pop, at twenty-four in 1933

borhood is Forest Park, on the city's northwest side. It's where Barry Levinson grew up to make his Baltimore films *Diner, Tin Men,* and *Avalon.*

Growing up, I didn't have much space. My parents and I, an only child, lived in a one-bedroom on the third floor of the big house, in what was but a crow's nest. Only our two kitchen windows faced the street. I took my own photo of home. I stood on the front lawn, tilted my head back, and pointed the camera directly up; what I got was the roof and gray sky that faded into the frame's edges.

The bedroom was my haven. It had one window and a door leading to an outside wooden stairway. The flight between the second and third floors frightened me at least until fourth grade. As an infant, I was told, I'd crawled out from the bedroom onto the third-floor landing, maybe three square feet, and was coaxed to be still by my mother until she got close enough to lunge and grab me. The bedroom is where I hung my Colts pennant, sticking three straight pins through its wool into the wallpaper. The pennant cost fifty cents at the stadium and came with a thin wooden stick that my mother, worrier that she was, confiscated out of fear that I'd poke one of my eyes. The green-and-gray pennant depicted a horse jumping over the crossbar of a goal post with a helmet flying up from its head and a football stuck between its front hoofs. In the evenings, I'd lie in my bed, up against a wall, gazing above me at that horse, then fall asleep while trying to visualize a time when that team would receive the acclamation of multitudes. I doubted that it would.

I covered the bedroom walls with pennants of the Colts' opponents in the All-America Conference. Each Sunday at the stadium Pop would let me pick one pennant at a concession stand, and I'd take the team we saw that day. The Cleveland Browns and San Francisco 49ers were the powers of the league, but on the bedroom walls I put the likes of the Brooklyn Dodgers and L.A. Dons, the Chicago Rockets and Chicago Hornets as well.

One day when I was sick in bed David Fairbank brought me my homework. His mere presence honored me because he was the toughest, and thus most respected, boy in the class. He wanted to know what my parents thought of their bedroom looking the way it did with all the pennants. I told him they hadn't mentioned it; until then, I'd thought of it as my bedroom. Looking at it now, I'd say that's how they wanted me to feel.

That bedroom is vivid in my mind even back to the war

years when we'd sit there on the beds in the dark after a siren would signal a blackout test. I found it eerie with the black shades pulled and the lights off, waiting for the all-clear. Pop had tried everything to get into the army. But pharmacists were needed on the home front. He persisted, even taking a written test that could have resulted in an override. Subsequently, he was told to report to Washington for a second test. He and three others took that test. One got to go to war.

In the bedroom I'd box with my father when he'd come home from work; I'd greet him with upraised little gloves he'd given me. Our feet would scrape across the linoleum as he would let me bore in while fending off my small blows. My mother would shush us, pleading that we were disturbing the family below.

In the bedroom I wrote my first sports article, in a marble copybook. It went about three paragraphs and must have been taken from an old newspaper or magazine account because it was about a Joe Louis victory over John Henry Lewis, and they had fought in 1939. In my version, which I came across years later, I'd overlooked the loser's last name and so had Louis beating John Henry.

In the bedroom I hung a toy basketball net on the door to the bathroom and scored over imaginary opposition with a miniature ball. To please my mother, I played in my socks and after laying one in tried my best to land softly.

Pop told me stories about Ruth and Gehrig, how Gehrig had died young, which was the saddest story. He told me how a whole country had rooted for Joe Louis the night he beat the German Max Schmeling. Most of his stories were about the Colts, and what improbable combination of events might occur that very Sunday to produce a rare victory.

Father and son in 1939 . . .

Most of our talks took place in the evenings as I lay in bed and he sat next to me in the dark. One night in 1947 before I went to sleep, my father promised to take me to a Washington Redskins–Green Bay Packers exhibition game to be played in Baltimore. All week he told me about the Redskins' Sammy Baugh.

By Sunday morning I was so keyed up I fainted at Mass. It was no ordinary slump into the pew at yellow-bricked All Saints Church. It happened at the communion rail, just as frail old Father Kenny approached me with the white wafer. I was told I threw my hands up, knocking the ciborium from his grasp. It fell to the sanctuary's dark red tiles with a terrible crash as hosts flew in every direction.

and in 1949 at 4412 Maine Avenue

The next thing I knew, I was coming to on the church steps with a man holding me upside down by the legs, dangling me. The first thing I said was to my mother: "Can I still go to the game?" I remember the reply verbatim: "Don't be silly, you're going to bed."

There I was that afternoon propped up in the pillows in my parents' bed after my father had gone alone to the stadium. Suddenly, I felt something sticking into my chest. My mother rushed in and under my shirt discovered a piece of Holy Communion. In those days a Catholic didn't speak at all in the presence of the Blessed Sacrament, much less touch a host. My mother immediately phoned the rectory, and a few minutes later one of the priests was there. He exchanged solemn nods with my mother at the front door, which I could see from bed. Then he plucked the broken host and placed it on a white handkerchief that he folded over.

When my father came back from the game there was quite a stir with my mother telling him about the priest's visit and he seemingly more interested in telling me that Sammy Baugh didn't get into the game until it was almost over with the Packers ahead, 31–0, but that Sammy was something. He led the Redskins to three touchdowns to make it 31–21.

When the Colts played away from home I listened to the games on a little white Philco on my mother's dresser. It was just a box with two knobs and a clump of wires falling out the back. Sometimes the wires would shock me when I tried to untangle them in hopes of getting rid of the static. One night I fell asleep listening to a Colts-Cleveland exhibition game from Toledo, having confused Toledo with Tokyo and wondering why they were playing so far away and how we could even hear them.

In 1948 my father brought home eight-by-ten glossy photos of two Colts rookies. I loved the jump-pass pose of Y. A. Tittle and place-kicker Rex Grossman holding a ball and pinned the corners of their pale green cardboard backing above my bed next to the Colts pennant. When I attempted field goals over the telephone wires in the yard, I kept my head dipped like the blond Grossman's when he kicked. In the years ahead I lost track of Grossman; I've never heard a single person mention his name. Tittle I followed in the newspapers and later on TV when he played for the San Francisco 49ers and the New York Giants and reached the Hall of Fame.

As a nine-year-old, I thought Tittle odd-looking. The quarterbacks I'd seen pictures of were handsome. The Rams' Bob Waterfield married Jane Russell. Tom Cruise could play Johnny Lujack. Even as a rookie Tittle was going bald. But I tried to look on him as beautiful in a more important way. He was ours, and he could pass.

In the contrived picture in the bedroom Tittle was leaping to throw, with a mountain in the background. The Colts trained that summer in Sun Valley, Idaho, an incongruously exotic setting for this baggy-pantsed team. I lay on my bed nights before turning out the light, wondering how Y.A. could jump so high against the brilliant western sky.

He was the first great Colt and my first hero.

◆

When I think of Y. A. Tittle, which is crazily often, I think of him in either of two photos: as the sensational rookie with the Baltimore Colts or as the New York Giants' crippled warrior, alpha and omega images of his seventeen-season career. My happier impression of Tittle, native of Marshall, Texas, and star at Louisiana State University, is the jump-passing rube kid of the 1948 Colts, number sixty-three, on my bedroom wall. The other photograph, better known, captures the heart-rending moment when time ran out on the quarterback. It's 1964 and the thirty-seven-year-old Tittle has been slammed to the ground by a 270-pound defensive end, John Baker of the Pittsburgh Steelers. Number fourteen is on his knees. His helmet has been knocked off. His mouth hangs open in a dazed look.

The *Life* photo spread on the besieged Tittle begins on page 141 of the October 2, 1964, issue, on a right-hand page opposite a Chesterfield King advertisement. It's the patented *Life* layout: three paragraphs of text, four photos, a big block headline reading HOW THEY RACKED UP THE GREAT TITTLE.

Frame one: A fist, taped so thick it looks like concrete, lands on Tittle's right jaw as he throws the football. His mouth is popped open like a bottle's, and his white-uniformed body is lifted off the Pitt Stadium grass so that the cleats of his high-tops are clearly countable.

Frame two: A wide-angle shot locates the point of impact three to four yards in front of the Giants' goal post. Tittle had been trying to spring the Giants free of trouble, but the ball is heading straight toward Pittsburgh's number sixty-four, tackle Chuck Hinton, who is pushing off the intended receiver, the late Joe Morrison.

Frame three: Hinton lumbers with the intercepted ball toward the end zone but even the official can't help looking toward Tittle lying in the end zone, his bald head on the grass, his helmet several feet away. Tittle has been propelled a full five yards.

Frame four: He's on his knees slumped forward, head bowed. Morrison leans down at his left shoulder and number thirty-seven, Ernie Wheelwright, kneels at his right side, his arm extended, his black fingers curling around the fleshy white underside of Tittle's forearm, one man reaching to tend the other's football death.

Then you turn. The whole next page is the prize photo enlarged. "Dazed and bloody, Tittle kneels in the end zone before players reach him . . ." Blood runs out of his bald scalp and down his forehead, disappearing into his left eyebrow; another current trails from his temple to the middle of his left cheek, ending in a fishhook. The palms of his thick hands, always so active during a lifetime of quarterbacking, rest peacefully on his thighs. His rump is lodged on the heels of his big black shoes. Toward the end of his football days Tittle had seemed one of us, a common man playing among behemoths. His hair was gone, his legs were creaky, his body was beaten into lumps. But he could still think and throw. The picture speaks to our own appointment with the inevitable.

Tittle played a bit longer, but that just about did it. There was the game against Washington just five nights later, a Friday night, when he demanded to be put in. He was, and he won it. It was like a wink from a dying man.

My New York friend Dave and I watched the second half on TV in a hotel room in Scranton, Pennsylvania. It was my wedding eve and I'd said good night early at my own party so we could go watch Tittle. By then he had talked himself into the game. Irwin Shaw would write in *Esquire* that someone on the Giants' bench told him that Tittle said, "If Allie [Sherman] doesn't put me in I'm just going to run out on the field and they'll have to come and get me to take me out." He did come out near the finish, slumped over and gasping through broken ribs as the Giants went the last one yard without him. Charlton Heston said that his inspiration for a movie on an aging quarterback called *Number One* was a picture of a dejected Tittle standing on the sideline later that season during his last game. After that, Tittle announced, "I've had as much fulfillment as I can expect," and took his family home to Atherton, California, where he still lives.

I met him at his office in neighboring Palo Alto. He's been in the insurance business since 1954, when he quarterbacked the 49ers. Arriving early, I found him pacing nervously in front of his secretary Melba's desk in an outer office while suggesting to her a way to arrange a future flight from

Canton, Ohio, to New York's La Guardia so he could use a senior-citizen coupon. He moved from point to point around the edge of the desk, as "wound up" as teammates used to say he got before a game. In his sixties the bit of hair above his ears is fluffy white. He wears dark-rimmed glasses. Still, I pictured him barking signals at the line of scrimmage: Tittle calling the play, Melba nodding reassuringly and swinging into action on the phone with their travel agent. "Tell her about the coupon," he said into her free ear.

Tittle speaks rapidly in a dialect of his native east Texas. If time is running out in a game, you have to score *raht cheer and now.*

His heroic career had its hilarious moments. At Louisiana State in the forties, in front of forty thousand people in Tiger Stadium, the belt from his pants was ripped loose while he was running back an interception against Ole Miss. He reached the fifty, the forty-five, the forty, the thirty-five . . . But his pants kept slipping. As he desperately reached for them, they dropped to his ankles, tripping him up with a clear field to what would have been the winning touchdown. LSU lost, 20–18.

"Here's another common, little ol' anecdote," he related a few minutes into our conversation, speaking animatedly with those thick hands. On October 13, 1957, the 49ers were playing the Bears at Chicago's Wrigley Field. The clock was running out, and the 49ers had just been pushed back from scoring position by a fifteen-yard penalty charged against an assistant coach, Tiger Johnson, for berating the officials. "I've known Tiger all my life," recounted Tittle. "Played against him in junior high school. Played against him three years in high school when he was at Tyler and I was at

Marshall. Played against him when I was with Baltimore and he was in San Francisco. Then we became teammates on the 49ers for six years. Then he was my coach for three years — my head offensive coordinator. Now the referee says Tiger's calling the officials all these filthy names. I say to the referee, 'I don't know who that big son-a-bitch is, I never seen him before.' The referee says, 'You mean that's not one of your coaches? What's he doin' on the sideline?' I said, 'I don't know, but I don't know that guy.' So he goes over to Albert — Frank's our head coach, and he'd heard us arguing — and he asks Frank, 'Who is this guy?' Frank says, 'I don't know who that drunk son-a-bitch is, get him out of here, he's been annoyin' the hell out of us.' So two policemen took ol' Tiger out of Wrigley Field, and the referee gave me my fifteen yards back. He walked them back, the fifteen yards! Those yards were important and I wanted 'em. But Tiger was really upset, he was almost fighting with the policemen. He was so mad, and they kicked him out of the whole Wrigley Field. R. C. Owens won the game with a catch on his knees in the end zone with twenty-seven seconds left. And so, man, we were happy. Meantime, Tiger had talked his way back into the locker room and he's sitting there and we're all celebrating and cheering R.C.'s great catch. Tiger says, 'Don't touch me.' I went over and hugged him. He says, 'Don't put your hands on me.' He says, 'I centered that ball to you all those years. I can't see out of my left eye from a forearm I took blocking for you. I can't move on my left knee — I've had three operations blocking for you. But I'm not worth a fifteen-yard penalty, that's what you think of me.' 'No, Tiger . . .'"

Y.A. told me about Tiger only after he'd determined I would appreciate the story. As we drove in his brown Mercedes to lunch nearby, he gave me a "Colts quiz." It amounted to a checking of credentials.

"Let me ask you this," he said. "Who were the Colts before they moved to Baltimore in 1953?"

"The Dallas Texans."

"And who were they before they moved to Dallas?"

"The New York Yankees."

He looked over with brightened blue eyes. "Okay, you know it."

We could talk.

I had to laugh: He could pick out a receiver in traffic easier than he could a table in an almost empty restaurant. He settled on a third one, suitably remote, and began telling me LSU stories. He told me his father saw him play for the Colts only once, an exhibition game in Shreveport, Louisiana, in 1948. Shortly after that he died. Absorbed in his recollections Tittle tried to order lunch a second time, but the waitress, as had Melba, soothed him. She read back what he had already asked for. Yes, he nodded, that was it. And, yes, Y.A. seemed fired up, the way he used to play. After we'd eaten, he introduced me to a tableful of colleagues. They smiled as he approached, but when he pointed at me and said, "I'm the oldest Baltimore Colt he could find," they looked a little vague. "Oh, yeah," one man said finally, "you did play for Baltimore." In California they think of Tittle as a 49er because he was one for ten seasons. Mostly everyone else thinks of him as a Giant. But in Baltimore he's still a Colt.

Yelberton Abraham Tittle was named for his father, a postman. Yelberton is an old family name, Abraham a good Biblical one. Tittle always was called Y.A., "Ya-Ya" — his sister Huline dubbed him that when he was two — or "Yat,"

Y. A. Tittle, as a Colts rookie in 1948

and later "The Bald Eagle." He played football since he was "head high to a cotton blossom." His older brother, Jack, starred at Tulane, and Y.A. grew up "fascinated by the spiral" he threw and "obsessed with getting better." After he'd agreed to play for LSU, University of Texas recruiters drove into Marshall and spoke to him of home-state allegiance. He went to Austin to enroll. Dana X. Bible was the coach. Bobby Layne was there as a sophomore quarterback. "Layne took me out on the town," Tittle said. "He was some drinker, and I had never had a drop to drink in my life. Alcohol didn't hurt him as a football player, but it shortened his life. Next to him I felt inadequate, like a little baby." Like cavalry, two LSU coaches appeared on the Texas campus. "I said, 'I want to go with you.' They said I was going to have to tell Coach Bible. I was scared. So I went into this phone booth with them watching and I faked it. I came back to their car and one of them said, 'What'd he say?' I said, 'He was sorry, but he understood.' Like that, we took off for Baton Rouge."

In 1948 Tittle was drafted by Detroit of the NFL and Cleveland of the All-America Conference. He signed with Cleveland, which had approached him first. When a Detroit official arrived in Marshall, Tittle was surprised. "I didn't know there were two leagues," he said. "It's hard to believe we were that ignorant." He never played for the Browns. They gave him to the Colts as part of a league plan to bolster the team. "I can tell you about 1948 because it's as clear as yesterday," Tittle said. "It was my honeymoon year." Y.A. and his auburn-haired high school sweetheart, Minnette DeLoach, set up housekeeping in Baltimore. It was an experience.

Before her arrival Y.A. and two teammates were desperately searching for an apartment. Finding one, they flipped a coin to see who would get it. Y.A. won. On moving in Minnette realized: no bathtub, no shower. "You had to go outside and down the steps to the basement," Tittle said. Minnette's mother came up and moved them out. A second place they lived had risks of another sort. "When we rented, the landlady told us that her husband had had some mental problems, but we didn't think much of it," Tittle said. "One day, he accused Minnette of stealing his milk. I was angry and went downstairs. I said, 'What's the idea of accusing my wife of stealing your milk?' He pulled a shotgun on me. I started backing up. I said, 'Oh, Minnette, why'd you have to take this man's milk?'"

Minnette still feigns indignation: "Y.A. didn't defend me. I haven't forgiven him yet."

The Tittles live more comfortably now. Y.A. drove up to a low, large house, fenced in and heavily shaded, with a pool in back. No one was home. In his memento-filled den he dug through heavy scrapbooks on a bottom shelf, looking for the Baltimore seasons he thought I should look through. "Here's one," he said, blowing dust.

I opened to a Colts-Browns game program — twenty-five cents. "The Colts take to the air . . . *Capital Airlines*. Again in '49 the Colts are flying *Capital*. The coaches and players know that *Capital* is the fast, comfortable way to travel . . . the way to arrive refreshed and ready for the game." Tittle said it wasn't exactly that way. He described a team flight from San Francisco to Ohio in 1948 when the plane "got lost somewhere around Wichita, Kansas, and we landed in west Texas."

They were bound for Toledo and the exhibition game with the mighty Browns in which Tittle produced a 21–17 upset and won the quarterback job from Chuckin' Charley O'Rourke. The rematch that counted in the standings was played on a Tuesday night in Baltimore during high winds and heavy rain. From that very night we referred to it as the "hurricane game," but that didn't stop me from begging my mother to let my father take me. She laughed off my pleadings. But Jack Kilner, who lived in the apartment downstairs, was going, I argued. He could take care of himself, she reasoned. He'd been a marine in the war, wounded, and a hero. He was heavily muscled and hairy-chested, the toughest person I knew. That night when he headed out his kitchen door wearing an olive drab poncho, the door slammed open against its hinges and he was blown back by wind and rain.

He rubbed some water out of his eye, and I thought he'd stay home for sure. But he dipped his head and went for it. Tittle almost managed to beat the great Browns that night. It was 14–10, Cleveland. Y.A. told me over lunch that he figured the first team to score would win because of the weather and that while the Colts did score first they weren't good enough to hold on.

The scrapbook kept boring straight into Tittle's past, and in a way mine:

A yellow *New York Times* clipping recalled his first pro game, against the New York Yankees in Baltimore. He threw four touchdown passes and ran for a score as the Colts won, 45–28. The *Times* man referred to him as the "blonde bombshell." A few more pages into the scrapbook I came upon a typed note from Charles P. McCormick, one of the Colts' owners. It was to Minnette. "An orchid to you — you and your husband deserve it! You have inspired him to greatness! The kids of Baltimore idolize your husband — so we cannot let them down! Here's victory ahead!"

Then, taped down: a ticket stub to the team's "annual banquet and dance" featuring Hayes Russell and his "Rainbow Music."

"Baltimore is really a small city even though it has a large population," Tittle said. "It isn't like L.A. If you're going to L.A., you have to know where somebody is to find 'em. But Baltimore, you can call a few hotels or restaurants and you can find who you're looking for."

Minnette liked to eat at Haussner's in East Baltimore after the games, and Y.A. would take her. The restaurant is chockfull with a valuable collection of nineteenth-century paintings, etchings, china, and sculptures. Amid naked busts galore, Y.A. stood out anyway. People would spot him in the gaudy maze and come up to him. Minnette remembers them as not being "pushy," just wanting to say hello in what she thought was a neighborly way. "They were so friendly," she said, "and they sure loved Y.A."

Dianne, the oldest of the Tittles' four children, was born in Baltimore. "She's writing this book, *Ode to a Hero,* and it kind of compares me with the Greek gods," Tittle said. "She's a Homeric scholar. I'm the father of a Homeric scholar and the grandfather of a Princeton student — can you imagine that? But I don't think she's got enough football stuff in the book. I don't know if you can sell a book about the Greek gods; people want to read about football or some sex story. I tell her, let me put some football stories in there, you know, like the Tiger story. Put it in that backhanded writing."

"Italics," I said.

He didn't seem to hear.

"Maybe she should talk to you. You know the football stuff."

By then he'd stacked scrapbooks next to me on the sofa of his den. He was loaning me the four Baltimore ones provided I didn't leave town with them. Here was this newspaper ad: On November 13, 1948, Y.A. and another Colts ace, Billy Hillenbrand, appeared at the May Company from 1:30 to 4:30 to sign autographs and promote the "Electric Football Game." "Electric lights go on and off as offensive and defensive plays click! Ideal gift for any youngster!" It was my favorite boyhood game. The most important piece to it was a heavy silver ball. Mine rolled away from me one Sunday night on a B&O train my parents and I were taking home from my grandparents'. It hit hard on the uncarpeted floor and disappeared just as we were pulling into the station in Baltimore. My mother searched frantically but couldn't find it, leaving my father to utter the fateful words, "We have to get off." I stepped into a night of dark disappointment.

I flipped some pages. *The Sun* did a baldness story in 1948 because four Colts were bald. (One was Lu Gambino, a fullback. In street clothes he looked like Robert Mitchum — wide-brimmed hat, long overcoat, baggy but creased trousers, a cigarette between his fingers, a craggy smile. Yesteryear's running back.) The story offered a number of hypotheses on why a team would have four bald players but could only conclude that it had "nothing to do with wearing a helmet."

Tittle mentioned that he wished he'd had hair, but said his baldness hadn't bothered him. He once joked, "I've been fifty-eight since I was twenty-eight." Still, a Louisiana newspaper clip from his LSU days reported, "Because of a rapidly expanding bald spot, he will allow pictures to be made from only the side of his face." He took to wearing baseball caps at practice, warming up for games, and afterward in locker rooms. On cold days he'd put on a dark blue wool cap. I came to a story headlined BORN TO PASS, and Tittle told me that was how he'd always felt, but that in Baltimore Cecil Isbell, the coach, taught him to be a "professional passer." Tittle was six feet, 192 pounds, and had a strong arm. Isbell counseled him to rely on his arm rather than intricate pass patterns and to throw more to the outside than over the middle. When Tittle got to apply those principles for a team as talented as the Giants, his place in the pro football Hall of Fame was secured.

As All-America Conference rookie of the year in 1948, he got the Colts into a divisional play-off. Although that game was lost, the final record of 7–8 was good enough to celebrate. But because of a horrid defense the Colts went 1–11 in both 1949 and 1950. In 1950, after the All-America Conference had folded and the Colts had been taken into the NFL, they met the L.A. Rams. This meant that possibly the worst defense in league history was matched against one of the most technically perfect offenses ever devised. Our heroes were up against the likes of Bob Waterfield and Norm Van Brocklin throwing to Crazy Legs Hirsch. The result: 70–27.

As I had listened to that game on the radio, I had grown flushed and feverish. I'd never heard of a score in the seventies. Sizing me up, my father looked sorry he had ever mentioned the Colts to me. Tittle remembered taking that defeat as badly. "I lived to win and hated to lose," he said. "But our defense gave up a record number of points that season. Our defensive backs were completely overmatched." It may have been ancient history, but his expression took on fresh pain.

When the Colts went out of business after 1950, Tittle was drafted by the 49ers. I felt even worse because in San Francisco Y.A. couldn't wear his number sixty-three anymore. The exciting little left-handed quarterback Frankie Albert already had sixty-three. Colt numbers were sacred to me then and for some reason have always stuck with me. I remember, for instance, that one of the most obscure names ever to play the game, a third-string quarterback for the early Colts named Sam Vacanti, wore sixty-seven. Anytime — every time — I encounter the number sixty-seven I think of Sam Vacanti, a black-haired, roly-poly fellow.

With the 49ers Tittle would have to wear number sixty-four. But eventually he took over from Albert and became idolized in the Bay Area. He never thought he'd play anywhere other than San Francisco. But on a Saturday night in Portland, Oregon, in 1961, he'd play his last game for the 49ers. It was an exhibition against the Giants. He'd been hurting physically and psychically. Red Hickey, the coach, had installed the shotgun formation, which required a mobile passer. Hickey was phasing out Tittle. What's more, Tittle was suffering from a severe groin injury that had carried over from the previous year. "I was so self-conscious about it I didn't even want the trainer to know," he said. "I'd go into a toilet with a roll of tape, rip off the tape, tape the son-a-bitch down, and flush the rest of the tape down the toilet. I taped it good for the Giants; I was fighting for my job. [John] Brodie played the first half. The Giants were all over him. He got sacked about seven times. I played the second half. My protection was perfect. I just ripped 'em apart. I thought I had saved the T-formation and preserved my job for the next five years. After the game the Giants' Sam Huff said to me, 'Hey, Y.A., we were told it'd be a hundred-dollar fine if anybody touched you.' The Giants players knew they were about to trade for me."

The next week, on his first play as a Giant, the Rams' Jack Pardee fell on him and broke two transverse processes. "It was the best break of my life," said Tittle. He spent much of the next six weeks in a whirlpool, sunk in up to his neck while worrying that his new teammates were sorry the Giants had traded their number-one draft choice for an old man. But the waters healed both the groin pull and his back, and Tittle stepped forth feeling almost youthful. Soon he discovered a favorite new receiver, Del Shofner, whom the Giants had acquired from the Rams. "I never had a receiver like Shofner. He could run, and he had great hands. It was like opening a Christmas toy."

We were driving on Route 101 back to his office as Tittle was talking about the experience of playing in New York and how "the roar at Yankee Stadium is a different type of roar, it seemed like. It's sort of a powerful thing to play at Yankee Stadium." And: "If you're winning in New York, that's the greatest feeling." He said that he loved his insurance work and always had but that "there's nothing like the great sports win." His glasses were perched on his head, and he was looking straight at the road, his hawk's nose in profile. "You can sell the biggest contract in the world," he said, "and it doesn't give you the feeling of beating the Chicago Bears."

In his office, Tittle showed me a copy of a photo of him coming off the field after his first game back in Baltimore when he was with the 49ers. He passed it across his desk. Fans who'd mobbed him had torn off his shirt. He was grinning, standing there in his shoulder pads. I looked up to see him reading a letter that had been in an envelope with the picture. "Hey," he said, "you sent me this."

He laughed, and I gave him back the picture. He looked at it for several moments. "I was still their hero," he said finally. "But I don't know why. We had such a lousy team."

◆

My grandparents moved to Aberdeen, Maryland, in 1918 after the Army's proving ground was relocated from Sandy Hook, New Jersey. My paternal grandfather was a civilian employee on the proving ground, a weapons assembler. John Gildea and Annie Moran, who ruled the home front, had a daughter and three sons. Pop was the third child and middle boy. He played shortstop for Aberdeen High in the twenties — a half century before Cal Ripken, Jr., played shortstop for Aberdeen High. At night Pop worked at Dell's Pharmacy

My Gildea grandparents, in
Aberdeen, Maryland

on Bel Air Avenue, the main street. He stocked shelves, made up orders and delivered them, swept floors, and jerked sodas behind a marble-topped fountain. Dell's was owned by Rudolph Spang, a veterinarian and druggist who had moved from Philadelphia. In a photo I've seen of him standing outside the old wooden E. Dell & Co. Druggists, Spang looked small and stern, a ringer for Calvin Coolidge. Apparently he was an amiable man, quiet and easy to work for. He became Pop's mentor.

From Doc Spang — the pharmacists were always called Doc — Pop learned that the neighborhood druggist was depended on for advice and minor remedies when the doctor wasn't available. Often customers had a question or needed reassurance about something far afield from pharmacy. Pop watched Spang mix ingredients, dispense pills, syrups, and ointments, patiently answer questions, make thoughtful suggestions.

Pop admired Mrs. Spang for her chocolate syrup that was used for the sodas. She prepared it at home, and Doc carried it to the store in gallon or half-gallon jugs. Pop spent a lifetime ordering "black and whites" — sodas with chocolate syrup and vanilla ice cream — and comparing the taste with Mrs. Spang's formula. The only ice-cream soda that ever came close was the jumbo double-dip, mild bittersweet chocolate that cost twenty cents at the fountain at Read's main store at Howard and Lexington streets, which my father managed from 1951 to 1955.

Dell's had a little ice-cream parlor by the front window. Thomas Arthur Cronin, a dentist, had his office on the second floor and while waiting for patients would come downstairs to chat with Doc Spang and customers and help out in the ice-cream parlor. The dentist added to the cheerful ambience, and Pop liked him especially because he was a sports fan who talked baseball.

Pop thought he'd play baseball in college, but when his mother took him on the train to Baltimore to enroll at the University of Maryland pharmacy school he was told that preprofessional students were ineligible for sports. "He was very disappointed," my grandmother told me. She pictured him sitting grimly at the registrar's desk making the difficult decision, pharmacy over baseball.

Doc Spang not only had recommended the profession but also had promised Pop a job filling prescriptions. The idea was he would work his way through school part-time, then become a country pharmacist and maybe even part owner of the store. He did return to Dell's after graduation for a few months, but while studying at Maryland decided that he liked the city. Walking a street in Baltimore one day, he encountered a friend who told him that Read's wanted another pharmacist. Read's was then a growing chain, spreading throughout the Baltimore area. He applied and was hired.

For years he worked at Read's stores in northwest Baltimore: Gwynn Oak Junction, Liberty Heights and Garrison, Pimlico. All were situated on corners. Sidewalks were crowded with people waiting for the lights to change. They'd push through Read's doors to an array of sundries and potpourri of perfume smells, moving along to the different counters, their feet scraping on the pink terrazzo. From the end of the pharmacy counter I'd watch Pop in his white jacket grind medicine to fine powder and delicately sweep it from a pill tile into capsules. He'd weigh the first capsule or two or three to insure equal content, but after he had established his rhythm he didn't have to use the small scale on the counter. He'd know.

"So, Doc, what do you think the Colts are going to do Sunday?"

He could tell them.

Pop liked Read's because it applied the principles Doc Spang espoused on a large scale. Each store was a no-nonsense apothecary where one also could relax at the soda fountain and enjoy a chocolate soda, cherry Coke, lime phosphate, or a Read's-baked apple pie topped with Hendler's vanilla ice cream. Hendler's ice cream, a Baltimore favorite, was known as "The Velvet Kind." Read's blue-and-silver-script logo, with the motto RUN RIGHT TO READ'S, blazed in the nights. Some evenings Pop would return to a store he managed, as conscientiously as if he owned it, to attend briefly to some matter, and I'd wait in the car in the wash of blue neon.

My uncle Len DeMoss told me Pop liked "the action" — that's why he left Aberdeen for the city and why he worked for Read's. Twice during his thirty years on the job he broke away briefly, once to own the small basement Blackistone Pharmacy on the corner of Thirty-third and St. Paul streets, near Memorial Stadium, once to work for Morgan & Millard, known for its Runyonesque clientele located as it was on "The Block," the section of striptease bars, porn shops, and the Gayety Burlesque house.

Mom and I were parked outside Morgan & Millard's one night, left there by Pop, who had gone in to do whatever he had to do, and being just a few feet from the Gayety marquee, my mother was prompted to ask, "Do you know what goes on in there?"

I'd been uneasy, feeling such a question coming on and not sure how to answer. I had read an account in the paper of a stripper trying to escape a raid at the Gayety while "wearing" only an umbrella. And I regularly perused the *News-Post*'s back-page display ads on Saturdays, devoted to establishments on The Block. Blaze Starr, who later owned The Two O'Clock Club, was a standout in her ad as she leaned forward with little or possibly nothing on, blowing a kiss with tantalizing lips.

"Well, they have pretty girls in bathing suits," I responded to my mother.

"Less than that," she said sternly.

I didn't say any more.

A Read's executive lured Pop back to the company both times he strayed — he was, for certain, hardworking and congenial, an asset. Al Aaronson, briefly a Read's pharmacist, suggests Pop stayed put mainly because "Read's gave you two weeks' vacation in the summer and a Christmas bonus, so you could never quit before the summer because your vacation was coming up and you could never quit after that because you needed your bonus."

The drug store of Pop's heyday was a place to congregate. Corner cops and athletes would come in for coffee in winter. White-haired Tommy Thomas, who managed the minor-league Orioles, hung out at Doc Ragland's drug store in Waverly. At whatever Read's Pop worked in an Oriole or a Colt regularly would drop in. "Al Klug's mother was in the store today," I remember him saying, Al Klug being a Colt offensive lineman.

Read's on York Road in Towson is where Pop met this lovely girl whose light brown hair fell in soft curls. She kept her hands clasped demurely in front of her flouncy skirt that extended well below the knee. He was on his first job for Read's when Mom came in. She'd graduated from Towson High and worked across the street at the front counter of the Mayflower laundry. She'd heard about the "new pharmacist" — dark-haired, slender, handsome.

He took her to the state fair at Timonium, and shortly after that they were married.

◆

No matter their station in life, Baltimoreans of the late forties and fifties shared certain values.

Good food on the table was important; everyone went to one of the city's big markets or had a favorite butcher or baker or knew where the freshest crabs were sold. People believed in taking life easy — "lazy-lidded" is how Anne

Tyler writes of Baltimore. No one in Baltimore ever wanted to "overdo it." People tried hard to avoid crowds.

The exception was on Sundays when the Colts played. You had to be at the stadium.

I think of four men who were always there: my father, a south Baltimore stevedore, a master sergeant who worked at the Fifth Regiment Armory, and a poet. They were as different as can be, yet remarkably similar to an extent. They loved the city while living in different corners of it. They were devoted husbands and family men who worked hard to put three meals on the table and attend their families' other wants. They were all drawn to the old stadium starting in 1947, and the Colts became their team. Had they known one another I'm sure they would have found plenty to talk about.

Joey Radomski grew up on the waterfront, where inevitably he would work. In time he earned a reputation; ship captains asked for Joey to load their cargo. Before containers were lifted on and off ships by crane, the movement of cargo depended on the muscle of men. At six feet two, two hundred pounds, Joey was an everyday Atlas. He also had a touch. He could arrange the huge crates so they would be secure. Sliding cargo could list a ship. There were no worries with Joey.

A striking man who resembled Ronald Reagan with swept-back black hair, Joey loved his work and its proximity to his brick row house, three blocks away on Towson Street. Locust Point — then and now — is a neighborhood of three thousand Poles, Irish, and Germans. Short of death, hardly anyone leaves the Point. Everything's there between Lawrence Street and Fort McHenry: neighborhood stores, corner bars. People walk. Trucks may roar along the tree-lined streets and grain dust sometimes rises like a sandstorm to blot out the noonday sun, yet people remain cheerful and optimistic. Joey was like that; he simply knew in the course of a week on the waterfront that he'd come up with two tickets to the Colts on Sunday, one for himself, one for his daughter Mary Margaret.

Hurst C. Loudenslager — Loudy — was raised in our Brooklyn, named for New York's Brooklyn. Like the better-known one, Baltimore's Brooklyn is separated by water from the city's central business district. World War II shipbuilding swelled the population in Brooklyn, which prompted Al Aaronson to buy an empty building on Hanover Street and open a Rexall drug store that proved immensely profitable and made his break from Read's a success. Loudy worked at the Carr Lowrey Glass Company.

During the war he joined the army and was stationed in the Philippines, where he steered an amphibious landing craft that transported troops from ship to beach. He painted his wife's name on the side: FLO. Back in Baltimore after the war, he drove a cab for a while, and a laundry truck. Then he joined the National Guard, becoming a supply sergeant at the Fifth Regiment Armory, a stone fortress in the city.

Bleachers used to be erected in the armory for various events. My parents took me there to see Sonja Henie skate. Eisenhower politicked at the armory. Box lacrosse games were played there and shown on early television, barely visible in the building's dim light.

Loudy was at the old stadium the night of the "hurricane game" of 1948. "It was more like a tornado," he said. "Practically blew you out of the stands. I never saw anything like that."

Cavernous Municipal Stadium could seat sixty thousand,

but it was mostly windswept benches that Tuesday night when the Colts almost upset the patent Browns in the fierce rain and awful slop. Municipal Stadium — it was rat-infested — was a place that made, say, Cleveland's barn of a Municipal Stadium seem like a sports palace. But Loudy loved the Baltimore stadium for no other reason than it was in Baltimore.

"Eighty-eight rows down, eighty-eight rows up. I counted 'em one day," he said.

His stubby legs were strong then, and he could take the climb. Five feet six, Loudy weighed 180 pounds in his prime when he played sandlot soccer and baseball. But after he had added considerable heft, a friend described him as having "the perfect body for someone seven three."

Loudy loved the separate building at the front of the old stadium where the locker rooms were located. The building was decrepit inside and cramped, but its exterior was dressed with Grecian columns.

Ogden Nash lived in north Baltimore, where row houses give way to noble Georgian mansions. I didn't know Ogden Nash. I didn't know anyone who lived in north Baltimore. He lived in a big stone house at 4300 Rugby Road in Guilford, the kind of place we gawked at on drives through the neighborhood. I read about Nash in the newspapers. In photographs, he usually had a cigarette in his hand and often was posed in his book-lined den. I found it curious that such an obviously dignified man enjoyed the horses and cared to visit Maryland's mile and half-mile race tracks, most of which I experienced at my father's side. Some I found dismal. At least, I thought, the state's thoroughbred traditions spawned the football team's nickname.

"Your father was the greatest long-shot player of them

all," Al Aaronson said. "He spent his lifetime looking for the long shot." More precisely, he was adept at picking winners that went off at odds of about five to one to fifteen to one. "A value player," explained my friend Vinnie, who goes to the track almost daily. "You have to bet against the chalk" — the favorites — "if you're going to make any money." One of Pop's "value" picks was High Chair, whose story is well known to our family. On a drug store tip, Pop rounded up a carload of friends and headed for Havre de Grace, where they bet on High Chair. Leading by about ten lengths in the homestretch, a lead that probably grew in the frequent retelling, High Chair fell with a broken leg and had to be destroyed.

Sometimes Pop would make two bets on a race and keep one a secret. Then after the race when I'd think he'd lost, he'd produce a winning ticket, slipping it up between his thumb and forefinger. He'd grin.

Nash's daughter Linell Smith told me that racing long had been a passion in her family. Nash's sister married an entrepreneur who raced horses at Saratoga. Nash's mother loved thoroughbreds, too. A Wellesley product, she tutored her son at home in Rye, New York, until he was about twelve and began his formal education. When she wasn't teaching him Latin, they often discussed horses. Later, he would take her to the tracks. He took Linell when she was a girl, and, like him, she fell in love with the races, eventually becoming a thoroughbred owner and breeder.

Pop was partial to Bel Air, a gem of a track with a sparkling white grandstand, tall hedges, and huge trees. I'm sure he liked it, too, because of its location in his home territory of Harford County. Havre de Grace was the county's big track. Some race-goers, not the locals, gave it the French pronunciation, Havre de Graw. On sleepy Sunday afternoons, when the Colts weren't playing and we'd be visiting my grandparents in neighboring Aberdeen, Pop would let me drive his car in the big empty parking lot next to the track. He'd walk me through the barn area and we'd peer inside the stalls at the huge animals. They might be lounging in the straw. Sometimes they'd be standing nervously with their heads protruding from the cubicles. I feared their size and bulging eyes and never would pat one on the nose as Pop would, even though there always seemed to be a small, unshaven man wearing a cap close by, encouraging me: "He won't hurt you." Pop showed me where one of the little men lived, above a stable in a steaming-hot room with a cot. My peek at a depressing side of the sport tempered Pop's romantic descriptions of afternoons at the races there. He would tell me how people came from as far as New York on trains, and he drove me up to a Pennsylvania Railroad siding that reached almost to the track's entrance. From high in the grandstand you could see in the distance where the Susquehanna River flows into Chesapeake Bay. Red Smith used to write about "The 'Graw" before its gates were closed in 1951, victimized by competition from New Jersey.

When Pop would take me to Marlboro, a small track in southern Maryland, my mother would say we were heading to "the end of the world." In winter the horses ran at Bowie. Babe Ruth took Ziegfeld Follies star Fannie Brice to the Bowie races. I could never get warm at Bowie, and the predictable sky of milky soup and backstretch panorama of naked trees and worn barns caused me to long for spring and baseball and Pimlico. Nash liked Pimlico. I liked it not only because of its spring meetings but also its location in the city. More than once when I was a boy riding in our car

Mom (left) and her best friend,
Celeste, enjoyed the races.

with Pop or Mom on the way home from my maternal grandparents' in Towson, we'd pass Pimlico on Rogers Avenue just as the horses were turning for home; we'd drive along parallel with them, magnificently close, or stop at the fence and watch. Before it burned in 1966, the track's yellow-painted Victorian clubhouse stood near the corner of Park Heights and Belvedere, cater-cornered from Read's. When Pop managed that store, he regularly slipped away for the last two races when the track's gates were opened and no admission was charged. Nash wrote a poem called "All Roads Lead to Pimlico."

Mom liked going to Pimlico with Pop. She'd already had one unforgettable experience there. Mr. Keevney, who worked with her at the laundry, liked to gamble, and one day when she was going to the track with her friend Celeste he gave her two dollars for an eight-horse show parlay. She was to bet each of Keevney's picks in the afternoon's eight races to come in third. As long as his horses finished first, second, or third, Mom was to collect the winnings and plow them back on his selection in the next race.

But in the first race Mom made a mistake — she bet Keevney's horse to place, so that she could collect only if it came in first or second. She realized her blunder shortly before the horse finished third. The parlay was dead.

But Keevney's picks continued to score. After two or three more of his horses came in, Celeste said anxiously to my mother: "Mary, what are you going to do?" Mom, who knew racing lingo, said, "We'll be okay. One of them will run out."

But one never did. By the end of the afternoon all eight of Keevney's picks had finished at least third. He was due more than seven hundred dollars on his parlay.

"What are you going to do, Mary?" Celeste asked.

"I'm going right in and tell Mr. Keevney."

She added: "Do you think I could get a loan at the bank?"

But to Mom's amazement, Keevney forgave her on the spot.

Pop, Joey, Loudy, and Nash were four of a kind. They all responded to the Colts' arrival with the enthusiasm of boys. My friend George Kelch, who was twelve years old and riding his bike when he heard the news that a team was coming, said, "It was like V-J Day."

In the book *Loving Letters from Ogden Nash* is a letter Nash wrote in September 1947 to his daughter Isabel, who was off boarding at Miss Porter's School in Farmington,

Connecticut: "Mummy and I are sitting in the living room wishing you were with us as line-ups for the first World Series game are coming over the air . . . We saw our Baltimore Colts in action against New York in the Stadium on Sunday — a crowd of fifty-one thousand and half an hour to find a place to park. The Colts lost 21–7, but put up a wonderful battle, and we look forward to seeing them against San Francisco next Sunday."

How easy, how natural, it was for Nash to refer to the Colts as *our* Colts. In their first month the team already was part of the city's fabric.

"He was interested in football always," Linell Smith said. "My mother's father was a great college football fan. Basically Princeton. I mean, he was really old-line Princeton. He and Daddy would always have a bet on the Princeton-Harvard game." Nash had attended Harvard one year, leaving with the explanation that his departure was by his own free will and stating that "I've the papers to prove it."

Eager to root for Baltimore's new pro team, Nash would drive to the old stadium in his black, prewar La Salle. Because it had four doors, his wife didn't want Linell and Isabel ever to ride in it for fear they'd fall out a back door — the same fear my mother had for me. That's why Mom persuaded Pop to get a two-door when he got his Ford in '46 and why Nash's wife insisted that he get a two-door in '43 when he had a little money from writing the lyrics to the Broadway hit *One Touch of Venus*.

Pop, Joey, Loudy, and Nash were four of a kind in another way — each fell in love at first sight, although of the wives, only Loudy's, Flo, took the Colts anywhere near as seriously as her husband. Pop fell in love when Mom came into the drug store, Joey when he saw Agnes McNeal with her father at a prizefight at the Coliseum, a small, glorious dump on Monroe Street that's still there, its marquee gone and a FOR RENT sign out front.

Pop and Mom and, a few years later, Joey Radomski and Agnes McNeal eloped to St. Mary's Catholic Church in Alexandria, Virginia. The Radomski girls — Mary Margaret, Helen, and Ceiley — and I never have figured out the coincidence of Alexandria and St. Mary's, but we know that our mothers' families were short of money and that Pop and Joey were shy enough to want to avoid the circumstance of a conventional wedding day.

But Joey's and Agnes's families considered their union a "mixed marriage" — never mind that both were Catholic. He was Polish, and she was Irish. He was from "down the Point," she was from "up the hill." Joey and Agnes had grown up one mile and worlds apart. To outsiders the areas may have blended imperceptibly, but in reality they were divided not only by the railroad tracks on Lawrence Street but by a fierce ethnic pride on both sides. Joey knew the marriage could mean trouble. Sure enough, six months later when Joey and Agnes confessed, Joey's mother, Frances Radomski (who had gotten off a boat at the end of Hull Street, walked two blocks, and there spent the rest of her life), wrapped her head in a towel to ward off spirits that might wreck the marriage and even destroy the couple. Agnes's mother, Mary McNeal, fell to silence and retired to her room, seldom emerging for years. "She never did recover," Mary Margaret said.

It may seem improbable to think of Loudy and Ogden Nash together because they expressed themselves so differently; Loudy could be vocal enough to knock a person off his stadium seat. But both fell in love at dances. Loudy first saw little dark-haired Flo in a Brooklyn dance hall. She couldn't help notice him because he was a big guy — not tall, but stout — and the only one who had on a suit and tie. That still didn't mean she would dance with him when he came up to her. "I don't know why I wouldn't," she said. "It was one of those girlish things. He asked me a second time, and I still wouldn't dance with him." Loudy sat disconsolately on a chair near a corner until she passed next to him, and he put his arm around her tiny waist and gently pulled her onto his lap. "I'm never going to let you go, not ever," he said. And she knew then that she never wanted him to. And she danced. Nash was down from New York City in 1928 — he had a job then writing advertising copy — when he met a Baltimore girl at an Elkridge Club dinner dance and, as a *Sunpapers* account has it, "promptly fell in love." He "surreptitiously switched placecards so as to sit next to the tall young society girl with whom he was smitten." She was Frances Rider Leonard. Following the warmest love letters a man could write, the two were married in 1931. Three years after that, Nash adopted Baltimore as his home.

While Loudy sometimes carried a record player and a forty-five rpm disc with the Colts' fight song on it, Ogden Nash used to hum that tune and sing the words. Nash could think up the most delightfully perfect verses. Loudy took purposeful stabs at poetry himself, handing out index cards with his heartfelt lines to Colts as they boarded planes for road games in hopes the words might inspire them to victory. "It just came out of my heart," he told me.

We are now into the season
And we're really on the prowl;

We're going to grab a great big Bear
And really make him howl.
After the game is over
And we've stomped them in the ground,
We'll let it be known to one and all
We're the best around.

Mary Margaret Radomski is reminded of the Colts daily. At night the blue light from the steeple of St. Mary's Star of the Sea Church — a marker on seamen's charts — shines through her bedroom window. When she turns off her lamp at night, the small room is bathed in blue. Colts blue.

Of course when Joey began taking Mary Margaret to the games, when Pop began taking me, the Colts wore green. "Y.A.'s shirt used to blend in with the grass when he was stretched out," she remembered. "He didn't have much blocking."

I told her that Y.A. had mentioned Baltimore's blue autumn skies, which he admired while flattened in the backfield. She remembered a snowy night when the Chicago Rockets played. She loved the white footballs with black stripes that were used then for night games. I did, too, and I had a white football and used it so much the black stripes wore off almost completely.

Joey would take Mary Margaret to the games on the "Football Express" bus, which still made getting there and back a journey — the longer the better to her, she said, because she could sit there next to Joey, shoulder to shoulder, and talk about the Colts or think about the game they were going to see or had just seen. I know how she felt.

◆

I loved riding the streetcars

The A. Aubrey Bodine Collection, Peale Museum, Baltimore City Life Museums

In 1948, Tittle's rookie year, Aubrey Bodine of *The Sunpapers* snapped what became for me a favorite photograph. It's a peaceful picture of a trolley motorman raising the pole of his 1913 vintage, canary yellow double-ender parked at the end of a line. On the back of car 5765 is a white cardboard advertisement for a Colts' game: FOOTBALL: BALTIMORE COLTS VS. CHICAGO ROCKETS. THE STADIUM. 2:05 P.M. SUNDAY NOV. 14.

As a boy of six or seven, I was fascinated by the sounds of the trolleys — the clanging bell, the clacking wheels crossing an intersection with another line, the grinding of steel as a car took a curve. I used to wonder where the shiny rails of the No. 33 line led. The No. 33s, also yellow double-enders, reached one end of their line at Gwynn Oak Junction. There, the motorman would walk through his car flapping the seatbacks so they would face forward before starting up in the direction I longed to explore. One Sunday when Pop was working, Mom and I walked to the junction from our Maine Avenue apartment and, to satisfy my curiosity, boarded a 33 for the "adventure."

It accelerated with what I thought a beautiful whine and rocked as I imagined a boat did, leaving me with mixed feelings of excitement: wanting to stop for passengers so I could hear the sweet start-up all over again, wanting to keep moving to build a speed that increased the sway of the car.

The cane seats were set high so a child could see out the big front windows and watch the ties in the roadbed be swallowed beneath us. The route included what I considered a magnificently secret stretch — the car gave off a whoosh as we sped into a sliver of space between tall hedges. After bursting out into bright sunlight, we passed through a leafy neighborhood of shingled houses with big porches and broad lawns until we stopped at a railroad crossing. We were coming to West Arlington, where Pop already had driven me on Friday afternoons every three weeks for haircuts at Sam and Elmer's on Belvedere Avenue. But to me, the trolley approached by a more exotic route.

On weekdays the barbershop was filled with waiting customers, talking and smoking. What a duo, Sam and Elmer! One tall and bald, one short and round. They did a soft-shoe and had a calendar girl over the cash register. The Sunday when we passed on the trolley was the first time I'd seen the blind pulled, the barber pole motionless. In fact, all along the street leading into Pimlico curtains were closed. It was winter and few people were out; it was as if we were passing through a remote shuttered village that somehow was part of the city.

Things were bustling, however, at Belvedere and Park Heights avenues, where the trolley turned right. People were out walking, some looking into the windows of little shops that sold Arrow shirts and Jarman shoes. To our left, a rider galloped a horse on the clubhouse turn of the Pimlico track. Read's was open on the corner. Pop was in there working.

We rode down Park Heights Avenue through Avalon with its rows of brick houses and kept going to Park Circle, which my mother had said was far enough for the outing. After coming down a slope into this confluence of streets, we got off and waited at a pylon for a trolley back home. I was awed by Park Circle — by the sight of the entrance to Carlin's Amusement Park, which had a rickety wooden "Mountain Speedway" roller coaster, a midway, an "Olympic pool," a dance pavilion where Rudolf Valentino once was mobbed, and an ice rink where the minor-league Baltimore Clippers played. Lamar "Racehorse" Davis, Y. A. Tittle's favorite Baltimore receiver, appeared in ads for the Park Circle Chevrolet dealership.

Mom's father had been a motorman on the No. 13 along North Avenue, but I had trouble imagining him in what I considered one of the most important jobs in the world. The older man I knew didn't move much from his living room chair, preferring to listen for the race results on the radio. Mom told me a number of times that her doctor had been killed during the war years, stepping off a streetcar in Australia; that's why, out there in the middle of Park Circle, we had to be careful.

The streetcars kept on rattling through our lives. When we lived on Maine Avenue we were only one block from the No. 32, which ran along Liberty Heights Avenue. When we moved to 5010 Gwynn Oak Avenue the same line passed our door. Because Pop drove to work, the No. 32 line was important. My mother took 32s — dark green, streamlined cars — when she went downtown shopping. My Aunt Catherine could visit us because after she'd ridden the Greyhound from Aberdeen to Baltimore she could walk one block from the bus station on Howard Street to Park Avenue and catch the 32. I went to high school at Calvert Hall instead of Loyola because the No. 32 took me almost door to door; Loyola would have required two changes. Once I rode the No. 25 with Pop, who had left his car to be fixed somewhere along the line. It was an even more woodsy route than the 33. The No. 25s also were green, but with forward-facing single seats on the right side. Pop sat behind me as we bobbed on the thick seat cushions on our passage through a forest.

Pop used to take Mom and me to dinner at The House of Welsh, a three-story brick building painted black — the

The House of Welsh, one of Pop's favorite restaurants in Baltimore, as it looked in 1947
The A. Aubrey Bodine Collection, Peale Museum, Baltimore City Life Museums

only black building I knew of. A large liquor bottle was painted on the side wall — WELSH'S BLACK BOTTLE, STRAIGHT WHISKEY. It was always warm inside Welsh's, and busy. Steaks and fries sizzled on the large round trays that the rushing waiters balanced on their palms. Going in and coming out of Welsh's, I liked watching the streetcars roll across the Guilford Avenue elevated, which was supported by a maze of black girders. The cars would inch up and down the trestle near the restaurant.

As a teenager, I fell in love with a girl who rode the 32. The blond-haired Ann, whom I desperately wanted to speak to but never had the courage to, got off at the same stop I did coming home from school. I always hoped she would drop one of the books she cradled in her arms, and I tried mightily each day to position myself behind her at the exit door. But she never dropped a book, and I'm sure never noticed me even when I was at her shoulder when we alighted. I'd even daydream that she might fall headfirst out the door and that I'd grab her coat and save her or hold her tenderly as she lay injured in the street.

I wished I was as fearless as this older guy who also rode the 32 on the way home from school. He was tough and wore a black corduroy jacket with dirty white trim and had swept-back dark hair, like Boogie in *Diner.* Some days at the stop before the streetcar turned left from Linden Avenue onto North, he would get off and sprint toward Druid Hill Park, then left past the trolley barn to the corner of Reisterstown Road, where the Red Fox bar was, trying to beat the trolley there and get back on. Sometimes he did. Sometimes we'd look up the avenue and see him beaten and breathless.

I loved one bus line — the No. 3 — because it went past the stadium. Most Sundays on the way to Colt games Pop would find a parking place on a street in Waverly, whose main intersection was Thirty-third and Greenmount. Montpelier and Frisby and Homestead and Independence — they were among Pop's favorite tucked-away side streets. But some Sundays Pop would pull up short. "Parking's going to be tough," he'd say, sensing not to drive any closer even though when we did we always found a spot. Instead, he'd park near Johns Hopkins University, and from there we'd take the No. 3.

It was always crowded on the bus in the hour before a game, but everyone was congenial, and we'd hang on in the aisle listening to Colt talk. Relatives or strangers, people talked to one another as they rode to see the Colts play. You could feel the anticipation.

In 1982 Roger Angell found his way onto a No. 3 after the final game of the baseball season when Milwaukee's Don Sutton beat the Orioles' Jim Palmer to decide the American League East in a classic game. In *The New Yorker* Angell wrote:

"Outside the stadium, I caught a bus that would take me downtown to the railroad station and my train home, and as the bus filled up with fans I noticed that most of them seemed less disappointed than I was about the outcome of the game and the end of their season. . . . A thin ten- or twelve-year-old boy in an Orioles souvenir batting helmet sitting on the aisle one row in front of me turned around to face his grandmother, who had the window seat beside me, and said, 'Well, they *killed* us,' and his father, from the row behind me, said, 'I *told* you Sutton would be tough for us,' and the boy said, 'Just wait till next year . . .'"

◆

Pop was always going to the fights, although he never took me. He went to New York for Joe Louis–Billy Conn in 1946. He'd drive to Philadelphia for fights. Mostly he went to the Coliseum in Baltimore. His favorite fighter was Archie Moore.

"It was my town, Baltimore," Moore told me when I happened to meet him in 1991. "I adopted Baltimore like one of those airports they call hubs. I made Baltimore one of my hubs for quite a while."

Before Moore became light-heavyweight champion of the world, but not before he was known as "The Mongoose" for his quick strikes, he fought twenty-two times in Baltimore, all but one at the bandbox Coliseum, where the Baltimore Bullets of the National Basketball Association played on a floor so highly polished it seemed to give off its own light in the gloom. Pop took me there to see George Mikan, Bob Cousy, Sweetwater Clifton.

I found Pop almost unhittable, frustrating, in our bedroom boxing matches after he'd go into Moore's crab-shell defense. I told Moore of Pop's admiration and how I grew up hearing stories of his legend.

Moore had just finished breakfast in the Trump Plaza coffee shop in Atlantic City and invited me to his room. He was there to attend the George Foreman–Evander Holyfield heavyweight title fight. "I'm so glad you want to talk about Baltimore," said the Sweet Scientist, pulling the curtains against the bright ocean light. "I'm tired of talking about this fight." Old George had signed on the older Archie to provide his unique wisdom, which Archie calls Mongoosiana.

The first boxer to incorporate himself, Moore once was asked why he kept Doc Kearns around as a sort of manager. "'Cause he's smart," said Moore. "What do you mean, smart?" he was asked. "Doc Kearns is so smart," said Archie, "if you give him two hundred pounds of steel wool, he'll knit you a stove."

Moore sat serenely in a chair like a contemplative monk, his hands folded. He has a round face with happy eyes and wore a crocheted white beret on which were affixed several airline pins, reminders of trips. He's spent much of his life on the road, having fought 234 times, from Piano Man Jones to Muhammad Ali and beyond.

The Coliseum in Baltimore, where the Bullets
played and Archie Moore fought
The Hearst Corporation

By his mother's account he was born on December 13, 1913, in Benoit, Mississippi, but he claims to have been born sometime in 1916 in Missouri. Years back he told the late San Diego sportswriter Jack Murphy, "My mother should know, she was there. But so was I. I have given this a lot of thought, and have decided that I must have been three when I was born."

Archie's age remains a mystery, and he chuckled when I asked what it was. He himself is one of life's mysteries —

he can remember things that occurred long ago as clearly as if they'd just happened. Like his Baltimore days, spent mostly in the late forties.

"There was this man named Sam Bruton," Archie said, "and one night he came backstage and into my dressing room. He was a fight fanatic. He said to me, 'Man, you sure can fight.' He was about my age, which wasn't too young. He said, 'Let's go out and have something to eat.' That's the first thing you want to do after a fight — I was hungry.

"So after we finished, I said, 'Would you take me to my hotel?' He said, 'Why don't you stay with me? I have an extra room.' He had nine kids — all boys — but somehow he had an extra room and I went down and stayed all night. I got up the next morning and felt right at home."

Ollie May, Sam's wife, fixed Archie breakfast, after which he adjourned to the living room, where he shadowboxed and wrestled with several of the boys. They punched him in the ribs and he tapped them on the sides of their heads and they jumped on him and pulled him down.

Like that: Archie belonged to a city and a family. It's how the Colts were made to feel.

Sam Bruton's house was near Welcome Alley, where the turn-of-the-century Baltimore boxer Joe Gans had lived, and Sam showed Archie where the house had been and Archie is pleased to have seen the spot. "Like any other boy," Archie said, "I would pick out a hero." Grantland Rice called Gans the greatest lightweight who ever lived, and Archie told me he grew up reading stories about Gans growing up in Baltimore working in a fish market and developing into a small Jack Johnson. Gans, smart in the ring, was called "The Old Master." From him Archie took his cue.

After Gans beat Battling Nelson in forty-two rounds at

Goldfield, Nevada, in 1906, he used his eleven-thousand-dollar purse to open the Goldfield Hotel in Baltimore. It was located near the burlesque houses and attracted crowds after the shows. They'd push through the swinging bat-wing doors by the first-floor bar. It's said that, except for Sundays, the doors swung all night, every night.

Gans died of tuberculosis at the age of thirty-five in 1910, but Goldfield's remained an after-hours spot for years before it was turned into a grocery store and the rest of the structure an apartment house. The name Goldfield Hotel endured in little blocks of tile on the worn front step until the building was torn down in 1960. Almost every visit to Baltimore Archie stayed with Sam and Ollie May, and Sam used to drive Archie around to see sights like the Goldfield, such as it was toward the end. They'd sit there and daydream about what it must have been. Archie told me, just as Pop had, about two of his unforgettable nights in the Coliseum when he beat Jimmy Bivins after Bivins had knocked him out in Cleveland. I could imagine Pop in there, craning to see in the packed room. Archie remembered "people up on tables and chairs, and I was told there were even people standing outside in the street trying to peep in for a glance. They came out in droves."

When Pop went to the fights I used to wonder why he'd still be out when I went to bed. "If there's three minutes in a round and ten rounds, why does it take so long?" I asked my mother. She was the one who explained to me there were many fights on a night — ah, the undercard. But Pop talked only about Archie.

"What'd your father do?" Archie asked.

I told him he'd been a pharmacist.

"He must have known Doc Levin," Archie said. "Doc

Levin worked at Doc Caplan's Drug Store." I asked why he liked Doc Levin.

"Caplan's was in the black neighborhood on a corner, and Doc Levin — his name was Bernard Levin — extended credit to the people. He trusted those who didn't have the money to pay for the prescription. One day this old black man came in with a prescription and no money and Doc just gave him the medicine. I used to see Doc talking to people. He was a counselor, like a neighborhood counselor."

When Pop managed Read's at North and Maryland, I remember us stopping in on one of his off days and Pop being commandeered in an aisle by an old man carrying a shopping bag. He was buying a truss and didn't know which one to buy. Pop heard out the history of the man's ailment. After that, the man could not decide on the brand or size despite Pop's suggestion. To me the drawn-out encounter was a remarkable display of Pop's patience, especially considering that we were on the way to the stadium and might be late.

But then in *The Terra Mariae,* 1929, the yearbook of the University of Maryland professional schools, it's written of William Joseph Gildea of Aberdeen, Maryland: "Wherever you see 'Bill,' there also you see a group of fellows seeking his good-will and good advice. Unflattering in all his attempts to help out those who wish help, he goes to all extremes to further his purpose."

Al Aaronson told me that from trusses to prescriptions, "You never turned down anybody in need. Your father felt the same way."

"Beautiful, beautiful," said Archie when I mentioned how Pop and Al regarded their work. Archie said again that Pop and Doc Levin must have known each other.

"There're two people I really loved and would like to see more than anyone else in the world — my mother, who's in Newark, and Doc Levin."

Right then, Archie wanted me to drive him to Baltimore so we could go around and look for Doc Levin. Last time Archie had heard, Doc was working at a hospital. Not Hopkins. He didn't know which one. But we'd find him, he said.

I asked Archie his mother's age.

"Ninety something," he said. "She has one leg. She lost the other to diabetes. Doc Levin was a big help to me — I talked to him about the possibility of getting her fitted with an artificial leg, and just him speaking to me about it was a help. I want to visit my mother and Doc Levin."

As much as I wanted to, I couldn't accommodate either of Archie's wishes. I had to write a deadline piece then on Foreman-Holyfield for *The Washington Post* and knew for certain that my editor wasn't about to let me substitute uncharted expeditions with Archie. Archie got George Plimpton, who also came in for the fight, to take him to Newark to see his mother. Plimpton wrote up the experience in *Esquire*.

It took me two years to find Doc. But I finally learned that Bernard "Bucky" Levin, eighty-two, was living in Pikesville. Doc, who had an unlisted phone, turned out to adore Archie. One day Archie had come into Caplan's Drug Store in west Baltimore. He had friends around the corner, on Carey Street. "It was like a marriage — spontaneous," said Doc Levin. "It happened. We've been tremendous friends. I owe him a letter."

Doc knew a lot of the old Colts, too. Eddie Block, the team's late trainer, used to come into the store for supplies.

By then Doc Caplan had died, and Levin had bought the store and kept the name Caplan's. Doc Levin thought for sure that Sam Bruton had died, but he didn't know about Ollie May. I'd found out that Ollie May had been a waitress at Read's; possibly she'd known Pop, although Doc Levin hadn't. "It's a four-wall job," he said. "You always worked. I beat the hell out of myself. I could be in there at three-thirty in the morning, closed for hours but still doing things, and somebody would rap at the door. 'My baby's sick. I've got to have this prescription.' And I'd open up."

Sometimes the phone in the store would ring and it would be Archie: "I'm at the airport. Send somebody out in the car." Next thing, Archie would be in the store; he and Doc would be sparring, playing. "He'd call me 'Kid Cream.' He always had some name. Archie's a beautiful man. Archie is unhurt. He never had a cauliflower ear. He's unmarked except for a little scar across an eye because he fell out of a highchair when he was a baby. I know of no fighter who could roll with a punch like Archie could."

Archie gave Doc a ticket for the second row the night in September 1955 when he met Rocky Marciano in New York. Archie battled Rocky, knocked him down, and almost beat the heavyweight champion only to be floored six times himself before the end came in the ninth round. Archie told me of another night after a fight in Baltimore when he went directly from the Coliseum to the train station because he wanted to get to New York. He lay down on the cobblestones next to the track as he waited for the train to pull in. It had been a hard fight; he was tired.

He told me about one of his last trips to Baltimore and being taken to Joe Gans's tomb. "It's another thing I had wanted to do," he said. "I don't know where I was, but there was a highway near it." He had been just inside a gate of the Mount Auburn Cemetery, overlooking the Baltimore-Washington Expressway. There, a headstone almost two feet thick and black with age bears one word: GANS. The sun was sitting low above some nearby row houses when I went there, and I thought of Archie's description of his "prolonged sunset": "I've been looking at the sun for a long time, but it still hangs there on the horizon. When it goes down, it will go down all of a sudden."

◆

In 1950 we moved into our new home on Gwynn Oak Avenue, which Mom and Pop had built to their specifications. Harry Subock was the builder; Pop found his name on a sign attached to a tree in front of a house being built a few miles away. Pop liked the carpentry work, as if he knew a lot about it. But he made a good pick. Mr. Subock was a tall, kindly man with a stutter. He was the first person I knew who walked around his house in his socks; he had us over many times to discuss the building of our home.

It turned out the way Mom and Pop had envisioned it. It was compact — two stories, three bedrooms. But it was built with specific materials they insisted on and had saved for: Paxton-240 brick, slate roof, hardwood floors. It had an entrance hall and coat closet, a side door and small rear hall, a back porch with a glider. Mom planted a dogwood tree in front.

One Sunday morning in 1951, Pop and I had just sat down at the kitchen table for breakfast. Mom was standing at the counter next to the sink, preparing something — she loved puttering in her new home. Pop turned to her and asked, "Do you think we should tell him?"

"What?" I asked.

Were the Colts, having folded after the '50 season, coming back?

Was I going to have a brother or sister?

"What is it?"

"All right, tell him," my mother said. Her tone indicated it wasn't the best time.

"We're going to get a television," Pop announced, looking pleased.

A television! We were the last people I knew who didn't have a television set. If I wanted to watch TV, I had to visit somebody. I saw a Preakness at the apartment of a friend on Liberty Heights Avenue. I saw a Hopalong Cassidy movie at a neighbor's apartment on Maine Avenue. Even my Gildea grandparents in Aberdeen had a set — for my grandfather in his last years. My grandmother never quite knew whether it was my grandfather's sense of humor, which in part was aimed at baffling her, or his failing mind when some woman on Channel 2 would be on and he'd say, "She's talking to me. Just to me."

"Does he believe that?" my grandmother would ask my father.

My father would smile. "He's just kidding."

The news that we were getting a TV, broken to me just as we were to begin breakfast, took my appetite away — just what Mom had feared.

"What made you change your mind?" I stammered.

"Your father won it," Mom said.

His store had sold a big number of some product — I can't remember what — and, as store manager, he would get the TV. What's more, it was a console. A Bendix console with no doors — the doors were a nuisance, Pop said.

A Bendix? I thought I knew all the brands. GE had "Ultra-Vision." RCA had "Rotomatic tuning." The Motorola brought "the station nearer," made "the picture clearer!" The Emerson was an "engineering miracle." The Philco had "Deep Dimension." I knew all that. But a Bendix?

"It's the best," Pop assured.

The only problem with the one he'd won was that it had a twelve-inch screen. I thought, that's bigger than Uncle Eddie's. But Pop said he was going to pay about fifty dollars extra and get a sixteen-inch. I couldn't have been more impressed. I also felt faint and excused myself from the table.

"We shouldn't have told him now," Mom told Pop as I was leaving the room.

The next evening, we drove to a store somewhere on the west side of downtown where we were to pick out the TV. It was a time when appliance stores put television sets in their windows, turned them on, and attracted crowds that would gather rows deep on the sidewalks, looking in. The place we went amazed me — it was a huge room filled with black-and-white television sets.

To boot, Channel 2's Bailey Goss, a big man with reddish blond hair, was in this store doing a live show. Bailey Goss — the big afternoon personality on early Baltimore TV whom I had seen on other people's sets! He was standing in the middle of the room interviewing people or, more precisely, simply bringing them on and asking their names. That was all there was to the program.

"Go ahead, line up," Pop told me.

I did, and shortly got on with Bailey Goss and said my name. But I never found anyone who saw me.

Pop was even more certain about getting a sixteen-inch

set after we'd stood there looking at all the identical pictures of Bailey Goss doing his interviews. He looked "washed out" on the larger screens, Pop pointed out. "If you get one any bigger than a sixteen, you won't get that sharp picture." Bailey Goss, Pop was certain, looked "sharpest" on the sixteen.

"How 'bout the twenty-one?" I asked, with faint hope.

No, it would be the sixteen — the sixteen-inch Bendix mahogany console without the doors.

The store delivered. A few days later a truck pulled up out front.

I'd sit on the rug in front of the Bendix and feel the richness of its finely woven loudspeaker fabric. In the mornings I'd spend a few moments checking the variations in the different channels' test patterns. The picture was as "sharp" as it had been in the store — Pop had gotten a roof antenna. Mom thought it detracted from the appearance of the house, but Pop prevailed: "You can't get this kind of picture without an antenna." I was proud of the antenna; it was evidence we had joined modern times. It was 1951.

Because Bailey Goss announced birthdays on his daily show, my Grandmother Gildea mailed in a photo of Pop. His birthday was February 3, the day after mine. Viewers sent in the necessary information with a photograph, Goss would give the names, and the camera would close in on small snapshots of the celebrants. In her letter my grandmother referred to Pop as "Doctor Gildea." Although pharmacists then often were called "Doctor" by customers, I thought she'd taken a liberty with the casual pharmacist's moniker of "Doc." Shortly after Goss got to the birthdays he called "Doctor Gildea." But Pop's picture didn't come up.

"Where's the Doctor?" Goss asked. It was very informal. "Can we see the Doctor? Can we get the Doctor up there? . . . There he is. There's the Doctor."

Then: "That must be his little boy with him."

I was mortified. My grandmother had sent in an old photo. I must have been five years old. I was wearing short pants and holding Pop's hand. I hoped none of my friends were watching, and as far as I learned none had.

Mom happily recounted the "Where's-the-Doctor?" bit after Pop had come home that night. He was still in the side hall, getting his coat off. "Aaah," he said, shrugging. He had no interest in having been on TV. He didn't care that much about TV, except for sports.

Nineteen fifty-one was the year when the Dodgers blew a thirteen-and-a-half-game lead and the Giants forced a three-game play-off for the National League pennant. They'd split the first two games, and I hoped to watch as much of the third game as I could on our TV.

But I had a music lesson scheduled that afternoon. Classical guitar.

My mother insisted that I take music lessons, which I agreed to if I could take guitar — a result of watching cowboy movies at the Gwynn on Saturday mornings. A man we called "The Professor" gave the lessons but, unfortunately for me, taught only classical. Late one Friday afternoon my parents took me downtown to a music store, where we picked out a guitar. It cost $127.50 — so much money I've never forgotten it.

Each Wednesday afternoon after school The Professor would drive up in his baby-blue Cadillac with big whitewalls and an ivory-colored steering wheel. We'd sit on two straight-backed dining room chairs in the middle of the living room for the half-hour sessions. He tried to teach me a piece called "Elegy," holding out the possibility of my playing in his summer concert. But I never could master it, and, on that October 3 especially, I didn't care. I wanted to watch the Giants and Dodgers.

The minute the front door closed behind The Professor I lunged for the TV. Minutes later, Bobby Thomson hit his ninth-inning home run — "The Shot Heard 'Round the World" — into the lower left-field seats at the Polo Grounds for a 5–4 Giants victory and the pennant. Ernie Harwell was announcing the game on TV. Later, he did Orioles games before moving on to Detroit. Harwell's voice was the best thing about the Orioles in the mid-fifties after they'd returned to the major leagues. "Ernie Harwell is a professional," Pop used to say when we'd listen to him at home or on the car radio somewhere at night.

We'd watch games on TV together, too. Pop purposely had had the antenna aimed to pick up the Washington channels. Arch McDonald and Bob Wolff called the Senators' games on Channel 5. On "Dugout Chatter," Wolff would give the player he interviewed a Countess Mara necktie from Garfinkel's. Pop pointed out to me how well Wolff did television play-by-play, using words judiciously to supplement the picture. If Mickey Vernon hit a ball off Griffith Stadium's right-field wall, Wolff might say, "And there's Vernon pulling into second with a double." "What we tried to do," Wolff told me years later, "was like putting captions on photos."

McDonald and Wolff split duties on radio and television, with the veteran McDonald taking the first and last three innings on radio, still the more prestigious medium. So after three innings on TV, Wolff might say, "I'm heading over to radio, and Arch will take you through the middle three innings."

A soundless interlude would follow. The camera usually showed the pitcher warming up. Then came the scraping of a chair, and you knew that Arch, a hefty man, was getting himself situated behind the mike. A pitch or two might even have been thrown before his gravelly voice was heard.

I also found *Captain Video* on Channel 5, weeknights at seven. As "guardian of the safety of the world," Captain Video regularly foiled the wily Doctor Pauli. Captain Video was the ultimate low-budget program on early TV. The sets were made of cardboard.

Before the Friday-night fights, Pop and I watched *The Big Story,* heroic deeds of newspaper reporters. A *News-Post* reporter's story was on one week. His investigation had taken him to a street off Garrison Boulevard, not far from our house. I thought more and more that someday I'd like to work on a newspaper.

◆

With the Colts gone during 1951 and 1952 I'd scour the *News-Post* and *Evening Sun* almost nightly for news that they might return. While searching the sports columns, I fell in love with the newspapers themselves. Especially the ten-star *News-Post,* the final edition, which Pop would buy at Gwynn Oak and Liberty Heights on his way home. Sometimes I'd be with him when Reds, the paperboy, no boy really but a big man with a cap, would come huffing out from the sidewalk into traffic, whip a paper from the dozen or so he had stuffed under his left arm, fold it with a slap against his knee, shove it through the half-opened car window, and take the nickel, all in one deft motion.

I used to spread it out on our sea-green living room rug and gaze at the block numeral "10" bedecked with stars in the upper-right-hand corner of page one and the masthead, an eagle perched atop a field of stars and stripes with the motto YOUR GOOD NEIGHBOR above. The paper had come off the presses an hour or so earlier. It even smelled fresh.

This long-gone Hearst paper (circulation 227,000 then) was powered by large headlines ('DEAD,' SHE WALKS OUT OF HOSPITAL; THE MIRACLE OF MEDICINE) and editorials ranting against communism and, locally, gangs of toughs known in Baltimore as "drapes." The front page was always a maze of bulletins, flashes, stories that started in boldface type, and the inning-by-inning runs scored in the still-in-progress afternoon baseball games, and, say, the result of the eighth race from Pimlico. A "0" in the Cubs' ninth inning, for example, would have been done in the pressroom, chiseled into that small, saved-to-the-last-second portion of the front page known as the "fudge box." Inside the paper were one-column photos of "pinup girls," teenaged boys joining the military, and missing dogs. I memorized a weather ear that made no allowance for error: "Fair most of today and tonight, but considerable cloudiness and scattered showers."

Pop was always buying papers. He'd buy the morning ones when they came up the night before. At Baltimore and Charles streets outside the old *Sun* building, I'd jump out of the car, pull a paper from the stack that sat unattended on the curb, and leave the nickel on the top paper. The first time I did that I picked up the top paper and scattered change people had left, feeling miserable at the sound of the coins hitting the pavement in the dark. When we'd take our annual summer week or two at Asbury Park, New Jersey, about fifteen miles south of Atlantic Highlands, where Pop was born, he and I would go for the morning New York papers — the *Herald Tribune*, the *Daily News*, and the *Mirror* —

a little after 11:00 P.M., when the next day's editions would come in on the train. Pop wanted the Monmouth selections to study before he went to sleep, and if the train was late we'd wait in the car outside Goldstein's newsstand on Main Street across from the station.

Without the Colts, Pop would take me to the tracks and to the minor-league Orioles, a way station for young prospects on the rise and former major-leaguers finishing up their careers. Watching games, we would speculate on players' futures and he'd relate tales of older stars I hadn't seen in their prime.

At Havre de Grace I saw Howie Moss, my first Orioles hero, finish up his career playing weekend games in the Susquehanna League. He'd been the one extraordinary player of the late-forties International League Birds. Broad-shouldered, with a sunburned neck flaring from his white-flannel shirt, the right-handed-hitting Moss made his living by belting home runs into the convenient left-field stands just 255 feet from home plate in the old Municipal Stadium. "The Howitzer," as he was called, launched fifty-three home runs one season. Once he hit the hot-dog stand at the top of the bleachers. This Ruthian clout convinced me that he should be called up to the major leagues immediately. But Pop gently explained that Moss would be around for some time. He couldn't hit like that in the majors. Saddened only momentarily, I kept rooting for my hero. "It was nothing to pick up an afternoon paper and see my name in a headline on the front page," said Moss, who died in 1989. "I don't think they even do that anymore."

By the early fifties, The Howitzer had faded from sight. Then, one Sunday afternoon as Pop and I stood in the high grass of foul territory at Havre de Grace, I saw a familiar figure playing left field just a few feet in front of us. It was

Howie Moss. I felt sorry that it had come to this, a weekend league for an aging hitter. But Pop saw the scene differently, telling me that Moss simply was keeping connected to the game he loved. At length I understood.

One evening in October 1951, Pop brought home two tickets — to the World Series. He had gotten them, as he had our Bendix TV, as a reward for sales — this time from Gillette, then the World Series sponsor. Pop was expert at calling attention to products; he got ideas for window displays and aisle arrangements from a magazine he subscribed to, *Chain Store Age.* As Read's manager at Howard and Lexington, he received the World Series perk from sales of Gillette's razor blades, "with the sharpest edges ever honed."

From a box seat, no less, just six rows behind home plate at the Polo Grounds, we saw Joe DiMaggio's long, looping swing connect. I can still see the ball rise in the smoky haze of that autumn afternoon and land in the upper deck in left. Years later, I realized that it had been DiMaggio's last home run.

But for me nothing could take the place of the Colts. Late in 1952 the Baltimore papers carried reports that the Dallas Texans were headed for Baltimore for the 1953 season. For some reason the winless Texans were on TV, and we watched on the Bendix as they won a "home" game played in Akron against the Chicago Bears. I was worried that with the victory the Texans might not come to Baltimore, but Pop assured me the outcome had nothing to do with their future home.

It turned out that he was right. On December 3, 1952, the page-one streamer on the ten-star *News-Post* screamed: COLTS RETURN, IF 15,000 SEASON TICKETS ARE SOLD. Pop held it up when he brought home the paper that night. He said the tickets would be sold, and of course they were.

Part Two

I'VE ALWAYS THOUGHT OF Bert Rechichar — pronounced "Wretch-ih-char" — as the toughest football player there ever was.

He was the youngest of ten children from Rostraver Township, a coal-mining area in western Pennsylvania. He was born blind in his left eye. When he was twelve, his father, Paul, was murdered with a massive hammer used for driving railroad spikes. A man sneaked up behind Paul Rechichar and beat him to death next to a lonely stretch of Pennsylvania & Lake Erie Railroad track on a mountain-bitter November night. The father had been carrying two hundred and fifty dollars when he stopped at Tonkie's Beer Garden on the way home from helping his oldest son, Paul Jr., plaster the second floor of his new house. Rechichar's father had planned to pay for a cow that day, but the man wasn't there to take the money. The murderer was in Tonkie's and saw the roll of bills when Paul paid for his drinks. It was a little after 1:00 A.M. on a Sunday, November 15, 1942, when he began his shortcut home, following the railroad tracks.

As Bert and his sister Helen went into Mass at St. Timothy's later that morning, he noticed an ambulance parked in the distance. Two men were lifting what appeared to be a body. In church Bert kept looking for Paul Jr. When he didn't come, Bert suspected something was wrong. After Mass, Bert and Helen ran to their brother's house, but no one was home. They walked back to Hamilton's Grocery Store, where each Sunday they bought milk and the *Pittsburgh Press*. Ruthie, who worked behind the counter, had tears in her eyes. "Your dad was murdered," she told them.

The news devastated Bert, although what idealism he might have had already had been shattered by the urgency of day-to-day living in the hard hollows between the Monongahela and the Youghiogheny. His father, a retired coal miner, would say at the dinner table, "Go easy on the butter, boys, it's up to sixty cents a pound." Then the war broke out, and four of Bert's brothers went into the service and his three sisters worked in a factory that made gun shells.

Everything was gritty and cold, the talk was about Hitler and Japan, coal mining and football, and now this killing. A little change purse with brass snaps that Bert had given his dad was found in a pile of cinders near a shack. Inside the shack the murderer was found hiding. Rechichar never meant it this way but the fact is: He played football as if every opponent were the man who beat the life out of his father.

The first time I heard of Rechichar was lying on our living room rug next to Pop, listening on the radio to the 1952 Sugar Bowl. The University of Maryland was playing number-one-ranked Tennessee. Hank Lauricella was the star tailback of Tennessee's single wing, but not the Volunteers' best player in Pop's estimation. That was the wingback and Lauricella's blocker, Bert Rechichar.

"He's tough," said Pop, emphasizing "tough." He told me

about how Lauricella got most of the glory but that Rechichar deserved as much. I never thought to ask Pop how he knew, maybe he just read it in the *News-Post.* But I would soon see how tough Rechichar was. After the Dallas Texans' franchise was moved to Baltimore the next year and became the new Colts, ten players were obtained from Cleveland in exchange for five. Among the ten was the hard-hitting safety who the previous season had been the Browns' number-one draft choice. That was Bert Rechichar.

My father brought the news home — his tan coattails flying as he hurried in the side door that March night. I spread out the *News-Post* on the floor and studied the one-column head shots of the new arrivals. One was Don Shula, the future coach. Rechichar had a squinty look; I could see a toughness as Pop reiterated his attributes. Opening day was in six months. I almost wished the summer away.

On September 27, 1953, the Colts, with their marching band already in place and fans singing the old fight song, began their reincarnation against the Chicago Bears. It was sunny and warm. Pop had tickets on the Bears' side close to some scaffolding. The second deck of Memorial Stadium was being built, and the season was going forward despite construction, conditions under which no NFL season would take place after the league became a slick corporate enterprise.

In that 13–9 Colts victory, Rechichar intercepted a pass and ran for a touchdown and made two other interceptions, a game-saving tackle, and a game-saving fumble recovery. I recall the disarray of the stadium and the bright beauty of the day and the play that ended the first half and the feelings that accompanied it. The Colts were lined up to attempt a fifty-six-yard field goal. A rookie from Oklahoma, Buck

McPhail, was back to kick, but he couldn't kick that far. Somehow I knew that even before Pop said it. I felt a hopelessness about that kick just as Pop tapped me on the leg. Rechichar, number forty-four, was running onto the field. He was struggling to get on a helmet and fasten the chin strap and at the same time was waving off McPhail. The two men crossed paths. Rechichar would attempt the field goal. He'd never tried one his rookie season with the Browns, who had Lou Groza, nor during the exhibition games with the Colts. As I would learn, his teammates were as surprised as we were to see him sent into the game.

"What are you doing here?" asked Tom Keane, the holder, still kneeling to take the snap for McPhail and now looking up to see Rechichar.

Rechichar didn't know where he was, fifty-six yards away.

He gave it an old-fashioned, straight-on boot. It wasn't a pretty kick. It sailed low, booming forward like a big egg toward the closed end of the stadium. But wondrously it stayed aloft. I still see it as if in slow motion, carrying and carrying and, at last, clearing the crossbar as the gun sounded ending the first half. We sat back down on the wooden bench and wondered how he could have made such a kick. Everyone must have been talking about it because a great murmur lasted until the Colts came up the steps of the baseball dugout and ran out onto the field for the second half. The ovation spoke to the attachment of town to team. We hardly knew such feelings and had had none like them since Tittle.

The kick remained a record for seventeen years.

The voice on the phone made me think AT&T had connected with hell.

"Yeahhhhh . . ."

It was an anguished, awful sound. Bert Rechichar had the flu, had it bad. Call him next week, he said. The receiver crashed, and I had a dial tone.

I could understand how Rechichar put fear into people. Just his voice made my heart skip. It's said that some of his coaches were afraid of him, as were younger teammates and opponents, especially wide receivers, who faced his ferocious tackles and forearm shivers. I had called him with trepidation. And I experienced the feeling again when I called back and tried to explain myself.

"Seventy and fifty-one," he said in a rasp. "There's a Howard Johnson's there. Seventy and fifty-one."

He seemed about to hang up, and I rushed to confirm that he had given me two highway numbers. I suggested a day and time.

"All right."

Click.

At nine o'clock on a December morning I was in Belle Vernon, Pennsylvania, sitting at the corner of the Howard Johnson's counter wondering if I'd recognize him. "Bert, the football player?" said a waitress, cleaning up a spill with a wet rag. "He's always in and out of here." Just then I saw him between the glass doors; he was unmistakable. A big man in a flannel shirt and gray jacket, he still had the squinty look, just an older one. His bushy eyebrows and sideburns were gray. The crew cut was gone; he had a small pompadour. He wore jeans and tan boots.

"Bill," he said warmly, as if we were longtime friends. "C'mon over here."

We sat at a table in a room of empty tables, and the waitress put down a pot of coffee without him asking. He

Bert Rechichar, at home in Rostraver Township, Pennsylvania, 1991

poured for both of us and used plenty of cream and sugar. He stirred and kept the spoon in his cup. "I appreciate you coming," he said, lighting a cigarette, snapping closed his lighter. He was all shoulders and elbows and big, rough hands.

Rechichar is the roadmaster of Rostraver Township. Two nights before, he'd been out in the snow in a yellow truck salting roads until 4:00 A.M. He worked out of a building that he said was "three football fields away," lived in a little house "five football fields away." He leaned over his coffee cup and said, "My wife calls it the chicken coop."

Her name is Marty — Martha Frances, the second Tennessee woman he married. He gives people nicknames, and because she has red hair sometimes he refers to her as "The Flame." He used to call Unitas "Peas." It's a name he gives people he likes.

As a high school senior, in the winter of '47, Rechichar was shooting hoops in the Rostraver High gym — his last football season had just ended, and he was eagerly attacking the next sport — when a short man came up to him and introduced himself. It was Hodges "Burr" West, a recruiter for Tennessee sent by the coach, Bob Neyland, to western Pennsylvania in pursuit of prospects. Neither Neyland nor West had heard of Rechichar until West, while looking for two highly touted fellows named Parimucha and Ciaramella up in Masontown, received a tip from the proprietor of a country store.

"This guy was back of the counter whittlin' on a damn stick," said Rechichar, "and he says to Burr West, 'Fella, you should go down to Rostraver Township and look that Rechichar boy up. There's a ballplayer you want.'

"So that night we were practicing basketball, and he brought out this damn grant-in-aid. Never seen me play. 'Sign that grant-in-aid,' he said. And he didn't even have a damn pen with him. I signed to go to Tennessee with a red crayon pencil."

After that, Neyland had Rechichar flown to Knoxville and worked him out. Rechichar had to be back that night to milk cows, but Neyland saw enough in one afternoon to assign West to Rostraver Township for the entire next summer. He rarely let Rechichar out of sight.

"I had him loading hay and stuff on the farm," Rechichar recalled. "He said, 'Hey, Burt, it ain't this hot in Tennessee.' But he wasn't goin' anywhere because Neyland told him,

'Burry, I don't want you to come back from up there in Pennsylvania unless you bring that Rechichar boy back.'"

What Rechichar didn't realize was that he'd never get to play tailback. While playing on the freshman team, he told Hank Lauricella to call formation left instead of right in the single wing because Rechichar thought that meant he could drop to tailback and get the snap from center. Lauricella did and the two shifted positions, but the freshman coach stepped up and broke the news: Whichever way the formation was, Bert blocked.

"I said, 'The hell with this,' and I had my damn ticket to leave out of there and they stole my damn ticket out of my bag."

I told Rechichar I was sorry his field-goal record as a Colt had been broken — in 1970 on a sixty-three-yarder by the New Orleans Saints' Tom Dempsey. But his response changed my impression of him as rough and, perhaps, unfeeling. Dempsey kicked despite having half a foot, and Rechichar said, "I was glad to see a guy in that capacity do what he did. You can't say enough about something of that nature. The guy was handicapped in the way he was; he done a hell of a job."

The Saints, he said, had arranged for him and Marty to visit New Orleans — "expenses paid, they paid the entire freight" — to be part of a celebration for Dempsey.

Rechichar's own record kick, as he explained it, was even more improbable than I'd thought. With the half about to end, he had left the Colts' bench early and was already down by the end zone when he heard people calling him back. He'd been anxious to get into the locker room to relieve himself. Since he hurried onto the field for the kick, he didn't have time to think of anything.

"Hell, I'd have probably missed it if I knew how far it was," he said.

Outside the stadium after the game he saw Bill George, who played linebacker for the Bears.

"You know what George Halas said during halftime?" Bill George asked Rechichar. "He didn't say a damn word. Finally, we're going back out and he says, 'Hell of a kick, wasn't it, fellas?'"

Rechichar went on to lead the team in scoring in 1953 and 1955, mostly on his place-kicking, in interceptions in 1955 and 1956, in punt returns in 1955 and 1957, and in punting in 1956. One game he even played middle guard when that position existed, and Unitas stayed up late the night before telling him how to do it.

What Rechichar didn't do was conform. His first off-season job was as a whiskey salesman, calling on package stores and saloons. He could go into a place, shake hands all around, and stay put. He was captain of the "dawn patrol."

"They said I was runnin' with ill-reputed people," he said. In the NFL that means gamblers rather than women of the night. "That's why Weeb" — Weeb Ewbank, who took over as the Colts' coach in 1954 — "traded me. He figured I was fuckin' around gambling.

"There was a friend of mine, he was a numbers taker. But he never asked me anything about a ball game or nothin'. He was just a hell of a nice guy."

But Rechichar never denied anything else. One Friday night he turned over his car near Gettysburg and a farmer pulled him from the wreck. A battered Rechichar phoned the team doctor, who went and got him, treated him, and let him stay overnight at his house without telling the coaches. Rechichar played that Sunday.

In time Ewbank heard enough Rechichar stories to want to trade him or replace him in the lineup — Weeb tried every kicker he possibly could to dislodge Rechichar. It didn't help Rechichar's cause that one Sunday afternoon he put his hands on the round little coach, right on the sideline.

"Unitas was just starting out with Baltimore, and he was lookin' for a play," said Rechichar, lighting another cigarette. "Weeb turned his back on Johnny. And I grabbed Weeb. I says, 'He wants a damn play. He wants a play out there. Don't turn your back on him.' He didn't like that. It was the wrong thing because you're supposed to listen to your superiors. I've always felt bad about that. But when you get that adrenaline flowin', you think you might know what's right."

It took a while, but Ewbank got rid of Rechichar. Or so Ewbank thought. He had him traded to the Chicago Cardinals before the 1958 season.

"Hell, the Cardinals didn't even have enough uniforms to go around," Rechichar said. "I mean, they're pathetic. So I leave, I go AWOL. I go to Atlantic City."

"Atlantic City?" I said. "All the way from Illinois? Why?"

"Who the hell knows? I just went up there and relaxed in the damn sun. I'm up there walkin' the boardwalk, lookin' things over. And who do I run into?" He blew his cigarette smoke upward. "Carroll Rosenbloom and Don Kellett and Bert Bell. There they were, just walkin' down the boardwalk."

Rosenbloom, a Baltimore native and clothing manufacturer who owned the Colts, and Bell, then NFL commissioner and Rosenbloom's old football coach at Penn, were neighbors near the shore. Kellett was the Colts' general manager. Bell and Rosenbloom both liked Rechichar.

"'Bert!' they said.

"I said, 'Yeahhhhh?'" He told them he wanted to return to the Colts.

"So they talk me into reportin' back to the Cardinals. They say, 'We'll see what we can work out once you report there.'

"So I drive from Atlantic City to Pittsburgh, catch a plane to Chicago, and the damn Cardinals are at the airport getting a plane to Texas because they're playing an exhibition game in Austin against the Colts. So I get on the damn plane with 'em and I start the ball game. Of course I know the Colts' checkoff signals, and before long Unitas comes up to the line and checks off and I know what the play is."

He paused, coming to the memory of what he did best on a football field. "Glen Dillon, a receiver for 'em, came down and hooked, and I gave old Dillon a fuckin' pop, you understand, his damn eyeballs read tilt when I seen him lying there."

Rechichar coughed as he exhaled. "But Weeb never talked to me after the damn game."

He had been looking for some sign that the two could patch things up. But it was off to the West Coast with the Cardinals to play the 49ers.

"Old Pop Ivy was the Cardinals' coach, and he worked the hell out of me," Rechichar said. "I had to run so many wind sprints and kick so many field goals and kickoffs. So we play at Kezar Stadium, and I have a hell of a first half — I recover a fumble, kick a field goal. I was doing really good. Second half I kick off and who comes in to replace me but King Hill, and he's a damn quarterback.

"I says, 'We ain't got the ball.'

"He says, 'Pop sent me in.'

"I said, 'For me?'

"So I come off the field and go over to Ivy, and he says, 'That's enough, you go in and get dressed.' I think they're going to trade me, but I ain't heard nothin'. So the game's over and we go back to Rickey's Studio where we were stayin' and in a little while the phone rings. My roommate answers. It's Pop. 'Is Bert there?' I go up to his room and he says, 'Bert, it ain't because you went AWOL. You came back and you did excellent. You were like a gentleman. I appreciate what you've done.' He says, 'You're going back to Baltimore. Here's your plane ticket. The cab will be waiting for you.'"

Rechichar tried to look surprised. He actually was when he saw the cab so soon.

"I don't even get back to my damn room and the cab's already blowin' the horn for me."

But making it back to Baltimore proved an adventure even after he got on the plane. "I get bumped off in Tulsa, Oklahoma, and it's a Saturday night."

Two things Rechichar loves are country music and Saturday nights.

"Sunday. Monday. Tuesday. I finally make it back into Baltimore Wednesday morning. I leave my damn clothes at the damn airport because I figure they might send me out somewhere else, and I get a cab to Charles Street and walk in the Colts' office and I says, 'Hey, Kellett, you got any damn money here? Cab guy wants his money.'"

Kellett wore fine suits, with a triangle of handkerchief jutting from the breast pocket, and had a ruddy, clean look as if he'd just had a facial. Nobody said, "Hey, Kellett."

But Kellett paid and assured Rechichar the Colts were keeping him.

"But my damn suitcase is out at the airport," Rechichar told him. Kellett even drove him to the airport and then to training camp. The team already was on the practice field, so Rechichar changed clothes and ran down to the field. When they saw him coming everybody began clapping.

Ewbank ignored the fuss.

But after Rechichar got into the drills and intercepted a Unitas-to-Berry pass, the coach called him off the field. He told Rechichar they'd talk that night. Rechichar said that Ewbank did most of the talking, for two hours, telling Rechichar what he expected of him, which, essentially, was somebody he wasn't.

For the next two years Rechichar tried to be that somebody. He tended to stay put in a basement apartment that he shared with center and linebacker Dick Szymanski, a straight-arrow roommate from Notre Dame. The apartment was on an alley not far from York Road, and some nights after practice defensive tackle Artie Donovan would drop Rechichar off. Rechichar would have Donovan let him out at the top of the alley. Donovan never did see where he lived, only the figure walking off alone into the dark. "Geez, he was like a man without a home," Donovan remembered.

Rechichar drank coffee in the mornings at the Govans Café, which used to be on York Road. He'd sit there at the counter and talk, smoke cigarettes, and take refill cups. He felt exceedingly restless trying not to be the restless person he was.

He made little money — $11,500 one season was the best. He drove a '48 four-door Ford until 1955 when he needed a little cash and George Shaw joined the Colts to play quarterback and needed a car. Shaw used it for three more years. Then, shortly before he got married, Shaw said, "Hey, Bert, I need a refrigerator. Where can I get one?"

Rechichar had just won a refrigerator in a church drawing. In Baltimore, people always seemed to be winning something.

"I says, 'Here's what I'll do, George. I've got this refrigerator down at Sears, at the warehouse. I'll give you this damn refrigerator, you give me that car back.' I kept that damn car until I got out of football."

That was in 1961, when he walked out on the New York Titans of the American Football League — he could hardly run anymore. He'd been on the Colts for their 1958 and '59 championship seasons, but Ewbank had banished him to the bench. In 1960 he traded Rechichar to Pittsburgh. This time Rechichar went quietly.

As he drove away in the '48 Ford he had a long cigar clamped in the side of his mouth.

Rechichar moved around for a while after football. He worked for a crane service in Knoxville and coached the Knoxville Bears of the Southern League, putting himself into the lineup occasionally. He ran a bar on Harford Road in Baltimore called "The Top Kick." But eventually he returned to Belle Vernon and settled in with the Westmoreland Paving Company. In 1986 he became the township's roadmaster. He paves roads in summers, plows snow from them in winters.

He took me along a narrow road in his Chevy, splattered with salt and dirt. "I live right up here," he said, turning into a long driveway. We pulled up alongside a one-story house with aluminum siding. "It's all we need," he said. "It's just me and her."

Marty, in her housecoat, was sitting on the living room sofa watching TV. She had the flu and apologized for being disheveled.

"How ya' feeling?" Bert asked her in a loud voice. He stood in the middle of the living room like a gunslinger, his hands in his jeans pockets. He seemed to fill the whole room.

"A little better," she said, huskily.

Ordinarily, Bert said, Marty would be working at her beauty shop in town.

"Come here. Look at this painting," he said, ushering me a few steps into their bedroom. He pointed to a portrait of Marty above their headboard. It had been done in New Orleans more than twenty years before when they were down there because of Dempsey's kick. Her hair was flaming red.

The only indication that Rechichar had ever played football was a black-and-white photograph Marty kept on her dresser. He's in his Tennessee uniform, crouched forward, wearing a helmet with no facemask.

"Now here's my son Donald's daughter, Lacy," he said, picking up a photo from a living room table. "Twenty-two months. Donald lives in the trailer court."

"I have a grandson, he just got a two-year scholarship to Oxford," Marty said. "The clippings are right there on the table. I got 'em in the mail yesterday."

"There's that little Lacy again, right there, see her," Bert said, pointing out another picture. "She's cute as a punkin'."

He led me to the kitchen. "Right here's my damn telephone. Right here's where I work out of."

After a while, he drove me past a two-story white house where he was born and down into a hollow next to the Youghiogheny. As a kid he'd trapped muskrats there by the water in hunting season. We looked across the river to barren trees and a deserted coal-mining town. It's where his father had worked.

Rechichar worked about a mile away. Road graders and snowplows were parked next to the building. At a map inside he traced the road-clearing routes each of his five men took on snowy nights. "If everything goes right, we got no breakdowns, we can get all the roads done in five and a half hours."

A few minutes later we drove back to the Howard Johnson's parking lot. He had to meet a township commissioner there. The man was waiting in his car when we pulled up. Rolling down his window, Rechichar shouted to him, "Get your ass out of there, I want you to meet somebody." The man laughed.

When I looked back in the thin December sunlight, the two were seated at the corner of the counter. Rechichar already had coffee in front of him, a spoon was in the cup, and he was lighting a cigarette.

◆

When Hurst Loudenslager heard that the Colts would be coming back to Baltimore in 1953 if fifteen thousand season tickets were sold, he bought a set for himself and a set for Flo. Full price for all six home games was $18.75. Immediately, Loudy began buying newspapers and football magazines so he could learn about the new Colts. Soon he would know them not just in print but personally.

At Memorial Stadium in the early fifties Loudy and Flo would sit about ten rows behind the Colts' bench. The players could hear him until he made himself hoarse. He'd wait in the corridor outside the Colts' locker room until every player had left. Buddy Young usually was last out; later on it was Unitas or Berry.

Loudy just wanted to tell them how good they were if they'd won or encourage them if they'd lost. If they'd lost, Loudy would trudge across the empty parking lot in the dark with Flo at his side, she knowing his thoughts: *Why did those plays go wrong?* He'd drive straight home and go to bed, feeling an emptiness that food couldn't fill.

The Colts loved Loudy like no group of athletes has loved a man. I'm pretty sure of that. Fans can be nuisances to athletes. Someone who dresses in a team's colors and carries around a record player to play a fight song would seem eccentric at best. But the Colts appreciated Loudy's sincerity. He was their friend.

After a particularly tough defeat during the Colts' final years in Baltimore, quarterback Bert Jones on his way to the locker room reached into the stands — Loudy was sitting in the front row by then — and held him in his arms.

"I'm sorry, Loudy," Bert Jones said.

Loudy loved each of the Colts individually, like sons. He felt the same way toward his National Guard troops. "There's not enough love in the world," he told me. He couldn't go far in Baltimore without hearing someone holler, "Hey, Sergeant Loudy."

Loudy became known around the Fifth Regiment Armory as "Mr. Impeccable." Like a fussy homemaker, he took great pride in the spotlessness and orderliness of his supplies. He coveted "superior" ratings on the Department of the Army's semiannual inspections and received them on all but one. A lone "excellent" rating left him sputtering furiously. He kept dust-free shelves of pressed uniforms, bins of polished wrenches, cans of ink in precise lines. He put his most identifiable touch on an array of military can openers. He lined up the little contraptions row upon row in stacks of ten that he wrapped with wide rubber bands. Inspectors commended him heartily when they came on this eye-catcher.

Except for the "excellent" rating, Loudy's only other setback at the armory happened in the mid-sixties when *Life* magazine showed up to do a story on pro-football players fulfilling their military duty. Loudy happily showed the *Life* people around, thinking the Colts who belonged to his unit would be portrayed as devotedly serving their country. Alas, when the report was published the gist of it was how NFL players were avoiding the draft. What really crushed Loudy was the photo of Colt receiver Willie Richardson, in Guard fatigues, washing Loudy's car.

Being married to Loudy required patience, but Flo had it. She chose to spend every Sunday with him at the stadium when the Colts were playing.

"C'mon, hon, we gotta get out of here," he'd call to her at home on Sunday mornings.

"It's only ten o'clock."

"We got to make sure we get that parking place."

They repeated that each week. And each time when they got to the stadium he could take his pick from almost all five thousand spaces.

Loudy loved Memorial Stadium, especially its curved facade with the stainless-steel lettering dedicating the structure to the war dead. TIME WILL NOT DIM THE GLORY OF THEIR DEEDS — the words made his eyes water.

"They may tear this place down someday," he said, "but they better save the front and put it someplace where everybody can see it."

While others might have considered the stadium a haphazard pile of concrete and brick, Loudy regarded it as a pantheon.

He liked to linger in the men's-room-green-tile lobby because of its glass-covered urn containing foreign soil where American soldiers fought. That and the bronze wall plaques to Johnny Unitas and Brooks Robinson.

He loved Memorial Stadium's location. It's a neighborhood ball yard situated at the base of a slope from stone-and-stucco Tudor row houses of Ednor Gardens up on Thirty-sixth Street. On Sunday afternoons in summer, right-handed pitchers enjoyed the advantage of a backdrop of white houses beyond center field that made the baseball difficult for batters to see.

As he began knowing the Colts better, Loudy learned their birthdays. He'd take them cakes. Now and then he'd be tempted to ask Flo to bake a cake for a player, but he didn't think he should bother her. He'd buy it. Then one afternoon when he was going out to watch a practice, he remembered he needed a cake but didn't have any money. Finally he asked, "Flo, I'm going to leave in an hour. Could you bake me a cake?"

"A cake in an hour? It'll be red-hot when it goes out of here," she told him.

She only had the ingredients for a walnut cake, which she made from scratch and took from the oven just before Loudy was ready to leave. The cake was steaming, and she told him not to put a cover over it so it wouldn't get soggy.

"That was the start of something," Flo said.

Before the team left Baltimore, she baked, by Loudy's count, 726 walnut cakes for the Colts. Some of the players gave her a plaque that read: THE BEST LITTLE WALNUT-CAKE MAKER IN THE WORLD.

◆

In 1953 Toots Barger — Mary Elizabeth "Toots" Barger — opened the Liberty Heights Bowling Academy in our neighborhood. Toots Barger was, and is, Baltimore's "Queen of Duckpin Bowling." Toots was a hero of Pop's.

Pop missed my birth because it was bowling night.

Maybe he really thought he could make both events — at least that's the story he told my mother. Mom, as far as I knew, never held it against him. But she did talk about it. She'd been in Mercy Hospital early, nearing the conclusion of a difficult pregnancy. Pop had fair warning to remain close by.

But when the moment came, he was rolling for Read's. His game was duckpins — the squat pins that take their name from Chesapeake Bay ducks. The game was invented in Baltimore, supposedly by John J. McGraw and Wilbert Robinson, whose careers took off with the turn-of-the-century Orioles and who became famous as managers of the New York Giants and Brooklyn Dodgers, respectively. Little Napoleon and Uncle Robbie. They owned the Diamond Bowling Lanes on Howard Street, which featured small balls and pins whittled down by a local woodworker. McGraw, who became Orioles manager, didn't want the players to strain themselves with the twelve-pound balls used in tenpins; the duckpin ball weighs no more than three and three-quarter pounds and, having no finger holes, is rolled with the palm. McGraw and Robinson liked to go hunting on the bay, and after they mentioned that their flying stubby pins resembled ducks scattering when fired on, a sportswriter named Bill Clarke coined the name "duckpins."

In Baltimore the game mattered. Pop and I watched Toots on television. The annual *Evening Sun* tournament went on for two weeks during the Christmas holidays, and Toots won almost every year when I was growing up. We'd see her during regular guest appearances on Channel 2's "Duckpins and Dollars."

She looked powerful as she glided forward over the polished hardwoods in her below-the-knee skirt, releasing the

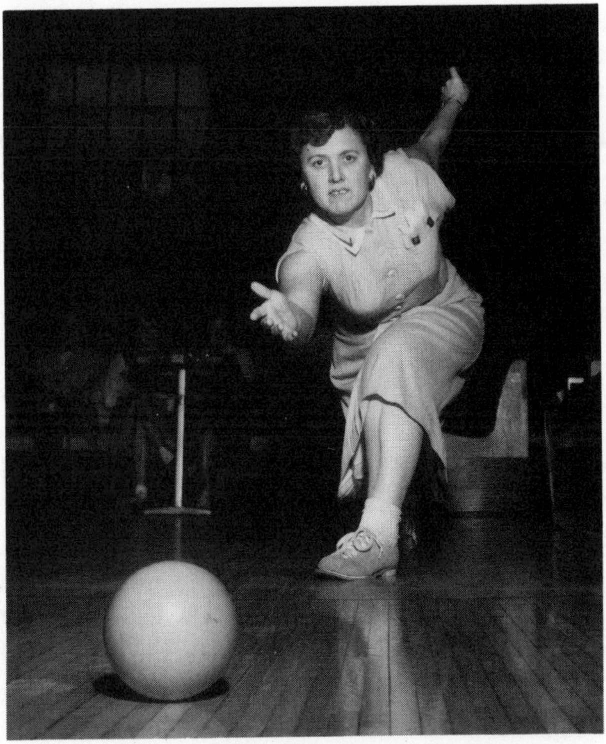

"Toots" Barger, duckpin bowling champion
The A. Aubrey Bodine Collection, Peale Museum, Baltimore City Life Museums

ball with more force than I'd ever seen. She could make the small ball do what she wanted with the slightest change of grip. Watching on TV, Pop would apply body English for her if a last pin was wobbling, and he'd sigh if it toppled. In 1947 Toots ranked number one for the first of thirteen times. Those were national rankings, but it would be a mighty stretch to say that duckpin bowling ever was a national sport. It spread a bit around the East Coast and into the Midwest, but that was it. Duckpins were almost purely Baltimore.

Pop's white bowling shirt hung in the bedroom closet. My mother used to iron it, putting up her board in the bedroom. She starched the collar. I didn't like the feel of it or the bagginess of the shirt itself — I tried it on and it hung just about to the floor. It had green lettering on the back — READ'S — and a scripted BILL on the breast pocket. I wondered how he managed to bowl while wearing it, but I knew he was good from the times he'd take me and I'd watch as he bowled with friends. The story is that he played well the night I was born, about eight o'clock. After his games, he came by the hospital, checked out mother and child, ignored the wrath of his own mother who had been keeping vigil, and set out to spread the word. He even spotted my Uncle Brad and Aunt Julia standing in line for a movie at the brand-new Centre on North Avenue and shouted the news from his car.

I don't know the lanes where Pop bowled that night, but Baltimore had a duckpin establishment in every neighborhood and he liked to move around. I loved the names: the Vilma, the Tivoli, Le Paradis. Some of these places were tucked away. The Vilma was in a basement. Others you had to walk upstairs to. The Arcade was above the North Avenue Market, a building with twin copper domes that also housed the Read's where he worked for a few years. One day Pop walked me up the stairway next to his store and I was impressed that almost out of nowhere there could be a room that size with so much activity, people talking and shouting and pins crashing. He also took me to the Recreation Centre on Howard Street, the mecca of duckpin bowling. Proudly, as if it were his, he showed me all four floors of this wondrous layout — a hundred lanes. There was nothing like it, he said, anywhere. I was sure of it.

It was at the Forest Park alleys on Garrison Boulevard that I had my first misgivings about the sport. Some of the bowlers made me nervous — youths with ducktail hairdos. Most had long combs protruding from their back pockets, cigarette packs in their rolled-up jersey sleeves, wooden matchsticks between their teeth. Some had upper lips of dark fuzz. It was my initial encounter with Baltimore's dreaded "drapes." When I was at Forest Park I kept my head down and bowled.

Toots always kept potential troublemakers out of her "house." The Liberty Heights Bowling Academy, strictly duckpins, was a homey place of a dozen lanes that you entered by walking down a long hall and up four steps. You could get hot sandwiches at the counter; they were premade, but Toots warmed them with a little heater. Schoolchildren from my parish, All Saints, bowled there, as did the kids from Howard Park Elementary School, located in the next block from Toots's. "The Howard Park classes from twenty, thirty, forty, fifty, and sixty years ago had a reunion and they invited me," she said. "Everybody was coming up to me, telling me how nice I treated them. They made me feel great."

Toots employed dependable, courteous, honest pin boys. She didn't want them demanding that the customers hurry. Some pin boys who worked elsewhere used to do this by pounding their hands or a pin against the side walls because they were paid by the game — three to five cents per. Wily as pin boys were, they knew when a big tipper was playing and often set the central and controlling five pin slightly forward, thus increasing strikes and spares and fostering generosity. Toots, though, was vigilant to such deception.

Pop had moved on from being pharmacist and manager

of Read's at Gwynn Oak and Liberty Heights avenues by the time Toots moved into the neighborhood or they would have met. She had come over from the Bel Air Road area ("Blair" Road, it's pronounced in Baltimore) where she'd grown up. Her parents called her "Tootsie." She had an older sister, Mickey. Toots got started in bowling by substituting for her cousin, who played in a league. Toots became renowned at the Vilma.

When she went into business at Gwynn Oak Junction she frequented the neighborhood shops: the jewelry store next door where she'd get her watches fixed, the restaurant up the street where she'd drink morning coffee, and Read's on the corner where she'd pick up her cosmetics and over-the-counter medicines to put in the first-aid kit she kept at the bowling alley.

There was a dentist's office across the street from Toots's place, and one day after an appointment with the dentist Governor Theodore R. McKeldin came over and bowled a game. "Mr. Republican" of Maryland, he was popular enough to be governor from 1951 to 1959 and twice mayor of Baltimore, although in the city his political party was very much in the minority.

I met him one Sunday morning after he'd attended services at the Howard Park Methodist Church, Toots's church, in the same block on Gwynn Oak Avenue as our house. A tall, sharp-featured man, McKeldin was known for his outgoing personality and flamboyant oratory. In 1952 at the Republican National Convention he gave the speech nominating Eisenhower for president. When I encountered him he was handing out campaign literature, which included black-and-white photographs of himself.

A kid on the sidewalk, I looked at the picture he gave me, glanced up at him, and said, "They should be in color."

"That would be too expensive," he replied with a loud laugh.

I walked home proud that I'd exchanged words with a governor.

Retired, Toots lives now in a small house on Chesapeake Bay. The bay comes up to her yard, and her glassed-in porch, filled with flowers real and artificial, offers a spectacular view of the water. The house is filled with shelves of knickknacks and glassware. A plastic white duckpin sits on a table. Ducks of another kind waddle on the lawn, waiting for her to feed them.

She's been there since she sold her bowling academy in 1968. Her husband died in 1982. She has a son and daughter, four grandchildren, and four great-grandchildren. At seventy-three she looked as strong as ever. Her hair was curlier than I recalled and her glasses threw me off for a moment, but otherwise she was the Toots I remembered. And she still bowls — three times a week, driving back roads in her '84 Pontiac to Dundalk on Mondays and Wednesdays for women's leagues and to Arbutus on Fridays when she rolls with war veterans. She goes to Pinland. "It's a nice scoring place," she said.

Her fame endures. When she walks through shopping centers in Dundalk or Arbutus people come up to her and say things like, "I grew up watching you on TV." Or, "You brought so much pleasure to me when you bowled."

Toots loved the Colts.

"At one game we put our feet into brown paper bags," she said. "It doesn't get that cold anymore."

She's been honored several times at Colt-related functions, and she's shaken hands with and spoken with numerous old Colts. Unitas, for one. She never considered being in competition with him when he opened his Colt Lanes in

Woodlawn. A huge horseshoe went up over the entrance. Pop and I bowled there once.

But the Colt Lanes failed a few years later. It was a tenpin house.

◆

Over coffee at John's sandwich shop in Locust Point, Mary Margaret Radomski and I were talking about the fifties Colts. Naturally, Buddy Young's name came up. We both held him in deep affection, for he was a tot of a player among the outsized men of football. He was five feet four and a half inches, 164 pounds at his heaviest. Eddie Block, the Colts' trainer, called him "The Little Giant."

"I liked his cute little round face," Mary Margaret said.

"He always had his chin strap unfastened," I added.

On the field, he'd zigzag fifty yards to gain twenty-five — pure excitement.

In the forties Buddy Young of the University of Illinois became the second black all-American, twenty years after Fritz Pollard of Brown. Young shared the most valuable player award of Illinois's 1947 Rose Bowl victory over UCLA and later that year was MVP of the College All-Star Game.

The first I read of Buddy Young was in a comic-book-sized football magazine when we were living in our third-floor apartment on Maine Avenue. The black-and-white cover photo beneath a yellow border was something thrilling to me — Buddy Young running at the cameraman with his cleats high, the ball cradled under one arm and the other extended as though to ward off tacklers, his chin strap dangling from his leather helmet. IS HE FOOTBALL'S FASTEST? the headline read.

At the time he played for the New York Yankees. I figured that Young was everything the photo and headline suggested because he played for some team other than our beleaguered Colts.

Years later I was stunned to learn of the reception he got during his first visit to Baltimore with the Yanks in 1947. Racists painted their faces with lampblack and shouted obscenities at him outside the locker room.

For good reason Baltimore was a worry to some baseball officials after Branch Rickey signed Jackie Robinson and sent him to the Montreal Royals of the International League in 1946, the year before he broke the major-league color barrier with Brooklyn. Baltimore was the International League's Southern stop. But Young took more abuse in Baltimore than Robinson.

"I didn't know whether I was here to play in a football game or in a minstrel show," Young said after he'd come to Baltimore in 1953 to play for the Colts. In 1953 Baltimore was a segregated city.

One of the first things he did was to have Colts tickets sold at a gas station in northwest Baltimore, where they'd be accessible to black fans. One time he accompanied a black florist to a floral design convention — all-white — being held in Baltimore. He got blacks jobs by befriending white business leaders and affably but persistently hammering at their discrimination in hiring. Geraldine, Buddy's wife, was with him more than once during conversations he'd have with some company's owner.

"But we've never had a Negro work for us," the businessman typically would respond.

"How the hell are you going to know if you don't try?" Young would say.

His clinching line usually would be: "All any man deserves in life is the chance — nothing more, nothing less."

As a freshman at Illinois in 1944 Young was turned away

Buddy Young, in his Colts
uniform in 1953
Courtesy of Ted Patterson

from a campus sandwich shop. He told his coach, Ray Eliot, and Eliot said, "Get on the scoreboard." It was Eliot's way of telling Buddy that he could combat racial prejudice through his ability as a football player. From then on, Young's short legs churned on football fields for more than one reason.

In Baltimore — preposterously, sadly — we grew up in a city of two distinct societies based on race — one of them subjugated. In the early fifties in Baltimore laws were enforced that kept blacks and whites separate: in schools private and public, in housing, in work.

One day — I was about fourteen — I took my three golf

clubs to the Forest Park public course near home — you needed three clubs to get on the course, and that's all I had. I was told, "You can't play today. It's 'colored' day." The man had to explain it to me. One day a week, I forget which one, was set aside for blacks to play.

In this environment Young set about on his course of persuasion. He had a catch phrase he'd use sometimes while explaining to businessmen that a person needed an equal opportunity to show he merited a job. Pointing to himself, he'd say: "It's not the size of the man in the fight but the size of the fight in the man." He'd usually get his way for two reasons: He was a Colt and he mixed irresistible charm and irrefutable logic.

The earlier Colt coach Cecil Isbell said, "If you don't like Buddy Young then you don't like people."

"Bert Rechichar would call the house," said Geraldine, a trim woman in her sixties. "He'd say, 'This is forty-four. Is twenty-two there?'"

Players would come over in the evenings, and long after everyone else had gone Unitas and Buddy would talk into the night. "They were always 'solving' all the problems of the Colts and the NFL," Geraldine said. "Finally, I'd have to put John out."

Just watching Young, you couldn't help liking him. For some reason I remember him in a 1954 night game at the stadium. The bright lights glistening on his helmet caused me to look closer. He wore his helmet tilted as if it didn't quite fit.

"Maybe it was the shape of his head," Geraldine told me, "but the leather helmet fit snugly while the new helmets didn't feel comfortable to him. He looked so funny in the new kind. He must have kept wearing his leather helmet three years after they went out. Finally, Bert Bell, who was still the commissioner, told him, 'Buddy, you've got to get rid of the helmet.'"

I keep this photo of him running around end for the Colts. He's wearing the "new" helmet. You can see spaces above his ears. It looks as if the helmet is about to wobble. Sometimes it would fly off his head. With the chin strap often unfastened, the helmet might pop up and roll across the field when he was tackled. He didn't like anything tight-fitting; when he wore a tie he'd always keep his shirt unbuttoned at the collar. His uniform shirttail hung out. But he looked neat in one respect: He was one of the first players to wear low-cut shoes.

"When I think of Buddy Young," Mary Margaret said to me, "I think of that run — 104 yards."

That was his kickoff return at Philadelphia on November 15, 1953. Mary Margaret's dad, Joey, and her Uncle Jimmy took the train up that day, except that they missed the train they'd intended to catch and took a later one. They ran from the North Philadelphia station to Connie Mack Stadium, arriving just in time. They were still breathing hard when Young took off.

"Thirty seconds later and they would have missed it," Mary Margaret said. "When Dad got home Mom said, 'Were you there for that?'"

Joey was still telling Agnes about Buddy Young when she fell asleep that night.

Mary Margaret listened to Buddy's heroics on radio that day. I saw it on TV. It seems to me he ran from left to right on the screen. So what if the Colts lost 45–14. There was only one Buddy Young, and the Colts had him. But when Buddy's brother Clarence was driving Geraldine from Chicago to Baltimore before the '53 season, she had her doubts about the city.

Buddy and Geraldine grew up as sweethearts at Englewood High on Chicago's South Side. Her maiden name also was Young, and sophomore year they were seated alphabetically — Claude "Buddy" Young next to his twin sister, Claudine, with Geraldine right behind Buddy.

Buddy went out for football, but encountered what he called "size bias." "Get away, you're too small," the coach said, shooing him.

Buddy used his father's address — his parents were separated — to transfer to Wendell Phillips High, where he made the team. He returned to score five touchdowns against Englewood and the coach who'd said get away.

During the war he played for a navy team near Oakland, the Fleet City Bluejackets, a powerhouse of professional players. In a star-filled game against the El Toro Marines at the L.A. Coliseum in 1945, Young made touchdown runs of ninety-three, eighty-eight, and twenty-five yards.

After scoring two touchdowns in the '47 Rose Bowl for Illinois, he played five seasons for the Yankees, who became the Dallas Texans in 1952 and the Colts in 1953. Geraldine arrived in Baltimore with three small children. She was eight months pregnant.

Roger J. Johnson took the Youngs into his home. Years before, Buddy had met Johnson briefly outside the stadium after a Yankees' football game in Baltimore. Before coming with the Colts, Buddy phoned Johnson, a realtor, to help him find an apartment, and for the duration of his search Johnson moved the Youngs into his row house on Smallwood Street.

"We stayed with the Johnsons until after Zollie was born," Geraldine said.

Zollie was named for Zollie Toth, the Colts' blond fullback from Louisiana State. Much was made at the time that a black player and white player could be roommates when the team traveled. But Buddy and Zollie were friends. It was that simple. Besides, Buddy had had a white roommate years before on the Yankees. He had told the talented tailback Orban "Spec" Sanders, a Texan, "I'd like to room with you so that you can get to know me and I can get to know you."

The *News-Post* said Young signed with the Colts for $12,500 in 1953 — but that came as a pay cut, according to Geraldine. Buddy told general manager Don Kellett, "If I earn it you can make it up to me."

Carroll Rosenbloom, the owner, did, with a bonus. Rosenbloom appreciated Young, too, not only because he could play but also because he recognized Young as someone special. At a 1953 team banquet at a downtown Baltimore hotel, Buddy and a tableful of friends were refused service during the cocktail hour. Buddy said to them, "Let's go."

When Rosenbloom and Kellett noticed Buddy was missing, they left the function immediately and drove to the Ten-Seventeen, a bar in a black neighborhood at 1017 Madison Avenue where someone suspected he'd be. They found Buddy having a beer with his friends.

"Come back," Rosenbloom pleaded.

Young declined, and Rosenbloom apologized. The prejudice made the Colts' owner livid, and he took his business from the one hotel to another. "The Colts along with Buddy played a major role in civil rights in the city," Geraldine said.

And just as he helped others, Young thought of his team before himself. Geraldine recalled him saying, "What good does it do to gain two hundred and fifty yards if you lose the damn game?"

In his third Colt season he was shifted from running back to flanker by Weeb Ewbank, and Buddy sensed he was being moved aside. Ewbank, like a coach, was no sentimentalist when it came to doing what he thought would win games. And he could be as stubborn as a man can be. Buddy hurt inside. But that didn't stop him from delivering to the team he loved his own replacement, Lenny Moore.

Moore, the Penn State star, had been drafted by the Colts but was talking of playing in Canada. Buddy went to Moore's home in Reading, Pennsylvania, and got the "Reading Rocket's" word that he'd come to Baltimore and sign. Buddy drove home that night in a snowstorm.

"Buddy was convinced Lenny belonged with the Colts," said Geraldine. Buddy, a star with a stunning absence of greed, had recruited Moore even though he knew it could end his career sooner.

In September 1956 Young found the roster crowded in training camp in Westminster, Maryland. One morning at seven o'clock he phoned Geraldine.

"Come get me," he said.

"What is it?" she asked.

"Just come on, now."

She picked him up, and he said, "I'm no three-plays-a-game player. I don't want to be pushed out. I'm retiring."

He announced it himself on WEBB radio, where he worked as a disc jockey. He was the morning man, six to nine. Count Basie's "Li'l Darlin'" became his theme.

When Geraldine listened to him she thought back to when they were younger: "He was always the smallest thing on the field. It was thrilling to watch him running from side to side, looking for an opening, then scooting up the field."

The Colts retired his jersey number and made him a scout. In 1964 Pete Rozelle, then NFL commissioner, hired him and he moved to Scarsdale, New York. He became the first black executive in any major sport.

He was known for sound advice. Gale Sayers was the most famous player to take Buddy's word and signed with the Chicago Bears instead of the then-rival American Football League. Sayers made the Hall of Fame and owns a computer company. Nothing satisfied Young more than discovering a black college player. He preferred roaming to being desk-bound. He'd drive America's back roads — some roads that weren't even on maps — in search of talented players. But once his job was done, often in some Southern town, he liked to get home as quickly as possible. He was a family man. He always went for the night flights.

"I would tell him, stay over in some hotel and get a flight in the morning," Geraldine said. "He would just roll his eyes."

On Labor Day weekend 1983, he represented the NFL at a ceremony in Louisiana honoring the memory of Joe Delaney, a Kansas City running back who drowned while attempting to rescue three children from deep water in a country pond. "He presented a check to go toward the education of Delaney's children," Geraldine said. "He could have mailed it. But Buddy wanted to give it personally. He was a hands-on person."

Before that event on Saturday he called home and told Geraldine, "Take some ribs out. I've found a new recipe."

Late that night he set out in a rental car for Love Field in Dallas, planning to take a 3:10 A.M. flight. It was to get in at 8:30 in the morning. But Geraldine never heard from him.

That afternoon highway police found his overturned car in a ditch near Terrell, Texas, about thirty miles east of

Dallas. Buddy was dead. He'd fallen asleep at the wheel. His watch had stopped at 2:25 A.M. He was fifty-seven.

Those who knew him, and those who didn't, grieved. "He had a lot of love in his heart," Unitas said. Buddy was buried in Chicago. Geraldine moved back to Baltimore, her consolation being that Buddy had been one beautiful guy and he'd been hers.

◆

Buddy Young was still scooting around defenders when the Colts first hit the newsreels in the theaters. Pop was a moviegoer, and if he wasn't enjoying himself at the stadium or a racetrack he was headed for the movies and taking Mom and me, sometimes just me.

Mel Allen used to be the sports voice on the *Movietone News* ("World light-heavyweight champion Archie Moore is challenged by middleweight king Bobo Olson at the Polo Grounds . . . Olson is down . . . Referee Ruby Goldstein picks up the count . . ."). And Marty Glickman did sports to wind up the *Paramount News,* "The Eyes and Ears of the World."

You could go from theater to theater and never see the same newsreel, although the reports were repetitious: Churchill or Stalin posing, Ike playing golf ("He tees off in a drizzle and uses an electric-powered cart . . ."), grim-looking heads of state shaking hands, reports from Egypt or Florida, the Cleveland Indians in spring training, barrel jumping.

When the newsreels mentioned anything about Maryland, Pop puffed up with provincial pride. He'd sit straighter anytime Glickman came on with dispatches about Jim Tatum's University of Maryland football teams or racing at Laurel.

Then one night — it was in 1955 — the Colts appeared to the blare of marching music. It went: "Dateline, Los Angeles. The Baltimore Colts versus the Los Angeles Rams, with thirty-seven thousand fans braving wintry weather to see the Western Conference leaders fight to hold their slender edge. It's touch and go, with the Colts roaring to the lead in the fourth period, sparked by Alan Ameche. But Tank Younger torpedoes the Colts . . ." The possibility of Colts footage heightened the prospect of a night at the movies. We were always going; one hot stretch of summer Pop took Mom and me eight straight nights because of the air-conditioned theaters.

Pop put adventure into it. He liked to drive to far-flung neighborhoods, all of them with fine old theaters decorated with chandeliers and lush tapestries. Sometimes two or even three of these edifices would dominate a single block. The multicolored lights of the marquees shimmered on the sidewalks. Lobbies had thick carpets, tropical fish housed in wall displays, and big circular marble water fountains that I would stand on my toes to reach as Mom tugged on me, warning not to let my mouth touch anything but water.

On Saturday mornings I'd walk up to the hole-in-the-wall Gwynn to watch a cowboy feature and a serial. It cost sixteen cents to get in, and you sat on hard wooden seats. My favorites were the Durango Kid, Lash LaRue, Johnny Mack Brown, and Buster Crabbe (Olympic swim champion turned "King of the Wild West"). Crabbe's sidekick was Al "Fuzzy" St. John; I liked his beard and sideways ten-gallon hat. One Sunday afternoon — out of football season — Pop took me to see a movie cowboy in person at the Pimlico Theatre . . . Monte Hale! Monte Hale told us from the stage that his horse, whatever the name, wasn't with him because he was out in a field teaching Trigger new tricks. I wanted to believe it.

A lot of Roy Rogers movies were in color, but I preferred cowboys in black and white. And cowboys who didn't sing. Roy and Dale and the Sons of the Pioneers always were breaking into song, interrupting the action. The Gene Autry films were mostly black and white, which offset his singing. That and a good right-handed punch.

Pop preferred Randolph Scott, Errol Flynn, John Wayne, Jimmy Stewart, Jimmy Cagney, Edward G. Robinson, and Alan Ladd. I was terrorized by Edward G. Robinson's portrayal of the sinister Johnny Rocco ("There's only one Johnny Rocco," Rocco rasped) and the storm in *Key Largo*. I couldn't sleep, I was afraid of drowning after *Wake of the Red Witch*. I cringed at the whipping Alan Ladd took in some movie that had him on a ship at sea. I cried to myself at *The Stratton Story* when Jimmy Stewart accidentally shot himself in the leg. But I still loved going to the movies with Pop because of everything involved: the different places he took me, the candy, the previews of coming attractions, which were numerous because the bills changed up to three times a week.

I knew the names of every Baltimore movie house. I'd memorized them in alphabetical order from the next-to-last page, last column in *The Evening Sun*. I'd dream of places we might go — the Aero (all the way to Middle River, which Mom said was too far), the Alpha, our neighborhood Ambassador, the Apex, the Apollo, the Arcade, the Astor, the Aurora, the Avalon, the Avenue . . . more than seventy neighborhood theaters. I always wanted to go to the Ideal because of the name; again, Hampden was declared too far. I never got to the Red Wing on Monument Street; it was a second-run house, but I was sure I'd like it because of the Rochester Red Wings, who played in the International League with the Orioles — I liked Rochester's blue caps with red bills.

Several times Pop took me to a narrow block of Lexington Street to the Valencia, a marvel to me because it was situated atop another theater, the Century. You could ride an elevator. Before the shows I'd sit with my head back on the seat staring up at the domed ceiling with a starry floating-cloud sky.

Sometimes on Friday nights Pop would take Mom and me for an early supper at Horn & Horn's cafeteria on Baltimore Street, then to Eutaw Street to the "Hipp" — the three-thousand-seat Hippodrome Theatre, which offered a vaudeville show and a first-run feature. The crowd would wind around a corner and down an alley. We'd come rushing along the sidewalk to buy tickets before the 6:00 P.M. price change from thirty-five cents to fifty cents.

Martha Raye onstage made an impression on me with a line about a skimpy dress that evoked rollicking laughter: "If it was any lower at the top or higher at the bottom it'd be a belt." It seemed racy.

Asbury Park, where we'd vacation, had a wondrous selection of theaters. "Philadelphia's Own Grace Kelly" got top billing over Gary Cooper in *High Noon* on the Lyric marquee in 1952. The Lyric was on a busy block that included Alice's Waffle Shop, Charlie's Bar and Grill, Vito's Hotel, Bo's Cigar Store, and Theo's Sandwich Shop.

The next year I fell in love with Audrey Hepburn. It happened at the Ocean, a white stucco box on Fourth Avenue near the water. Pop took us to see *Shane,* but it turned out to be a double feature and we walked in on *Roman Holiday.* Gregory Peck reaching out and undoing the tie, nothing more, on Hepburn's blouse sent a new sensation through me. It was the summer my face broke out.

I got over Hepburn. But never Unitas. We'd see him on Sundays and later in the week in the newsreels: "Baltimore, quarterbacked by Johnny Unitas, trounces L.A. . . ." With trumpets sounding, Mel Allen spread the Colts' fame on the *Movietone News.*

◆

On a Monday morning in December 1991, I walked up the sidewalk to a modest red-brick rambler on Patrick Drive in Oxford, Ohio. It was sunny and bright but as still as a snowy night. Wilbur Ewbank, known in pro football as "Weeb," came to the door — the only coach to win championships in both the NFL and the American Football League.

Weeb!

I had mentioned his name in the office one day, and a friend said, "Weeb! Is he still alive? You've got to go see Weeb. How old is he?"

Weeb, eighty-four when I visited him, looked fit except for a limp. He'd slipped down some stairs at a high school gym and pulled a ligament in his foot. Otherwise, Weeb was Weeb: short and round. His burr cut was grown out and combed, his hair whiter than when he coached the Colts. He wore brown checked slacks and a brown shirt. Light-rimmed glasses had replaced the dark-rimmed ones he wore when he finished up coaching with the New York Jets.

He had said he wanted to see me at ten o'clock because his wife, Lucy, usually fixed him a big breakfast at nine. Meals always were important to Ewbank. He gave his Colts "Saturday-night snacks" — hamburgers and even a couple of beers if the players wanted them before going to bed on the eve of road games. He figured they were going to drink anyway, so "snack" time would enable him to keep track of them at least for a while. Everyone had to stop in for the "snack" whether they wanted anything or not.

But the most important meal to Weeb was the team's pregame meal four hours before every kickoff. Weeb was intent on everyone getting a steak, but in the interest of team harmony allowed some variations in the meal. "It could get right confusing," said a droll Buzz Nutter, who played center for the fifties Colts. He told me that every summer during the first week of training camp Ewbank would hold a meeting that could drag on for more than an hour. Ewbank would ask each player individually what he wanted to eat at the pregame meal, and he'd write down the orders himself. What the player asked for, and Ewbank approved, he got before each game that season.

"'All right, today we're going to go through your pregame meal. Now what do you want to eat? Ameche, what do you want?'

"'Well, I want two eggs over light, baked potato, scrambled eggs — and bacon!'

"It got to be a sideshow. Everybody was in there sayin', 'Can you believe this?' It'd get down to Big Daddy, and he'd say, 'I want steak well done and I want a root beer float.'

"Weeb would say, 'Root beer float? You know we can't have all this stuff. Donovan, what do you want?'

"'Weeb, you know I don't eat before a game. I don't want anything.'

"Pellington would jump up and say, 'Weeb, you know damn well he wants hot dogs, but he's afraid to tell ya.'

"One year Weeb came down to me, and he said, 'Buzz, what do you want?'

"I said, 'Weeb, I want steak and eggs. I tell you what, I want one brown egg and one white egg, I want you to scramble the brown one and fry the white one.'

"He said, 'Aaaah, we can't do this . . .'"

"It ended up where you had all of the well-done steaks at one table, medium-well-done at another table, a goddamned rare at another table."

Most often Ewbank was the serious teacher, the product of a formal football background. He'd learned his X's and O's at Miami University in Oxford, known as the "Cradle of Coaches" for sending forth so many renowned ones, and especially from Paul Brown of the Cleveland Browns. Ewbank was strict and especially effective in one-on-one sessions with players. Some he'd threaten to fire. No player liked to hear, "Weeb wants to see you after practice."

His strength was his organizational ability, which he learned from Brown. He also was amazingly lucky. In 1954 he took charge of the Colts after they had won only three of twelve games the previous season. The New York Jets were as bad if not worse when he became their coach in 1963; as the hapless New York Titans they had finished last the year before and drawn only thirty-six thousand people to seven home games. But as he upgraded both teams, bringing in players and releasing others, he happened onto two of the most illustrious quarterbacks ever, John Unitas and Joe Namath.

Ewbank's good fortune, I learned, has continued in his private life. Since retiring back to Oxford in 1976, more than twenty-five years after leaving, he has enjoyed a bucolic existence. He gardens. He watches football games on television. He travels now and then to football gatherings. The oldest of his three daughters lives in town with her family. "Lucy belonged to two bridge clubs when we lived here the

Weeb Ewbank, in his home in
Oxford, Ohio, 1991

first time," he said. "When we got back the faculty one no longer existed. Everyone had died or moved out. The other one was still going."

For several years he suffered from myasthenia gravis, in his case a muscle weakness of the eyelid that causes the lid to droop. But the problem went into remission.

We were sitting in his living room, which has two televisions so he can watch two games at the same time on Sundays. But he wanted to show me his basement. Down there he has years of stuff, much of it in boxes. He has reels of football film stacked high; books, scrapbooks, loose photographs. The rest of the memorabilia is on display: He has a

Jets' wall, a Colts' corner, a section on his early days when he played three sports for Miami. He was a five-foot-six quarterback and a forward on the basketball team. "Today they'd say go home and grow up," he said, laughing at the photos of himself.

Baseball probably was his best sport. He began to play it as a boy in Richmond, Indiana, twenty-eight miles northwest of Oxford. "I could have had a tryout with the Cleveland Indians," he said, "but I didn't want to leave Miami University." He played semipro baseball for years, starting his sophomore year after he was married. He was still playing on the college team, but he needed the money. For the games that earned him five dollars he used the name Shorty Thomas.

Weeb looked handsome as a youth; he had a dimpled smile and combed his hair slickly. It was the first time I'd ever thought of him as young. Because to me he always seemed old. With the Colts he dressed for practices like coaches of the day: T-shirt, gray sweatpants or low-hanging football pants, a cap, a whistle around his neck. In one sense — tactics — he might have been ahead of his time, but he looked squarely a part of it.

Now he got comfortable in an easy chair near the middle of the basement room, propping up his bad foot. On the wall over his left shoulder was a '58 Colts team photo with a National Bohemian beer advertisement across the bottom.

In Baltimore Weeb and Lucy lived on secluded Murray Hill Circle off North Charles Street. On Friday nights he'd take her to dinner in Towson. Sometimes they'd venture as far as midtown Baltimore to eat, but "we didn't go all the way downtown too much. We didn't go into traffic."

He sounded like one of those overly cautious Baltimoreans. When the weather gets cold they say, "We'll see you in the spring."

In Baltimore Weeb rarely lapsed from this sedate life. One night, however, he went out with a guy named Sam, a bakery owner. Sam said to Weeb, "Let's go on down to Baltimore Street." That meant to a strip joint on The Block.

"Oh, I don't know," Weeb said.

"C'mon, Weeb, relax."

He tried to. "I thought I was doing pretty good. There was a U-shaped bar, and I kind of got down there away from the bar a little bit where I didn't think anybody could see me. Then two girls — strippers — came out there, and when one of them came down she turned to me and says, 'Coach, you think I would make a good guard?' I wanted to get out of there. 'Sam, see I told you.'"

Weeb wanted me to know that this did not happen the night before a game. "In fact," he said, "it was the off season."

Ewbank was superstitious and had his idiosyncrasies. "I wore this brown suit one time and we won, and I kept wearing the brown suit." Brown suits and a brown hat were his Sunday favorites.

"One Saturday night he went to church with the Catholic players," Nutter told me. "Then he had to go again with them because we won."

He believed in an occasional trick play, not only because it might be effective in a game but because he thought working on it would break the boredom of practice. He wanted perfection in practices. He'd jump in and stop play — and lecture — if anything went wrong. Once a fumbled snap from center sent him rushing up to find out the cause of the problem. "Ah, we were just practicing in case it happened in the game," Unitas said. "Oh, okay," said Ewbank, as players tried not to laugh.

Yet they'd work for him, and the best players would work the hardest. Ewbank loved Unitas and Berry for toiling long after practice had ended. Sometimes he thought they overdid it.

"One day I said, 'John, you've thrown enough.'

"He said, 'Coach, I just work here. You better tell him.'

"It was Raymond who was keeping John out there. Raymond always had a list of special things he wanted to accomplish each day. 'I just got two more things I want to do,' he'd say."

Ewbank stood up and walked over to the photo of the '58 Colts. He moved his finger along the picture, stopping at Unitas. I knew he had never stated whom he thought was better, Unitas or Namath, but before I would think any more about it he already was saying, "I never had to tell who was the greatest and I never will — I love both of 'em, John and Joe. But the '58 Colts, I think they're one of the greatest teams. The '58 team was better than the Super Bowl teams, better than both the Jets and the Colts of '68. And '59 was as good as '58. We had an easier time in the '59 championship game."

He was looking into the faces along the rows of players. "Just go down through there." They were posed on the grass at Memorial Stadium. "Look at Mutscheller there. Old fifty, the center, Buzz. Jim Parker. Look here, John, of course. Dick Szymanski. Pellington. Raymond. Leonard Lyles — he gave me his card, he's down in Louisville. Andy Nelson. Alan. Ray Krouse — he was a good pickup for us. The kid here, I can't say his name." It was Jack Call, from Colgate. "Ol' Rech . . ." That was Rechichar, but Ewbank stubbornly wouldn't talk much about him. Just: "He didn't conform. And, of course, that's the reason Paul Brown let him go, too."

Then: "Thurston!" And he added, "I told him the only reason I traded him was because I needed a linebacker and I had two good guards." That was Fred "Fuzzy" Thurston. He and Jerry Kramer became Green Bay's pulling guards who ran interference for Paul Hornung and Jim Taylor. Vince Lombardi won that trade.

"The linebacker never panned out," Ewbank said. "I'm sorry about it."

"Still?"

"Still."

Ewbank has outlived several players from his Colts teams. Remembering Sherman Plunkett choked him up. A huge offensive tackle, Plunkett was a reserve for the Colts. Ewbank later took him to New York, where he became a starter for the Jets. When Ewbank was in Baltimore for a touch game featuring players from the Jets and Colts Super Bowl III teams, Plunkett was close to death with cancer. The coach and two former Jets, Verlon Biggs and Winston Hill, went to the hospital.

"Biggs went in the room and shook hands and Hill went in, and here came old Weeb. I stuck my hand out and he said, 'Man, it . . .'"

Plunkett couldn't find words. Ewbank couldn't find any now. He dabbed at his glistening-sad eyes and turned to more pleasant thoughts. Lenny Moore. Moore could run and catch and break open a game in an instant. "I said to John, 'I don't care how you get the ball in his hands, you can toss it out to him or you can throw it to him or you can hand it off to him, but get it in his hands.'" Ewbank laughed. "Just get it in his hands," he repeated dreamily.

It took Ewbank five years to build a championship team, but at the outset no one dreamed it could happen. Pop and I were hurrying across the parking lot that September Sunday in 1954 when Ewbank made his debut. It was 2:07 P.M. We were two minutes late. The speaker at the open end of the stadium boomed, "Los Angeles 7, Baltimore 0." For some reason we'd parked on the east side of the stadium. Normally Pop used the streets on the west side. We would never park on the east side again, nor would we be late again.

"They must have run the kickoff back," Pop said.

It was more dramatic than that, and Ewbank said he'd never forget it. The Rams used the hidden-man trick on the first play from scrimmage. They huddled only ten players as the speedy Skeets Quinlan stepped unnoticed about a foot onto the field and stood in defilade with teammates on the sidelines.

A quick snap, and Quinlan was gone down the right sideline toward the open end of the stadium to gather in Norm Van Brocklin's pass and keep going. Quite a welcome for Ewbank as an NFL head coach. About twenty yards behind Quinlan was the primary victim, the not-so-speedy left cornerback Don Shula.

Driving home after 48–0, Pop didn't say much. "The play killed them," he allowed. We watched it on TV, on "Corrallin' the Colts," that Monday night, read about it all week in the papers. "They won't miss something like that again," Pop said. And they wouldn't. And after that season, the league banned the sleeper play.

Pop believed Ewbank would be successful because he'd been an assistant coach under Paul Brown. Pop could get awfully serious talking about Weeb Ewbank, but if Mom was around she'd silence him with, "You mean Eub Weebank."

Settled again in his chair, Ewbank affirmed that coaching under Brown "was the greatest thing that ever happened to me."

The two met after Brown had transferred from Ohio State to Miami of Ohio. Brown was a sophomore, Weeb a senior. In 1943 both were in the service at the Great Lakes Naval Station in Waukegan, Illinois, and Brown asked Ewbank to assist him with the football team. Ewbank coached the offensive backs. In 1948 Brown phoned Ewbank and asked him to coach the offensive tackles on his Cleveland Browns. "God, Paul," Ewbank remembers saying, "you don't want me to coach your tackles. He said, 'Don't worry about it.'" Ewbank learned every aspect of football as Brown taught it. After Ewbank got to Baltimore, the Colts took on a resemblance to the Browns. They lined up like the Browns. They ran plays like the Browns; the fullback delay was an obvious copy. But the results often were the opposite — they were swarmed over. They still were the Colts.

Then things changed. Along came Unitas, and unlike Brown, who called each play for his quarterback by shuttling linemen, Ewbank let his quarterbacks call their own plays. Unitas found a freedom he'd known on the Pittsburgh sandlots. At least that's how it looked. But if Unitas did as he pleased, he did so within the covers of Ewbank's playbook. Ewbank taught Unitas the plays and how to change them at the line of scrimmage. Each game Ewbank worked up a list of what he called "good plays" — ones he thought had the best chance of working against the opponent. Thus armed, Unitas ran the game.

More often than not, Ewbank wouldn't call a specific play even when Unitas asked for one. Marchetti, who'd be standing there on the sideline, remembered conversations between Ewbank and Unitas when Unitas would come over looking for a play during a break in the action.

"'Whadya got?' John would say.

"'Whadda you got?' Weeb would say.

"'Ah, c'mon, Weeb . . .'

"'Well, John . . .'

"And Weeb would hesitate on what he would want to call, and I seen John say, 'I'll get the first down,' and go in without any direction at all."

Unitas would turn and trot — with little steps, head and shoulders bent — back to the huddle. He was apt to call any play no matter how obscure — as long as it was in the playbook. Ewbank might have put it in back in training camp, but as long as it was in there Unitas would summon it up and his teammates had better know it.

"If somebody would miss a block," Ewbank recalled, "he'd say, 'Goddamnit, what are you trying to do, get me killed? C'mon, do your job.' He was different. He'd give 'em hell if they didn't do something. He'd beat me to it a lot of times. He was a fighter, I'll tell you."

I asked Ewbank if he believed the story Donovan told in his book *Fatso*. ". . . During the 49er game in 1958 here in Baltimore, Unitas kept calling Lenny Moore's number in the huddle, and Moore kept slashing through the San Francisco defense. So after about half a dozen straight runs by Moore, Lenny came back to the huddle and told John, 'Hey, man, cool it. I'm getting tired.' Whooa. Nobody tells John Unitas to 'cool it.' Parker says Unitas's face turned into a flinty stare, and his eyeballs nearly burned a hole through Lenny's head. 'Listen, asshole, nobody tells me to cool it,' Unitas said. 'I'll run your ass till you die.' He put the fear of God in him, and by this time Lenny's stammering, 'Forget it,

John. Forget I said anything. Give me the ball, please. Give me the ball on every play.'"

Weeb chuckled. "I don't doubt it," he said.

"John likes to tell this story on me. He'll say, 'Yeah, Weeb used to send in plays once in a while. Like he told me, "Get a first down."'" Weeb actually did.

"John had the habit of going for the touchdown when he'd get down around the twenty, and he'd get intercepted once in a while down there. I always said, two times ten — go for two first downs. I remember a third and about eight at the twenty and I sent in a guy: 'Tell him, get a first down.'" Unitas threw for a touchdown.

In 1973 Ewbank retired from coaching. He stayed with the Jets two more years as vice president and general manager, and after that went back to Oxford. He had a regret. "I had neglected my family so long," he said.

He mentioned Charley Winner, his former quarterback at Washington University in St. Louis who married Weeb's middle daughter. Weeb hired his son-in-law as an assistant coach with the Colts but worried that others would think he favored Winner. "I was mean to him, really," Ewbank said. "When it'd come to Christmastime, I'd make Charley go to the bowl games. I really made it tough on Nancy. But if somebody had to miss a Christmas at home, poor Charley, he was the one who had to do it."

Taking the stairs slowly, Weeb suggested that football required sacrifices and had its uncertainties, as if trying to come to terms about his treatment of Charley.

I reminded him of what Pop had told me was Weeb's finest move, just after he'd done it. It was one of the first things he did after signing his $17,500 contract for '54. He switched Marchetti from offensive tackle to defensive end.

Marchetti knew all along what position he should be playing but was never inclined to say much. Then Ewbank told him the plan. Here is the entire conversation:

"Gino, play defensive end," Ewbank said.

"Thank you, sir," Marchetti replied.

Ewbank had only one complaint with Marchetti: "We had a hard time getting a necktie on him. He didn't want to come to banquets because he didn't like to dress up."

But if Ewbank asked Gino to stay after practice and help an offensive lineman he'd stay — gladly. "He'd give you everything, he'd just give you all he had," Ewbank said. "One day our assistant coach Johnny Bridgers wanted to help this rookie with his blocking, and he got Gino to give him some hard rushes. Gino would come in, grab him, and throw him.

"'Get lower, you're too high,' Johnny Bridgers would tell the rookie. He'd get lower. Every play the kid kept getting lower and lower and finally Gino came in and went right over the top of him. Leapfrogged him. The kid says, 'Now what do I do?' Johnny Bridgers says, 'Just applaud.'" Ewbank laughed again at his recollections. "Just applaud," he said.

We were at the front door and I had my coat on, buttoning it. But I was just standing there. Weeb was silent. He was journeying in his mind half a lifetime back to Baltimore, where Gino was crashing into quarterbacks, back when it seemed as if he'd do it forever.

◆

One evening Mike Gregor picked me up in west Baltimore and drove me around the beltway toward Glen Burnie. We talked about Gino Marchetti. In 1982 Marriott paid $48.6 million for the Gino's empire — 313 Gino's fast-food stores, 43 Kentucky Fried Chicken outlets, and 113 Rustler Steak Houses. Only one Gino's remained, and we were headed toward it.

Mike, a police officer at Baltimore-Washington International Airport, grew up as an only child of a broken home, and when he was five or six years old his mother, Doris, thought it would be a good idea to get him around a ballplayer who would be a good influence. At the time, Gino Marchetti was opening up his new fast-food places, and the drawing card was Gino. He would appear in person at every opening.

"My mom and I went around to the openings and stood in line just to get his autograph," Mike said. "We went to the openings in Dundalk, on North Avenue, on Edison Highway and Sinclair Lane. We went to every one where Gino was going to be. After a while he began recognizing me. Gino started making the statement that his places weren't officially open until I got there. The way I was brought up, I wasn't a smart aleck. I stood, I was quiet, I was mannerly, and I guess he noticed that. I guess because of that Gino started taking me into the locker room."

Gino took Mike into the Colts' locker room every Sunday when the team played at home. He took Mike in not just after the game, when assorted hangers-on crowd into teams' locker rooms. Gino took Mike in before the games. Each Sunday for years Gino did it. It was hard to believe — and a lot of Mike's boyhood friends were skeptical. Mike himself could hardly believe it.

There was Unitas on one side of the room, loosening up, zinging passes to Berry a few feet away. Mike remembers the sound of the spin Unitas put on the ball.

Mike Gregor and Gino Marchetti, photographed by Charles Hart of the old *Baltimore News-Post*
The Hearst Corporation

"If Gino left his locker to go into the training room or someplace, he'd just say, 'Wait here,' and I'd wait right in front of his locker. I wouldn't move. Gino was larger than life, a massive man, and there I was, right with him."

Marchetti was swarthy, with coal-black hair that fell across his forehead. He stood six feet five but seemed even taller. In the beginning Mike only came up to Gino's belt. He wasn't much taller when he "officially" opened the Gino's we were going to on Mountain Road, off Ritchie Highway, the last place you could get a Gino's Giant, the double-decker burger.

Driving along, Mike was saying, "The old players, they didn't work out like football players today. The most they lifted was like Donovan, twelve ounces at a time. But they were strong and tough. A lot of them had been in the war. Gino had just turned eighteen when he was in the Battle of the Bulge."

When Mike was growing up he also visited Gino during the off-season at his offices in Towson Plaza. Gino was partners with teammate Alan Ameche, who had his own drive-ins. Ameche's featured a hamburger called "The Powerhouse," similar to the Gino's Giant. Ameche's places had the little figure of Ameche in his Colts' uniform with the number thirty-five rotating slowly on the sign out front. I used to go to the one on Reisterstown Road.

Mike would watch Gino and Ameche at work.

"They were hands-on owners, just getting started. They were in every day or they were out at the stores. I think the biggest thing about Gino, the one thing that I could put into my own life, was that there was no foolishness about him. He knew when to have a good time, but he was all business whether he was working or playing ball."

Mike turned left onto Mountain Road — we were getting close — when he said something about the way Marchetti played that came as a surprise to me.

"Gino was double-teamed every play" — that much I knew. And then: "He lined up offside."

"You think his helmet was over the line?" I wondered.

"His whole body was over the line," Mike said emphatically.

"You think?"

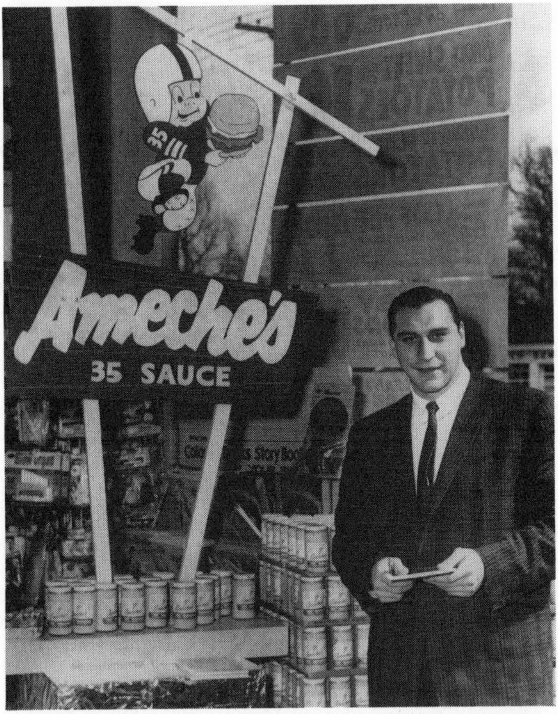

Alan Ameche, who wore number thirty-five, taking orders for his Ameche's "35" Sauce. The photo was taken by James Lightner of the *News-Post*.
The Hearst Corporation

"Oh, yeah. If you ever saw pictures, you'd see it. You could pick it right up."

"How could he get away with it?"

"No official was going to say anything to Gino."

This I would have to be convinced of.

"He was quick off the snap," I said, changing the subject slightly.

"Oh, amazing. His first step was just amazing. And I'll

tell you, the guy who played alongside him was fast off the line, too. Donovan. They had a first step like Brooks Robinson's. Their reaction time was like that" — he snapped his fingers. "Of course, Donovan ran a two-minute ten yards."

As he kept driving, I said, "I never would have found this place."

"It's not a place you just drop by," he said. "You've got to want a Gino's Giant to come here."

Finally, there it was. The last Gino's in America. GINO'S. HOME STYLE HAMBURGERS, the sign said. The building was set back, partially obscured by a frame house next door. It was across the street from a used-car lot with lights blazing down on the cars.

"I'll take a Giant and a small diet Coke," I said, following Mike's lead.

We sat at a table at the front window. Mike talked.

"One day I was in the locker room and a security guard came up to me and told me I'd have to leave. I was going to walk out the door and Gino yells, 'Where are you taking him?' And the security guard says, 'He doesn't belong in here.' And Marchetti comes over and says, 'As long as I say he belongs here, he belongs here.' The security guard and I became very good friends to the day he retired. His name was Smitty."

Sometimes at the stadium Mike would go out on the sidelines for warm-ups; if it was cold he'd go back into the locker room. "It was like being at home," he said. Some games he sat on the bench; most of the time he sat in the stands with his mother. After the game he'd go back inside the locker room with Gino. Mike said he never will forget the riveting moments inside the room before kickoff.

Donovan, the fun guy usually, spent time in the bathroom, throwing up from anxiety. "The intensity in Gino's face was unbelievable," Mike said. "People talk about players having a 'game face.' Gino had 'game eyes.'" Marchetti smoked in a little room next to the locker room.

Just before the introductions the players would all pile out the door, not too much with the rah-rah stuff, just breathing hard, Mike said. During the games Mike would watch Gino more than the other players. "He would come out of the defensive huddle, and he'd get down on one knee and wait. Then he'd crawl on both knees to get up into his stance. He would stay there, like a snake just coiled and ready.

"Then he'd just throw people aside to get to the quarterback. Throw 'em aside, just that simple. On the sideline, he was always walking. Never stood still.

"But as mean as he was on the field is how gentle he was when he took off his uniform. He played a game in '64 when he was kicked in the head and knocked unconscious. They took him off the field on a stretcher, and his arm was just flopped over the side. The next night he was supposed to do an appearance at Hamburgers clothing store in downtown Baltimore. He made the appearance, and it wasn't for the money because the money was next to nothing. He'd made the commitment to be there.

"Gino retired after that season, but in 1966 the defensive line was decimated by injuries and Rosenbloom asked him to come back in the middle of the season. The Colts' offices were on Howard Street then, across from the bus station. When Gino walked in, Rosenbloom said to him, 'I've signed it. Just fill in what you want.' I never asked Gino what it was."

Gino gave Mike a job when he turned sixteen, and he worked his way through senior year at Northern High School and two years at the Community College of Baltimore behind the counter at Gino's. The last time he saw Marchetti, who'd relocated outside Philadelphia, was in 1986, when Gino was inducted into a Maryland football hall of fame. Marchetti was signing autographs before the event, but stopped when he saw Mike and his mom. He came over and hugged them, kissed Doris. Gino was as great as ever to them.

"I think in 2019 when they name the first team for the first hundred years he'll be the best defensive end. I fully expect it — I guess I'll still be here."

I thanked Mike for bringing me to the last Gino's.

"The Giant still tastes different from the Big Mac," he said.

As I put my tray on the stack, Mike turned. "Let me get one of these for Mom."

"You bringing her a Giant?"

"Yeah."

Walking out, Mike carried the Giant in a bag. He looked happy.

"I'll drop it off to her on my way home."

A few months later, the last Gino's closed.

◆

Gino Marchetti went a long way in life without a plan. He survived a world war he might have avoided. He never sought fame, and after it found him he didn't have much to do with it. He became a multimillionaire in a business he initially knew nothing of and had to be talked into.

Marchetti had a midlife crisis; in fact, it almost killed him. He'd get to that as we talked in the noonday quiet of his modest Wayne, Pennsylvania, town house. But first he said,

"God, I've been lucky, believe me." He looked relatively unchanged from his playing days — of course he played until he was forty-two. At sixty-five his sideburns were white, but the head of hair still was mostly black. He seemed very much at peace. It was a peace he'd known most of his life, lost, and found again — in part through the fifty-seven-pound white marlin that hung on his rec room wall. He'd get to that story, too.

His parents, Ernest, and his tiny mother, the five-foot-two Maria, were born in Italy. As was the custom, the oldest brother set out for America in search of a better life. That was Ernest's brother, John, who found mining work in West Virginia. John wrote home, Ernest followed. Gino was born near Smithers, West Virginia, in a town that no longer exists. He was the sixth of seven children. Shortly, John set out for California in search of something still better. He settled in Antioch, near San Francisco, wrote, and once more Ernest followed.

Gino grew up as the scourge of Antioch. "I was what you call, maybe, a little wild," he said. "Compared with what they do now, I was an angel. But I had gotten into a little trouble with one of the teachers. So they were going to throw me out of school. I had a choice: If I got thrown out of school, I'd have had to go home and face my father, or I could join the service — they automatically gave you your diploma if you were a senior and went in the service. I joined the service. I was thinking of the moment, not realizing what was on the other end, that, Jesus, in four or five months, I could be over there shooting at somebody or somebody could be shooting at me. I never once gave that a thought. I didn't realize it till we were right there on the front line."

He was among the American forces colliding with the

German offensive near the Meuse River in Belgium. It was the Battle of the Bulge. "I'll never forget, artillery shells going psssssst, whistling. Me and this guy McKinney hitting the mud. Me looking at him, him looking at me. You know, 'Get us out of here.'"

But within days the Germans were being pushed back, and Gino's division was the first to make contact with the Soviet troops. Along the way Gino carried a machine gun "through the fields and up the hills. It was a challenge — there was a guy on one side of me named Miller, and he was carrying a gun. He was six feet nine, a little bigger than me. I used to look at him and he'd be carrying that son of a bitch and as long as he kept carrying it, I kept carrying mine. If he put his gun down, I'd put mine down. That was the competitiveness in me.

"Over there really changed me. When I heard the shells that first time, I thought about all the things in life that I did wrong to my mother. I thought about everything, including the time she threw something at me and hit her new stove and nicked it. I made a vow that if I ever got home that my life would change, which it did. I became more responsible, a better family member than I had been."

He came home during the summer of '46, "took my uniform off and put my Levi's on and it was like I was never away." He went to work as a bartender for his oldest brother, Leo. And he played a little football. Another brother, Itsie, and a friend, Nick Rodriguez, put together a sandlot team. "They were great athletes, at the time much better than I was. But I guess the biggest break of my life was one day when a couple of us were on the way to play in San Francisco and I was driving by my house and I seen a red Chevrolet parked in front. I said, 'Geez, let's go see who's at the house.'"

It turned out to be two football coaches from Modesto Junior College. They were in the living room talking to Itsie and Nick, recruiting them. Gino sat down and listened.

"They must have talked about thirty minutes," he said. "Never said one word to me. As they were leaving — I'll never forget this — one of them, Stan Pavko, the line coach, looked at me and said, 'You look like you're big enough to play. Why don't you tag along?' His exact words."

Gino did. He was the only one of the three to stay. While there, a University of San Francisco scout saw him play. When the scout came looking for him, Gino was tending bar at Leo's.

"I was smoking a cigarette," Marchetti said. "He introduced himself — his name was Brad Lynn — and he said, 'How'd you like to come to USF and play football?'"

Gino never imagined such an opportunity. "I dropped the cigarette. I stomped on it, I swear to God, I stomped on it."

All he had to do was meet the coach, Lynn told him. That was Joe Kuharich, who later coached at Notre Dame and in the pros.

Marchetti roared onto the campus on his motorcycle.

His hair was long, and it flew in the breeze. He wore a black leather jacket and boots.

"In those days," he said, "if you had a leather jacket, the more zippers you had the cooler you were. I had seventeen zippers. So I was pretty cool.

"After we'd had our meeting and I'd left, Lynn told me that Kuharich called him in. Kuharich said, 'Where'd you get that Okie?'

"But I guess Brad said, 'Wait a minute, he can play football. Give him a chance.' Thank God, they gave me the chance."

USF might have been the best little-known college team there ever was. Nine of its players made it to the pros. Two made the pro football Hall of Fame, Marchetti and Ollie Matson. The New York Yankees football team drafted Marchetti for the 1952 season, then the team was moved to Dallas. After playing the 1952 season with the Texans, Marchetti arrived in Baltimore when the franchise was moved again. The Colts' coach in 1953, Keith Molesworth, made Marchetti an offensive tackle. He hated it, but didn't think it was proper to complain. Gino loves Ewbank for shifting him back to defensive end in '54: "I owe all my success to him. The offensive-line meetings were so goddamned organized. It just wasn't me. It was like putting me in a shirt and tie in a bank, counting money or something. I went crazy."

Marchetti affectionately calls Ewbank "Wilbur."

"He was a great organizer; when you went into a game, you felt very well prepared. He was a great judge of talent; he put players in the right position. But his problem was trying to be too nice a guy — and I told him that at one of those parties where you have a couple of beers and you feel kind of brave. You can't be a nice guy because the team will die on you. And that's what happened to him eventually in Baltimore."

Marchetti considers Ewbank's successor, Don Shula, to be tougher.

"The first game we played for Shula, 1963 against the Giants, and they beat us, Shula sent in the field-goal team a couple of times and John would motion them off the field. John would do it to Weeb all the time and get away with it. But I'll never forget, Shula grabbed John and said, 'Listen, I want to tell you something. I'm the coach. If things go wrong, I get fired, not you. Anytime you see the field-goal team coming in, come right off the field. I don't want to see that anymore.' Never seen it anymore either."

On those Sundays when the defensive unit was introduced, Marchetti always was first onto the field.

"It was just such a feeling. That noise lifted me, like thirty feet in the air. You'd get up to the top dugout step and you're nervous and you hear them say, 'From the University of San Francisco . . .' and you come out of there, snot coming out of your nose and steam coming out of your ears. Wow. Every week, every Sunday, to get that excited . . . I was as excited at the end of my thirteenth season as I was at the first. I think of coming out onto the field. I think of the band playing the fight song. I thought I was the luckiest guy in the world."

And then: "My whole secret, if you ever watched, I guess almost ninety or eighty-five percent of the time I played offside. I got into the neutral zone, as they might call it."

I asked him if he ever lined up across the neutral zone, on the other team's side of the ball.

"Oh yeah. Yeah."

I told him that's what Mike Gregor had said.

"Oh, Mike Gregor. God bless him. God bless him. Mike and his mother — super people. Well, he was right. Somebody noticed me anyway."

I asked him why the officials didn't penalize him.

"I got warned a lot," he said.

"But they never dropped a flag?"

"No. Because I'd get warned and I'd say, 'Jesus, thanks a lot.' Or after a play I'd say, 'How'd I look that time?' I tried to be nice. But I got as much as I could get. Don't get me wrong, I wasn't way over. And it wasn't as if I jumped offside; they would penalize me for that. But I was right on the border, just over the border. I was to the point where they could have called me. So close, just so close."

Special players in any sport often benefit from an official's doubt or a reluctance to make a call against a star. Sometimes the star goes scot-free and the outmanned opponent is penalized. Against Minnesota once when the late Norm Van Brocklin was coaching, the Vikings had their right offensive tackle line up about a step and a half back to give him a better chance to get set for the charging Marchetti. A flag was dropped against the Vikings. The tackle was ruled to be in the backfield.

"I was very, very, very quick," Marchetti said, and there was no doubt in his voice. "I loved to get my hands on a ballplayer. An offensive lineman has to set up. If I could get to him before he gets his strength, then I had an advantage. That's why I always loved bigger guys than smaller guys because bigger guys couldn't set up as quick. Or during a game they'd get lazy lifting all that weight. So my whole act was getting my hands on somebody. When I got my hands on him, he was mine. Because of my finger strength, or whatever it was. I could wrassle him around and make him go the opposite way of where I wanted to go."

But Marchetti's father worried that his son would get hurt. He never went to see his son play. He even was afraid to watch on television. Each season when the Colts played in San Francisco, Gino would "sneak home" the forty miles to Antioch to see Ernest.

"And every time I was about to leave he'd give me the same piece of advice for the next day's game. He'd say, 'Gino, whatever you do, stay out of their way.'"

"I said, 'Yeah, Papa, but Danny' — Gino's brother — 'broke his leg falling off a barstool.'"

In 1958 the Colts were in San Francisco and Gino's hotel room phone rang. Carroll Rosenbloom, the owner, wanted to see him.

"Naturally you get all nervous," said Marchetti, as if the Unitas of the Colts' defense had reason to be nervous. "I'm thinking, maybe I got traded."

As directed, he went to the owner's suite.

"Carroll comes out and sits down and says, 'Hey, listen, Gino, what are you going to do with your life?'

"I said, 'What do you mean?' I was playing football and thought I was king of the world.

"He said, 'You ought to move to Baltimore year-round. You ought to go into business, and I'll help you.'

"I said, 'Oh, geez, I don't know. I'll think about it.'

"But he talked to my wife, Flo, and first thing you know we're moving to Baltimore."

Rosenbloom recommended that Marchetti go into the bowling business — tenpins. But fullback Alan Ameche, former teammate Joe Campanella, and a friend, Lou Fischer, asked him to join them in the restaurant business. In the summer of '57 the three had started Ameche's drive-ins featuring the meaty Powerhouse.

Now Fischer thought up the idea of the fast-food chain they would call Gino's. They'd offer a fifteen-cent hamburger and a bigger hamburger like the Powerhouse only with a different sauce to be known as "The Gino's Giant." John Steadman in the *News-Post* first called Marchetti "The Giant."

It sounded good to Gino. And soon after, the first Gino's opened in Dundalk.

"But the one that really got us started was number two, on Pulaski Highway," Marchetti said. "The owner of the property wanted a ten-year lease for ten thousand dollars a year — one hundred thousand dollars. I went home and thought about it and called Carroll. 'He wants somebody to sign this lease guaranteeing payment if we go broke,' I told him. He said, 'Will my name do?'

"All I was wondering was, 'How many fifteen-cent hamburgers would we have to sell before we made any money?' But right off the bat we did twelve thousand dollars a week there selling fifteen-cent hamburgers. That's a hell of a lot of hamburgers."

In the early days Gino even drove a truck and delivered meat patties to the stores. "I'm just a frustrated truck driver," he said. "I loved working with the people."

In 1964 Marchetti made all-pro at age forty. He retired and was given a "day" along with Bill Pellington at the last home game of the season.

"I don't want a car," he told the organizers. "I can buy my own car. I'd like my dad here."

Ernest still had never seen his son play in person.

"That was really the greatest day I ever had because he was there," Gino said. "When the game was almost over I sat by him on the bench. He said, 'Gino, maybe you did know how to play this a little bit.' The last game he says this."

Meanwhile, Gino's Inc. spread through the Northeast. Because its headquarters were in King of Prussia, Pennsylvania, Marchetti moved to the Philadelphia area. In 1982, when the company was sold to the Marriott Corporation, Gino was rich beyond anything he could have imagined.

A few months passed, and he began feeling "terrible."

"Yeah, terrible. I'd been lucky. Loved football. Football closed. Loved the restaurant business. I went from one to the other. Going from one to the other wasn't so tough for me. Because I played as long as I could. I would say I had a pretty good career. Really nice. Then I go right to the restaurant business, which I loved because I loved the people. We had a good time, we worked hard, and we enjoyed it. I was lucky.

"But when I left the restaurant business I could understand the experience of some athletes who wake up one day and that part of their life is over. They don't have anything else. I can understand how some of these guys wake up and say, 'Jesus Christ, what am I gonna do? Where am I gonna go? I miss it.' Listen, you want part of that action."

He didn't have that action anymore.

"I ate a lot and drank a lot. I blew up to three hundred and thirty pounds. I was drinking a lot. V.O. and water, light beer. V.O. and water, mostly. I had a heart attack."

He looked up at the fifty-seven-pound white marlin on his wall.

"See that thing right there. That's what I do."

"That's what I do, too," said his wife, Joan, who'd come downstairs. She is Marchetti's second wife. After a divorce from Flo, who has since died, Gino married Joan in 1978. He'd owned a boat since 1969 and fished occasionally, "but mostly," he said, "it was social — flying the cocktail flag."

After his heart attack he knew he had to do something. Together, he and Joan took up competitive fishing. In 1986 they bought a bigger boat, a forty-four-footer. They were competing in a tournament when he caught the fish on the wall.

"If it had weighed three more pounds," he said, "I could have won a hundred thousand dollars. When I caught it, I knew it was close. When we were coming in with it, I kept thinking, How can I put a few more pounds on it? I kept putting water in its mouth. I covered him up nice with a blanket because I didn't want him to dehydrate. I wet the blanket down so the sun wouldn't dry him out."

He said I should see his boat — *My "O" Lady.* He keeps it at the Jersey shore.

I found Gino again a few months later at the southern tip of New Jersey, at a marina off Delaware Bay. From the parking lot I saw him halfway down a pier, hosing off the deck of his boat. He had on big yellow boots. It was June. He and his wife had brought the boat back from Florida, where they spend winters. He'd already been offshore a half-dozen times to the Baltimore Canyon, deep water sixty to a hundred miles out in the Atlantic. He fishes the canyon walls for marlin. The best time, he said, is the end of August and first part of September.

"A seventy-five, eighty-pound white marlin is a big fish," he said. "A blue marlin can run five hundred to seven hundred pounds. I've never caught a blue. I've had one but I've never been able to land one. They're really hard to bring in. Big, powerful. They fly out of the water, twist and turn, and that way they're able to spit the hooks out. Any slack in the line at all and you might as well give up.

"My neighbor here is Bernie Parent" — the former hockey goalie. "He just got his first blue marlin last week."

This sort of fishing, Marchetti said, is "like throwing the quarterback for a loss, third and ten, and two seconds to go. It's exciting — the anticipation and then seeing the fish's head, the jumping . . . I think that's been my savior, you might say."

My "O" Lady had two staterooms and everything on board one might have in a small modern apartment — TV, VCR, microwave. Sometimes Gino and Joan relax by fishing in the bay. "Turn off the engines. Put the line around your toe, as my wife says. If the fish comes, okay, if it doesn't, okay." But Marchetti can take only so much of idling in the bay. He never was a spectator.

"Matter of fact, Shula wanted me, when I first retired, to travel with the team and sit on the bench, help the younger kids or give them some advice or whatever. So I said, sure, and the first trip was against the Green Bay Packers in Milwaukee. God Almighty, I went through hell. I felt like I wanted to run in every time. After the game I went in and found Shula. I says, 'Shula, I'm just not going to do this anymore.'"

The boat rocked from the wake of a boat speeding through the inland waterway as Joan poured some coffee. I mentioned that fame hadn't seemed to affect him in the least, and she agreed that he was a man with no sense of self-importance.

She hadn't known him as a player and said, "I still can't get over when I'm in a store and take out the credit card the salesperson will say, 'Gino Marchetti!' Or a telephone operator, same reaction, when you give the name."

"Fame? I think it's just realizing who you are," Gino said. "It's a game. One time a guy says, 'Jesus Christ, you're talking to me.' He was an electrician. I said, 'I don't know anything about electricity. You don't know how to play football. So we're even.'

"When we were playing there was no such thing as outside interests, except for one or two guys. You couldn't find outside jobs. That was the amazing thing about Rosenbloom setting you up in business. Most owners back then wanted to keep you poor so you'd play harder. You had time after practice to go to Andy's bar and drink beer and talk about Sunday's game and just have a nice afternoon.

"Sometimes we'd have a party after the games. 'Bring five

dollars apiece for the beer,' we'd say. 'Whoever wants to come, come.' We'd have thirty guys out of thirty-six. Then you could see later on in the sixties guys couldn't come anymore. They had outside interests. This guy represents this company: 'My boss wants to take a couple football players to his party.'

"I remember when I went back to the team in '66, the first guy to come up to me was John. John said, 'Jesus Christ, Gino, I'm glad you're here.' I said, 'Why?' He said, 'I got somebody to have a beer with after practice now.'"

Joan went off to daily Mass, and Gino, who has three grown children, mentioned that he had adopted the younger two of her four children.

"Before we were married I used to like to go to the Little Paddock, a shot-and-a-beer joint in Philly. Lancaster Avenue. All the workers come in. I'd say to Joan, 'Let's go down to the Paddock and have a beer.' She'd come, no problem. I'm so thankful she likes fishing."

He recalled his three-and-a-half-hour battle with the six-hundred-pound blue marlin. "He took his last dive, and I swear to God I thought he was going to dive into the cockpit. He did a big loop, and he caught his tail around the wire leader so that he went in the water headfirst. I'm holding the pole, and he goes all the way to the bottom. For another hour I reel him in, and I got him just about to the top. Then we see this big shark grab him and take him right off. I swear to God, took the line and everything."

Gino was standing out on the flying bridge. His black hair was blowing. He still ached to compete — what he wanted was a good fight with a fish.

"I'd really love to catch a blue," he said.

◆

When I was eight or nine years old and Pop was taking me to the old stadium to watch the minor-league Orioles, we'd sit in the grandstand about a dozen rows up just to the right of home plate. Another dozen rows or so behind us was a green woodshed built right into the seats. This was the radio booth. A white sign was tacked to the front: WITH. It was a bare-bulbed cubbyhole that I used to turn toward and regard with awe. Bill Dyer called the games; he sat in a green chair. After the games someone would close the flap on the front of the booth and lock the back door on the way out.

WITH — 1230 on the dial — was one of Baltimore's five radio stations at the time, all of them AM. As my grandfather DeMoss in Towson listened every afternoon for the race results, I'd ask him things like, "Where is Narragansett?" He'd only answer when a song was on. Bill Dyer played the records and in between brought the "up-to-the-minute" results from the nation's tracks off a ticker that clacked in the background. "Here's the fifth from Tropical Park . . ."

"Boomie" — that was the name I stuck on my maternal grandfather because when I was small he'd entertain me by throwing walnuts against the side of a barn next to his white asbestos-shingled duplex at 10 West Joppa Road. Each time a walnut would hit the barn he'd shout "Boom"; "Boomie," I said, and that's what he became to everyone in the family.

Boomie would shush me as he scribbled the race results in pen across the entries for that race in his *Morning Telegraph*. The breast pockets of his heavily starched, short-sleeved white shirts were all ink-stained. He wore dark-rimmed glasses, and I knew the gray stubble of his face was sandpaper-rough from all the times I'd stand next to his chair and put my cheek against his. Before noon each day he'd bet the horses with a man in the neighborhood, and on those late afternoons when he'd have something to collect he'd take me along as he walked down the street. The half block was as far as he ever cared to go after retiring as a streetcar conductor.

WITH advertised on a big billboard on the roof of a building in Pimlico, a great white sign that I'd look up to whenever I was with Mom or Pop and we were driving past. The sign had the WITH emblem of a Greek god (Zeus or Hermes?) with lightning flashing from his mouth. Joel Chaseman's name was up there in black block letters — he did the afternoon show, after Dyer had left town, and play-by-play of the Bullets' basketball games. I marveled at Chaseman's dulcet-toned, swift accounts of the games and to this day compare basketball play-by-play announcers with my memory of Joel Chaseman. When the billboard was changed, Buddy Deane's name usually was put up.

Buddy Deane was just about every Baltimore kid's hero. I began listening to him on WITH in the early fifties. His voice had an unfamiliar twang. Born and raised in St. Charles, Arkansas (population, about 150), Winston J. "Buddy" Deane grew up listening to Little Rock radio, dreaming about being on radio himself someday. On WITH Buddy Deane played rock 'n' roll when nobody in Baltimore and hardly anyone in the country played rock 'n' roll. For the longest time I thought he discovered the music, but actually it found him. It found him early.

Deane had come up from Memphis, where he used to hang out at the Peabody Hotel when he wasn't doing his radio show. The Peabody brought in big dance bands, Ray Anthony's being one. Buddy befriended Ray Anthony's manager, and the two would get together when Anthony played at the Peabody. The last time they saw each other the man asked, "Is there anything I can do for you?" To which Buddy, eager to be a radio star, said, "Sure, find me a better job." Next thing Buddy knew a man from WITH in Baltimore was on the phone.

Buddy had heard of WITH, although he certainly hadn't heard it — it was, at the time, a mere two-hundred-and-fifty-watt station. It sold itself to advertisers with the slogan "Pinpoint Power," avoiding mention of the minuscule wattage.

"The reason I knew of it," Deane explained to me, "was because WITH was one of those rare, local independent stations that lived on its own wits, a mix of music, sports, and the personalities of the disc jockeys. We knew where these stations were located, all over the country. They were the kinds of places where you did everything and you could shine, not like the network-affiliated stations with network programming and all you were was the voice doing the station identification."

I imagined WITH to be located gloriously somewhere in the heavens, but actually it was at 7 East Lexington Street in a building that seemed old even when it was new. WITH had cramped offices on the second floor and a small studio on the third. In 1951 Buddy was handed a time slot and the freedom he had hoped for. "But it was made very clear to me," he added, "that I had to produce. And the first year I didn't get very far in the ratings."

To spread his fame he starting doing record hops on Sunday afternoons in the Famous Ballroom on Charles Street near North Avenue. "Who's going to pay to see a guy play records?" people asked him. But he played records that kids were asking to hear: Little Richard, Chuck Berry, Fats Domino. These were white kids wanting to listen and dance to black music. No disc jockey in town except Buddy Deane was paying attention to them.

While others played orchestra music or jazz exclusively,

Buddy on WITH would drop in an occasional Fats Domino, and his ratings began to rise. It was 1953.

"The thinking at the time was that you should not play what people could buy at the record stores — just the opposite of what soon became obvious, that you played what people wanted," Deane said. "Instead, stations would go out of their way to play songs that had never been heard. They'd even play transcriptions of tunes by an orchestra that wasn't associated with a particular song."

One week Buddy began talking up a "House Rockin'" contest he would hold that Sunday at the Famous Ballroom. "I called it a 'House Rockin,'" he said, "although I'd never heard the term rock 'n' roll." That week he got a call from a guy who wanted to promote his tune by bringing his band and singing and playing for the kids. Buddy said sure. That Sunday the place was packed. "But a lot of the kids who showed up were 'drapes' — hepcats, you might call them," he said. "The band was strictly country — guys in cowboy boots and buckskin cowboy clothes — and you have to remember at the time that pop and country music never mixed. I was in trouble.

"These guys clanged out things like 'San Antonio Rose,' and the kids started complaining. They didn't want any country band. Some of them even wanted their money back. I thought there was going to be a riot. So I went up to this guy and pleaded, 'Look, I advertised a "House Rockin'" contest.' He said, 'All right, I got somethin'. Well, he did this number, and the kids went up the wall, across the ceiling, down the other wall, across the floor.

"Then the guy comes over to me and says, 'We've got 'em rockin' 'n' rollin' now.'

"That was Bill Haley and the Comets."

The Bill Haley of whom Elvis himself said: "No matter how big I get to be he will always be the king."

Buddy played "Rock the Joint" and "Crazy Man Crazy" on WITH. And then: "Rock Around the Clock," rock 'n' roll's first anthem.

"Bill Haley was the first to incorporate a black beat with white melodies," Deane said.

Buddy brought Haley to town four or five times after helping make him famous, and down at the Valencia a crowd filled the place and overflowed outside and some even tore at Haley's clothing and jostled him as he tried to pry his way inside to perform. That night in Baltimore in 1954 arguably was the first rock concert in history.

The next year Keith's movie house closed down because of dwindling business. Haley put on a final show there, rocked Keith's out of existence. To the amazement of the owner and the theater moguls of Baltimore who were struggling with their Broadway shows, two thousand packed Keith's for Haley, more business than the theater had done in months combined. A parking garage went up in place of Keith's, but rock 'n' roll was here to stay.

Buddy played it full-time. In music stores you could pick up his handout, "Deane's Disc Digest," which touted a top ten. His record hops — called "sock hops" — spread throughout the city. We listened to the station for his "pick hit of the week" and his "wax to watch." Occasionally he'd play rhythm and blues, by, say, the Cadillacs: *"Some people call me Speedo, but my real name is Mr. Earl."*

One of Buddy's first converts among deejays was his WITH colleague Joel Chaseman. "He'd been playing Glenn Miller and Benny Goodman," Deane said. "Before long he was one of the first to play Elvis records."

Buddy would walk into the studio when Chaseman was playing records and pile up five-dollar bills that he'd empty from his every pocket, admission money he'd taken in for a rock 'n' roll show down the street at Loew's. "Lookee here, Mr. Joel."

Chaseman had never met anyone like Buddy. And to Buddy, Chaseman was different "because every deejay wanted to be a radio star. But he wanted to get into management."

Spinning rock 'n' roll records and doing play-by-play of Bullets' basketball games gave Chaseman a chance to observe how a station was operated. He wanted to be in charge and would become as adept at that as he had been on the air. He spent more than twenty-five years as chief officer of major broadcast groups and production companies. From 1973 to 1990 he was chairman and CEO of Post-Newsweek Stations, Inc., and a vice president of The Washington Post Company.

When I was growing up, Chaseman's honey voice gave me chills. It came out of our little Philco as he described Bullets games. He broadcast from the last row, center, in the Coliseum; bookies sat up in the corner to his left, and money changed hands every game. Chaseman remembered the place correctly: "Small, very urban, dingy, crowded, loud, fairly low ceiling, busy."

Something a little nutty always seemed to be happening there. Once, during a game when the Bullets were playing in the Eastern League, my friend Steve Gavin and I saw a player named Danny Finn of the Hazleton Hawks duck off the court unnoticed by the Bullets and the game officials during a Bullets' foul shot, run down an aisle behind some stands, and dash back onto the court at the other end all by himself. He took a long pass for an uncontested layup to the bewilderment of the Bullets and laughter of spectators.

Chaseman traveled with the Bullets, once by train as far as Grand Forks, North Dakota, for a game with the Minneapolis Lakers. A Grand Forks cabdriver greeted Chaseman with news that it was minus three degrees, "a warm spell." All I knew was that he brought the games from Fort Wayne and Syracuse and Rochester, and although the Bullets of the 1953–54 season went 16–56 to finish a distant last, I fell asleep nights listening to the rhythms of faraway games and a symphony of Bullets names long forgotten: Leo Barnhorst, Rollen Hans, Connie Rea.

For a time the Bullets were coached by Clair Bee, a pink-cheeked gentleman with white hair — I had some of his books for boys, *Backboard Fever* and *Touchdown Pass,* and read them repeatedly. I had an autographed book of his that my parents gave me for a birthday present; Pop joked that Mom had gone down to the Coliseum to get it. Bee listened to a tape recording of Chaseman's play-by-play and offered some valuable advice: Give the score often, locate the players on the floor, and describe the matchups of individuals and how they were reacting to them because, Bee pointed out well ahead of his time, basketball is a game of individual matchups. With his game descriptions Chaseman, a near-sighted man with glasses, let me see Paul "The Bear" Hoffman twelve feet out from the basket, or just to the right of the key, or at the baseline using his broad shoulders to shrug off a defender — a knack for description that made you feel you were there in a way only the best announcers can. Except it was almost better than being there, at least for me, because of that voice. I wanted to be Joel Chaseman, play-by-play man.

One time when he was in the midst of his afternoon record show on WITH, the station's owner phoned him. Tom Tinsley. Tinsley rarely spoke to the disc jockeys. But here he was calling Chaseman, who was sweating in this beastly hot studio on a summer Saturday afternoon.

"Yes, sir, Mr. Tinsley, what can I do for you?"

"Your voice shakes the speaker in my car," he said. "I'd appreciate it if you could do something about that."

"Yes, sir. Yes, sir. I'll do my best."

An English major at Cornell, Chaseman had done a little baseball play-by-play in Scranton by the time Channel 13 in Baltimore went on the air in 1948. Chaseman's mother was a cousin of the station's owner, and at the age of twenty-two he hooked on with then WAAM-TV, doing a little of everything, at twenty-five dollars a week. A few years later, when Chuck Thompson went over from WITH to WCBM radio, Chaseman was offered the job as afternoon man. He took it "to save up a little money" because he was offered twenty-five thousand dollars a year, an amazing salary — plus $1.25 for every commercial he did, and he would average twenty commercials an hour, four hours a day, six days a week. It was enough to detour him temporarily from his career path.

"I didn't know my ass from third base," he said, "and Buddy at the time had a lock on being the music maven. He had this very popular, kind of raucous morning show — he had a personality that came through the radio and grabbed you by the lapels. He was a promoter with these sock hops. He was a power. But Buddy came to me. He'd heard the music I was playing and was certain I was doomed to death. I liked jazz. I was playing Eddie Fisher.

"He wondered, very deferentially for some reason, whether I was going to continue to play this type of music. The sense of it was, you ought to realize what's going on out there. I considered that a valid thought. So I began to listen and I realized: Many people believed World War II was just an interruption of a continuum that went back to World War I. Others saw a new era breaking through. The fifties were a transition time. Buddy knew the world was changing — he was an agent of change. So I began playing what was popular from two o'clock to four and then using my promotional knack took it a step further; from four to six I'd play what was really popular — the very latest — based on random phone calls we'd make to record stores to see what was selling."

Even if Chaseman planned to quit broadcasting the basketball games he loved, he never had to make the decision. The Bullets quit on him. Their funds dwindling, they went out of business on Thanksgiving Eve 1954. They were revived in a new arena in the sixties.

"Just two years ago," Chaseman said, "I got a flight into BWI and my car was at Dulles, so I took a cab and the driver and I talked all the way, just generally, not about sports or radio, and when I was getting out, he said, 'You're Joel Chaseman, aren't you?'

"I was amazed. 'How did you know?' I asked him.

"'I recognize your voice,' he said."

In 1957 Chaseman returned to Channel 13, no longer WAAM but WJZ, as program director. He hired Deane to do on TV what he'd been doing on radio. "The only trouble was, we couldn't figure out what to do when the record was playing," Deane said. "We tried dance instruction. We had a caricaturist come in from *The Sunpapers* and draw a picture of the musician while his song was playing. Then we hit on the idea of kids dancing. Dick Clark started up at the same time in Philadelphia, but we didn't know about him. But even when he caught on, the station kept me on."

We all got a look at Buddy Deane. Stocky. Round face.

Always smiling. Always moving with the microphone and cord, giving long, tantalizing introductions to the latest hits that you'd guess the title to before he'd announce it to squeals and applause. Like "Rag Mop." Buddy loved Brenda Lee and seemed to melt away in front of the camera when he introduced "I'm Sorry" and the teen dance partners — boys with buzz or greaser haircuts, girls in poodle skirts and saddle shoes and hair like spun sunset — fell into loving embrace.

Alan Ameche used to appear on the show to advertise his restaurants. Deane coaxed guest appearances from the likes of Frankie Avalon, Fabian, Chuck Berry, Bobby Darin, and the Everly Brothers. During his six TV years he presided over assorted dance crazes: the twist, the mashed potato, the locomotion, the limbo, the frug.

Many parents took exception. It got so that Buddy had to give up shopping with his wife and eating dinner out because adults would berate him as the cause of their children doing such things as the frug. Eventually, that which gave Buddy fame took it away. He went off Baltimore television in January 1964. The station said his ratings had become "soft." But Deane said at the time that he had been "victimized" by what he called an "insoluble" problem. "Integrated dancing is more delicate than schools or jobs," he said then. The station had been bombarded by complaints — from segregationists, after the station and Deane's decision to integrate younger dancers, and from others because the show wasn't integrated altogether. The Baltimore writer-director John Waters had Buddy Deane's show in mind when he made his 1988 movie *Hairspray,* an offbeat treatment of integration.

Deane returned to WITH, but by October 1964 his big days in Baltimore were over. He headed back to Arkansas and, taking a cue from Chaseman, became a successful businessman. Occasionally he goes back to Baltimore. And a few years ago while visiting, he went down to 7 East Lexington Street and found the building that housed the station, still there, still old-looking. It was vacant, but for some reason the entrance was open and he walked inside. There on the floor was the only sign of his halcyon days, a dusty Greek god with lightning flashing from his mouth.

◆

EDDIE: Was George Shaw a first-round draft choice?
ELYSE: First-round draft choice? . . . True.
EDDIE: Wrong. He was a bonus pick . . . Okay, that concludes the true-and-false section of the test. Let me get the short-answer stuff in order.
ELYSE: Could I have a glass of water?
EDDIE: No . . .

— Dialogue in *Diner*

"A bonus pick?" George Shaw asked. He'd never heard of it, but that's what the Colts had made him.

It was January 1955. Shaw, a senior at the University of Oregon in Eugene, was speaking long distance from his frat house, Alpha Tau Omega, with Colts general manager Don Kellett. A graduate of the University of Pennsylvania, Kellett was articulate and persuasive. He would need his charm to lure Shaw to the Colts. A textbook-perfect quarterback, Shaw also was an all-American baseball player pondering a career with the New York Yankees. He played center field and imagined roaming Yankee Stadium like DiMaggio and Mantle.

"Yes, the bonus pick," Kellett repeated. Shaw knew little about pro football, his only exposure having been a few

49ers and Rams games on television. Kellett told him that each year before the NFL's draft of college players, the name of a team was drawn from a hat and that that team was awarded an extra selection before the draft's first round. That year the Colts had won the bonus pick.

"Who's the coach?" Shaw asked. And: "What color is the uniform?"

The Colts in 1955 were little known beyond Maryland and close-by parts of Pennsylvania. Shaw had an idea where Yankee Stadium was. Baltimore he'd never thought of.

Kellett turned sympathetic. Baseball had been *his* first love. He'd played at Penn and even made it up to the Boston Red Sox for nine games in 1934. He knew how Shaw felt. But Kellett added emphatically, if Shaw signed with the Colts he would not have to spend time in the minor leagues as in baseball. He'd be "big league" right away.

Kellett explained how fortunate the Colts had been in the draft. After they'd taken George as the bonus pick, they'd selected Alan Ameche on their regular turn in the first round. Shaw was flattered. Ameche was well known, the fullback from Wisconsin who'd won the Heisman Trophy. Shaw couldn't understand why the Colts hadn't taken Ameche as the bonus pick.

"Because," Kellett said to Shaw, "you're three players in one. You can play quarterback, defensive back, and flanker."

Shaw was impressed that Kellett knew about him. Shaw had rarely left the field when he played football at Oregon. He played the positions Kellett mentioned, plus running back, and he kicked off and punted and returned kickoffs and punts. He was the all-round athlete. At Grant High School in Portland, Shaw had been playing in a baseball game one afternoon when the track coach came up and begged the baseball coach to let George run the hundred-yard dash in a track meet on a nearby field. Because the baseball team was far ahead, the coach took Shaw out of the lineup and turned him over to the track coach. Shaw pulled off his baseball shirt and ran a 9.9 hundred in his baseball pants and spikes.

Shaw thanked Kellett on the phone and promised to consider Baltimore. In fact he went down to the bus depot and bought a *Sport* magazine to learn what he could about the Colts. He learned that after consecutive 3–9 seasons they needed a quarterback and a lot more.

In May, Kellett flew to Eugene to close a deal with Shaw. First, he had to watch Shaw play center field in a doubleheader. After that, he took Shaw and teammate Jack Patera to dinner at the Eugene Hotel. A suave host, Kellett sold the idea that the Colts had concluded one of the best drafts in NFL history; indeed, it was extraordinary considering that it was based largely on one reel of film.

After the Colts had taken Shaw as their bonus, the Chicago Cardinals picked Max Boydston, an end from Oklahoma. Ecstatic over their opportunity, the Colts then took Ameche. On the second round they took Dick Szymanski, Notre Dame's center; the running back L. G. Dupre from Baylor on the third round; the Oregon linebacker Patera on the fourth round; on the fifth offensive lineman George Preas from Virginia Tech. Louis George "Long Gone" Dupre became a familiar figure with his nifty jaunts through the opposition from 1955 through 1959. Szymanski played center or linebacker in Baltimore for thirteen seasons and later became the team's general manager. Preas was an eleven-year fixture at tackle. Ameche became "The Horse" of the Colts' backfield.

What's more, Raymond Berry reported with the rookies. He'd been selected the previous year, but had stayed in college at Southern Methodist and played his remaining season of eligibility. Berry had to be the most remarkable twentieth-round draft choice.

After signing with Kellett for a whopping eighteen thousand dollars for 1955, Shaw landed in Baltimore that July. Everything seemed crowded to him. The houses were jammed together, block after block of row houses. Then came another surprise: In a few hours, he was being driven in a bus to training camp in Westminster. Just forty miles northwest of Baltimore, Westminster seemed to me at the time a journey to distant country. Shaw thought the same. The farmhouses, the fields, horses grazing gave him a sense of going home. Once there, he felt at home.

"I'd never been around anyone more organized than Weeb Ewbank," said Shaw, now a stockbroker in Portland. "Taking tests on what was in the playbooks was completely unfamiliar to me. But I think he liked me because I was pretty organized myself. I kept on time, knew the playbook, and asked questions."

Shaw found the team's new publicity man, John Steadman, similarly efficient. Steadman had been a young sportswriter on the *News-Post,* and 1955 was his first of three seasons working for the Colts. One of the first things he did was drive Ameche from Westminster to Sagamore Farms in Worthington Valley, outside Baltimore, so photographers could take pictures of Ameche, The Horse, with another horse, Native Dancer. The gimmick shot of the young Colt and the old gray appeared in papers across the country.

"Buddy Young took a liking to me right away," Shaw said, "because I was from Oregon. His father had been the head guy in the dining car on the train that ran from Chicago to Portland — the Portland Rose. The waiters wore tuxedos, and Buddy's father wore a white dinner jacket. As a boy, Buddy made the run sometimes with his father. Buddy, though, was almost impossible to hit with a pass because he was so tiny. You'd have to throw it out there and hope."

In Baltimore, Shaw settled into a row house off Loch Raven Boulevard, near the stadium. That's where he and his wife, Patti, began to raise a family. He walked to the stadium to play in the games. Pony-drawn wagons carrying fruits and vegetables would come down the alley behind the Shaws' house.

These were Baltimore's nomadic hucksters, known as Arabbers or Arabs (pronounced "A-rabbers," with a long "a"). About 350 of them, mostly older men, worked the city then; they rented the horses and wagons for four dollars a day and bought their goods at a produce center. They carried strawberries in early summer, cantaloupes and watermelons in August, citrus fruits throughout autumn. During quiet moments Shaw would hear an Arabber's call or the tinkling of bells on the wagon, go outside, buy a melon, exchange pleasantries. Then he'd watch the old man climb back up to his seat and start his horse with just a touch on the reins.

Shaw's first game for the Colts was an exhibition against the Philadelphia Eagles in Hershey, Pennsylvania. He played safety. Next to him at cornerback was Don Shula. "I was covering Pete Pihos, and he caught three balls against me," Shaw said. "He wasn't fast, but he was clever as hell." Shaw hasn't forgotten what Shula told him after the game. Already thinking like a coach, Shula suggested, "I think you'd be better off sticking to quarterback."

That's where Ewbank put Shaw. And that's where he was on opening day of the season in Baltimore against the Chicago Bears. Almost everyone I knew went to the stadium that day to see all this talent that was being touted. We were stunned when Ameche took a handoff from Shaw on the game's first play from scrimmage and ran — raced, actually — seventy-nine yards for a touchdown. "I didn't know he had speed," Pop said to me.

Shaw said the play was called in the huddle by Alex Sandusky, a second-year guard from Clarion State Teachers College in Pennsylvania. "Alex pulled to the right," Shaw said, "and their defensive tackles ran down the line of scrimmage after him and took themselves out of the play. The hole in the line was huge, and Alan was quick."

The Colts won their first three games — they'd never won three straight games. But reality hit in game four in Chicago. Big Ed Sprinkle tackled Shaw low and hung onto his legs. Standing vulnerably, Shaw was leveled by another "Midway Monster," George Connor. Connor crashed his right shoulder into Shaw's face, broke his plastic, single-bar facemask, and knocked out his top four front teeth. Shaw had to be helped from the field.

On the sidelines, blood poured from his mouth. He was dizzy. Everything felt gray and cold.

"Sizzy," Shaw said to Szymanski, sitting next to him, "how do I look?"

"George," Szymanski answered, "you never were going to be a matinee idol."

Trainer Eddie Block, a short, inventive man, jammed several sticks of gum into his mouth and chewed them into a big, juicy ball. Then Block took the wad of gum from his mouth and put it into Shaw's mouth, flattening it along his upper gum to protect the exposed nerves. Wrigley Field, Wrigley's gum.

After a 38–10 trouncing, Shaw's brother Tom, who happened to be in Chicago, came to the Colts' dressing room. Sizing up the mashed face, Tom said with concern, "George, are you sure you want to pursue this business?"

At home in Baltimore, neighbors brought Shaw soups and soft foods. He was back in the lineup the next week.

Two months later, as was customary, the Colts ended their season on the West Coast with games against the Rams and 49ers. As usual, they lost both of them. Most of the players were eager to get away for the off-season. That year, linebacker Doug Eggers talked Buzz Nutter and Alex Sandusky into joining him on a hunting trip to Eggers's native South Dakota. It was a cockamamie idea.

"It's December, we'd been on the coast for two weeks, and we ain't got no clothes, no nothin'," Nutter told me. "But, okay, let's go. We get the guy from the airlines to change our tickets and give us tickets to Sioux City, Iowa. And Eggers says, 'It'll probably be a little cold up there.' But, shit, we're gonna go anyway.

"So we fly up to Sioux City, Iowa, and as we're flying in I say, 'Fuck, Eggers, it doesn't look too goddamned cold. Look, the goddamned ground is hardly covered with snow.' We get to Sioux City and we have to take a bus up to Yankton, South Dakota. And the further we go, the deeper the goddamned snow gets. I mean, it's in the middle of the plains. I mean, it's in the middle of nowhere.

"So we're on this goddamned bus going from Sioux City, Iowa, to Yankton, South Dakota, and Sandusky and I are sittin' there — and we're always on Eggers's ass anyways; Eggers is a country boy, nicest guy in the world — we're sittin' there and Eggers is sittin' in the seat in front of us with this guy. The guy looks at him and says, 'Aren't you

Fred Eggers's boy from Wagner?' That's Wagner, South Dakota, where we're going after we get to Yankton.

"Eggers says to the guy, 'Yeah, yeah. I'm from Wagner. Yeah, I'm *Doug* Eggers.'

"The guy says, 'Oh, yeah, where have you been? I haven't seen you for a while.'

"Eggers says, 'Well, I been down in Baltimore playin' with the Colts.'

"'The Colts?'

"'Yeah, you know, professional football.'

"'What are you, the coach?'

"'No, I play professional football for the Colts.'

"And the guy says, 'Well, did you play Iowa last year?' He says, 'They had a good team.'

"Goddamn, Sandusky and I are rollin' on the floor. This is unbelievable.

"Eggers says, 'No, no, *professional football,* you know, the Baltimore Colts.' The guy never heard of the Colts.

"Well, we get up to Yankton, and we get off of like a Greyhound and get into a van, a five-seater van. That's the bus to go to Wagner, South Dakota. We get to Wagner, they've been snowed in. They have not been out of the house for a week. It's like twenty below zero, the snow is up to your damn knees.

"We go out to the farm, stay like two days or somethin'. We take all of Old Man Eggers's clothes, you know, everything he has to wear, and go out and hunt around. It's freezing. Everything's out of season. We have no licenses. We go all that way for one laugh: 'Did the Colts play Iowa last year?'"

The Colts had finished with a 5–6–1 record, the best they'd done, and Shaw was named the NFL's Rookie of the Year.

A few years ago Shaw was relaxing at home one evening when his son John came home from a movie store with a rental. Shortly he began shouting from the other room, "Hey, Dad, you're in this movie." It was *Diner.* Shaw hadn't heard of it, but there he was, part of the *Diner* quiz. As the Baltimore boy named Eddie is about to get married, he worries that life will not be the same if his wife cannot understand his love for the Colts. He threatens to call off the wedding if she fails his Colts' trivia quiz. It's a wacky scene, as is the wedding with the bridesmaids dressed in Colts blue and the bride walking down the aisle to the slow strains of the Colts' fight song.

The Shaws watched the film together, the father telling the son what it was like when the Colts belonged to Baltimore.

◆

The summer of 1956 was hot and slow. The pace of Baltimore life was noted by the 320-pound Divine, who before his death in 1988 played female roles in John Waters films: "When you live in Baltimore, you don't think anything could ever happen."

I worked that summer in a loft that opened onto the Central Avenue alley in East Baltimore, a few blocks from the Domino Sugars sign on the city's skyline. We made storm windows — cut the glass, put insulation around the edges, and used a rubber mallet to pound on the metal frames. It was almost always ninety degrees or hotter. The first night I came home from work, covered with dirt, my fingers cut and burning, I went upstairs, showered, fell into bed, and went right to sleep. The next day my mother told me she'd thought I was dying but that Pop had assured her I was only being introduced to real work.

That summer I searched the sports pages of the *News-Post*

and *The Evening Sun* for some encouraging sign. Hugh Trader, who covered the now major-league Orioles for the *News-Post* and whose job I'd determined to be the finest there could be, wrote from Detroit of promise shown by a young third baseman, Brooks Robinson. Recently called up from Triple A ball in Vancouver, Robinson had gotten into the lineup at third base in the late innings and made a one-handed diving play. He also doubled. "The kid," Hugh Trader prophesied, "has it all. His only flaw could be lack of speed."

At the time I thought Tony Baldoni might be our sports salvation. He was a stocky middleweight who'd settled in Baltimore and trained under Al Flora, who owned the Florentine Club, two blocks from our house on Gwynn Oak Avenue. It would become the Club 24 after Flora sold it to number twenty-four, Lenny Moore.

In the summer of '56 Baldoni fought Ralph "Tiger" Jones on a Friday night at St. Nick's in New York. I was enthralled that a guy from up the street could appear on "The Gillette Cavalcade of Sports." Pop and I turned it on at ten o'clock. But after Jones had scored a knockout in the sixth round, Baldoni had to be carried to his corner, and it was at least ten minutes before he was able to walk to the dressing room.

What impressed me about Baldoni's next debacle, a one-round knockout by Joey Giardello, was how flat his back looked on the canvas in the next day's *Evening Sun* and how the paper reported the eclipse of a local hero. The previous day's story had built him up as "the pride of Forest Park"; the account of his demise referred to him only as a native of Wilkes-Barre, Pennsylvania.

In the *News-Post* and *The Evening Sun* everything seemed to be happening somewhere else. Capital Airlines was advertising "vibrationless" flights; a world out there that I had only a vague notion of seemed to be speeding up. I read about the circus rigging its big top off Pulaski Highway — for *the last time*. I thought about the night years before when my father and his father took me there. I remembered them hurrying me across a field of high weeds so that we'd have time to see the sideshow before going into the tent, then sitting in green bleachers high enough to see all three sawdust rings, the pounding elephants, a lion tamer with his whip. But nothing remains as clear as the three of us — my tall grandfather, my father, and I holding onto Pop's hand — crossing the empty, silent field with the colored lights of a Ferris wheel glowing up ahead, my sensing an anticipation in their lengthened strides and my struggling to keep up.

In 1956 I got my driver's license. I could take Pop's Dodge — Colt blue — to Reisterstown Road, which was where Ameche's was and where the diner was. In the movie it was called the "Fells Point Diner." Actually it was the Hilltop Diner. "Food Served at Its Best," it said on the menus. What could beat the hot turkey sandwich with mashed potatoes and a fifteen-cent Coke?

Pop's Dodge had fluid drive, a technological miracle. You didn't have to shift if you started up on level ground or downhill. Of course the '50 Dodge accelerated about as fast as a bicycle.

We'd go to the Crest movie, then across the street to the diner. Cars, rock 'n' roll, the Colts — that's what we talked about, my friend Paul Dill and I, as we'd sit lingering in the booths. Each booth had a jukebox, and Elvis — he made a million dollars in 1956! — crooned to us on weekend nights: "Ah wa-ha-hant yew, Ah nee-hee-heed yew . . ."

That was the summer the Bengies Drive-In movie opened. Instantly it became the most notorious passion pit we'd ever heard of. The Bengies' ads in the newspapers promoted such double-feature fascinations as *Hot Rod Girl* and *Girls in Prison.* But for us the Bengies existed only in lurid thoughts because it was too far to get to, being all the way over on Pulaski Highway. Even if we'd known any girls to take there, I wouldn't have wanted to answer to Pop if he found out. When I was driving him one Sunday afternoon that summer he gave me a tongue-lashing for not coming to a complete stop at a stop sign. He told me he *never* wanted that to happen again, striking all fear into me.

There'd be no "make-out" sessions for me at the Bengies or two other fabulous teen-necking sites, Lake Montebello near Memorial Stadium, and Druid Lake Reservoir. I'd secretly thrilled to the Druid Lake passage in Leon Uris's *Battle Cry,* which for some reason found its way onto our bookshelf at home. Danny, the Forest Park High football star, took Kathy to the reservoir in *Battle Cry:*

"After a few dances in the decorated gymnasium, they stole away from the well-wishers and back-slappers. As they drove, her soft golden hair brushed against his cheek and he smelled the fresh sweet scent of perfume. She hummed the tune of the last dance softly . . .

"He turned the ignition key over and tuned in an all-night music station. The car stood by Druid Lake Reservoir between cars parked every few feet circumferencing the lake. She came into his arms and they kissed and she nestled there, tucking her legs beneath her. He sighed as he kissed her cheek again and again."

During the summer of '56 Buddy Deane staged an outrageous promotional contest in which he offered "the shirt off

Elvis Presley's back." Deane got this sports shirt *supposedly* worn by Elvis when he recorded "Don't Be Cruel" and "Hound Dog" and a statement *supposedly* signed by the singer saying that, indeed, this was the shirt. Buddy had the statement enlarged and placed in the window of an empty store next to a dummy garbed in the shirt. Every day enormous crowds gathered to peer in at the dummy. Extra police had to keep people from pushing and fighting for a look, and the fear was real that someone would be shoved through the window. Downtown merchants were relieved when the contest ended and the doldrums resumed.

Then it happened. In late summer of '56 Johnny Unitas and Lenny Moore and Big Daddy Lipscomb all joined the Colts. My friend George Kelch went up to the Westminster training camp that summer. At lunchtime everyone sat around outdoors talking, and George fell into conversation with a fellow who introduced himself as John. When it came time to move on, George asked John his last name.

"Unitas," he said.

"Geez, you're on the team."

George came home thinking not, Wouldn't it be something if Unitas turns out to be a pretty good quarterback? No, George swears he thought, Wouldn't it be something if Unitas turns out to be the *greatest* quarterback there ever was?

A week later the Colts played their annual intrasquad scrimmage at the stadium. It was called the Blue-White Game. For this people would almost fill the place. One year the Associated Press in New York queried Baltimore AP: Wasn't that attendance figure supposed to be five thousand? No, Baltimore AP fired back, fifty thousand was correct.

Before those games the players took part in various competitions. The quarterbacks threw footballs through a spare tire. Unitas put every ball through the tire. The new number nineteen had this pronounced overhand delivery, as if he were reaching way up for something on a shelf, then snatching it down.

That night Unitas worked with the reserve offense, the white-jersey team. He passed for three touchdowns. Late in the game he was told to change out of his white shirt and get on a blue one. Shortly, he connected for the first time with Raymond Berry. It was a deep pass down the left sideline. Berry jumped and caught the ball between defenders. A few plays later Unitas sneaked over, and the game ended 20–20. He had tied up the game we thought he'd won for the other side.

A few days later the *News-Post* came out with a photo spread of Unitas. Even if he hadn't yet played a real game the caption extolled him as a "pass master." That was Hearst journalism, which I took as gospel. That time it was.

◆

He wore number twenty-two on what was an odd-looking uniform to say the least. It had red-and-black-striped sleeves and a white front — that part was modeled after the University of Pennsylvania football jerseys of the time. But his helmet was scratched and dented — the last one to be given out. And his pants didn't reach his knees because they belonged to a friend several inches shorter. This was how John Unitas looked in the fall of 1955 when he played sandlot football in Pittsburgh for the Bloomfield Rams.

Unitas had returned home from college that spring, missing his graduation ceremony at the University of Louisville because his first wife, Dorothy, back in Pittsburgh was about to have their first child. Some of Unitas's friends were surprised his car held together on the long drive from Kentucky. He had a '41 Plymouth, the color of pea soup. Friends called it "The Green Hornet."

"It was ugly," said Fred Zangaro, who also lived in Pittsburgh and played football with Unitas at Louisville.

"I thought it was rather pretty," said Unitas, laughing. We spoke at his office in Timonium, Maryland, north of Towson. He had a new job with Matco Electronics Corporation and was trying to work his way out of debt. In February 1991 he had filed for bankruptcy after bad business judgments led him to financial ruin. Still, he seemed upbeat, cordial, whistling as he'd come off the elevator at his floor. Nearing sixty he looked years younger. Though hunch-shouldered as ever, he was trim, and his brown hair, parted on the right, had not a fleck of gray.

Zangaro was a freshman when Unitas was a senior, although Zangaro, who'd been in the service, was three years older. He was married and had two children, and the Zangaros used to have Unitas over to their apartment in Louisville for spaghetti. Unitas and Zangaro went to the Kentucky Derby together in 1955 and combined for a five-dollar bet on Swaps. "That was a lot of money," Fred said.

Swaps, the California horse, had won a local sprint and come to their attention, and they watched excitedly as Willie Shoemaker kept Swaps in front of Nashua and Eddie Arcaro by a length and a half in a classic race in the darkening afternoon at Churchill Downs. The Louisville gamblers, Zangaro and Unitas, split nineteen dollars.

Fred never went back to the university after one year because he had to support his family. He got a job in Pittsburgh in construction through his brother Dom, a union steward. Dom also owned a pizza place — Dom's Lunch on Federal Street — and Fred worked there as well.

One day Fred saw in the paper that the hometown Steelers, who had drafted Unitas on the ninth round, had cut his friend. Unitas had done well in scrimmages but had not been put in for a single play in the exhibition games. Near the end of training camp, at St. Bonaventure in southwestern New York, the coach, Walt Kiesling, called him in and told him the team had room for only three quarterbacks and he was number four. "I was ticked off is what I was," Unitas said to me. "I got a little hot and told him, 'You know, it'd be different if I screwed up, but you never gave me an opportunity to play.'"

Art Rooney, who founded the Steelers in 1933 and ran them until his death in 1988, used to say with a sad, wry smile that his best remembrance of Unitas in a Pittsburgh uniform was "playing catch with my kids on the sidelines."

Unitas hitchhiked home. That morning Dorothy had bought tickets to the Steelers' opening game only to return home and learn that her husband had been cut. In a 1958 *Saturday Evening Post* article titled "The Passer Nobody Wanted," Jimmy Breslin quoted Dorothy as saying that John looked like "half past six" coming up the walk. They sat and looked at each other the rest of the night.

On Sunday they went to the Steelers game, John sitting there restlessly, knowing the plays that were being run. That week he wrote to Cleveland Browns coach Paul Brown asking for a tryout. Brown wrote back that Otto Graham had decided to play one more season, but that Unitas was welcome to come out to training camp the next summer if he didn't hook on with another team.

Unitas was desperate for work when Zangaro phoned him. "He didn't have any money, he was in pretty tough shape," Zangaro recalled.

Zangaro said that with Dom's help he got Unitas a job on a pile-driving crew — although as Unitas remembered it his high school coach arranged the job. The work was hard and not exactly safe. Unitas elaborated: "On the pile-driving outfit I was the monkey man. Which meant that every day I had to go up as high as a hundred and twenty-five feet. They had an eight-ton hammer, I guess it was, and in between the hammer and the piling there was an oak block so you weren't hitting steel on steel, you were hitting steel on wood and driving the piling down into the ground. The monkey man would go up and change the block. It went into a beveled piece of steel — you'd put the block in between the hammer and what they called the dick, which was a long piece of steel. Once you got the oak block in between the hammer, here, and the dick, here, the hammer would hit the block and the block would come down. So much friction would be caused, the block would burn up in there. I'd work at different heights depending on how hard the driving was. They'd drive and get down to where it wouldn't go any farther and you'd go up and change the block. That went on eight, ten, twelve hours a day. Numerous times a day."

Fred Zangaro also gave Unitas a suggestion about football. "If you lay out a year, you'll be in trouble. Come on over and play with us."

"Us" was the Bloomfield Rams, a sandlot team that played at the grassless Arsenal Junior High field near the Bloomfield section. The Rams were organized and coached by Chuck Rogers, who, like Zangaro, stood about five feet six and weighed 210 pounds. Rogers, a beer distributor then and now, was known as "The Bear."

Although he wasn't built like a quarterback, The Bear was

the quarterback of the Bloomfield Rams. He appointed himself the team's signal caller, his rationale being that since he gave the orders off the field, he might as well give them on the field. He ran the team out of the basement of Parise's restaurant, a sandwich shop on nearby Liberty Avenue.

Rogers made a follow-up call to Unitas, suggesting they meet on the corner of Liberty and Edmond. Rogers knew Unitas was serious when he showed up because he had to come a distance. The season already had begun, and money was tight. The Rams' top players were making fifteen dollars a game. Rogers told Unitas he could make only six dollars a game. Unitas agreed. He accepted the beat-up helmet without complaint, and Fred gave him an extra pair of pants that he'd used with a team called the Superior Bulldogs.

Unitas played his first game for the Rams as a defensive halfback, scoring the game-winning touchdown when Zangaro, a linebacker, intercepted a pass and lateraled him the ball. Having established himself, Unitas was given the chance by Rogers to play quarterback.

The Arsenal Street field, like other Pittsburgh fields, was sprayed with oil by a city truck a few days before the season to keep the dust down. After four or five days, the oil dried and the field turned hard as brick. It was strewn with rocks and glass. A concrete wall stretched the length of one sideline just a few yards out of bounds. The stands were elevated above the concrete wall. Some opponents who knew of Unitas because he'd been mentioned in the papers tried to drive him into the wall on plays that ended up on that side of the field. Their message: "Welcome to the Steel Bowl Conference."

"But John was determined," Rogers said. "He could take anything that was given."

That was the way he'd been raised by his mother, Helen. Born in Pittsburgh on May 7, 1933, he was baptized John Constantine Unitas by his Uncle Constantine, a priest. Johnny was five when his father, Leonard, died from pneumonia, leaving Helen to run a small coal-delivery business to support herself and her four children. When business was slow in warmer weather she cleaned offices downtown, four nights a week, 10:00 P.M. to 6:00 A.M. For this she was paid three dollars a night. Later, she took an accounting course and got a job with the city.

John played quarterback for a small Catholic high school, St. Justin's. Jim "Max" Carey was the coach. Carey arranged a tryout for Unitas at Notre Dame, but the assistant coach who worked him out, Bernie Crimmins, sent Carey a letter saying that the boy was too small and might get hurt. Unitas then was six feet tall but weighed only 145 pounds.

It seemed as if he would have to go to work until Carey got the University of Louisville interested and the school offered a full scholarship. It was luck. A Louisville assistant coach, John Dromo, was in Pittsburgh to scout a college game. He would need a ride to the airport afterward and decided to call a friend. That was Carey.

"I told him I was going to scout the game and asked him if he wanted to help," Dromo said. "He said he wanted to, and I told him to meet me at the press gate. I still hadn't told him I needed a ride to the airport.

"Jim then said, 'Oh, by the way, can I bring my quarterback with me?' I thought, 'Oh, no, the usual stuff,' and then I said, 'Okay.'

"So the next day I'm waiting at the press gate and I don't even remember what Jim looks like. All I'm looking for is a guy to come up to me and smile and say hello. And sure enough, here comes this guy, and behind him was this great big tall kid hunched over. Jim introduces himself and then says, 'John, this is my quarterback. I want you to meet him, John Unitas.'

"So I shook hands with John, and when my hand disappeared in his I took another look at him."

Over the next four years Unitas remained obscure because Louisville was no football power. He had his moments — in one instance, he completed eleven straight passes in the rain, three for touchdowns, against St. Bonaventure. But in his junior year Louisville lost consecutive games by scores of 59–6, 44–6, and 41–0. Unitas took a pounding.

Then, as later, he was a passer who would, if necessary, hold the ball before releasing it until just an instant before being hit by a defender. He didn't hesitate to run the ball, with it planted under his arm, and he didn't step out of bounds or slide in front of a would-be tackler to avoid a hit. At Louisville he also played defensive back. After some games, his shoulders were so sore from tackling he couldn't raise his arms and his uniform shirt had to be cut off.

Pencil-legged, Unitas looked ungainly. But he would develop nifty footwork, so-called happy feet, like Joe Montana's. Unitas lacked Montana's nimbleness, but nevertheless he was mobile enough and rugged. Old Colt films, for example, show a Colt running back reversing his field and suddenly Unitas coming into the picture to level an opponent with a block.

Unitas's teammates on the Bloomfield Rams could see how good he was even if the Steelers couldn't. The Rams would practice two or three nights a week, and Unitas always liked to put in extra work.

"Go down six yards and cut over the middle," he'd tell Zangaro.

"Kiss my ass," Zangaro would reply.

"He threw the ball so hard," Zangaro explained, "I didn't want to catch it."

Although there were five or six set plays that went either to the right or left, Unitas made up most of the plays in the huddle. Sometimes after practice, John and Fred would stop at Vodde's on the North Side for a beer.

"He never drank much," Fred said. "Didn't smoke. Didn't talk loud."

Chuck Rogers, who'd happily stepped aside as Bloomfield's quarterback and concentrated on kicking extra points, still thought that a tackle on the sandlot team was the top pro prospect. So the coach got his wife to go downtown to the library and get the address of the Baltimore Colts and a name he could write to. He wrote Don Kellett and received a reply.

Rogers wishes he had the letter — and the canceled checks for six dollars that he paid Unitas with. But the gist of Kellett's letter was, We'll give your tackle a tryout, but we're looking for a guy named Unitas. Kellett, a general manager who knew that a team could always use another quarterback and how little it would take to try out one more, had seen Unitas's name on an old waiver list. Kellett asked Rogers if he knew where Unitas was.

Rogers immediately called Baltimore and gave Kellett Unitas's phone number. Unitas was living with his in-laws. In February 1956 a three-minute toll call from Baltimore to Pittsburgh was eighty cents; hence, the legend that all it cost the Colts to get Unitas was an eighty-cent phone call. Unitas was at work when the call came, and Dorothy waited anxiously for John that evening to tell him the news. He took it with a characteristic shrug. He hadn't thought about Baltimore.

He was making $125 a week with overtime, and — although this certainly wasn't going to keep him in Pittsburgh — Rogers had upped his pay per game with the Bloomfield Rams: first to eight dollars, then to ten, then to fifteen dollars for the championship game against the Arnold (Pennsylvania) Athletic Club, which the Rams won when Unitas got hot in the second half.

He and Dorothy talked it over before Kellett called back. Flitting out of town for another football tryout went against everything about work and family responsibilities that had been ingrained in Unitas. But Dorothy encouraged him to try Baltimore. And so he accepted Kellett's invitation to come down for a one-day workout in May. A few days later the mail brought what would be Unitas's first "National Football League standard players contract," which he signed and returned. If he made the club he would receive "the sum of $7,000 to be payable as follows: 75% of said salary in weekly installments commencing with the first and ending with the last regularly scheduled League game played by the Club during such season and the balance of 25% of said sum at the end of said last regularly scheduled League game."

In May Unitas got a ride to Baltimore with the tackle Rogers had recommended. The tryout, held on the grass of Clifton Park near the stadium, lasted about two hours. Weeb Ewbank took a look and realized the Colts might have stumbled onto a quarterback coaches only dream of. Certain things about Unitas hinted of something unexpected: the way the kid dropped back to pass, a canniness with which he glanced at one receiver and threw to another, how quickly the ball reached its destination. Tall and long-armed, he ambled up to take the snaps from center like a natural.

The coach hid his exuberance. He told his son-in-law/defensive assistant Charley Winner to tell Unitas some minor things to work on back home. A clue to their thinking: Unitas rated a plane ticket to Baltimore that July for the start of training camp. He flew down with Dickie Nyers, a running back who'd played at Indiana Central and would make the Colts for two years. The pair reported to the Colts' offices in the city, then boarded a bus with the other rookies for the one-hour ride to Westminster.

Unitas wasn't optimistic as the bus took them into the gently rolling farmland. George Shaw, Baltimore's returning quarterback, already had established himself in 1955.

"I thought it would make sense for them to bring in a veteran to back him up, not a rookie like me," Unitas said. "And you just never knew how the people were going to treat you. I knew the kind of treatment I got in Pittsburgh. You just assumed this would be the same type of situation."

He got an inkling of something different after walking into the locker room. It was modest even by standards then. But cramped as it was, things were clean and orderly. "For instance," he explained, "when we were at St. Bonaventure, whenever you'd go into the locker room to get your 'whites,' you know, your socks and your jocks and your T-shirts, they were all in piles. This pile here, that pile there, this pile. You'd have to go scrounge for yourself. Pick up a pair of socks, get a shirt, get a jock. In Baltimore you went into the locker room and everything was rolled into the T-shirt — jock, pair of socks — and it was in your locker."

He thought: If they just give me a chance . . .

◆

"John, where's John?"

It was Weeb Ewbank on the sideline at Chicago's Wrigley Field, looking for his rookie backup quarterback. Unitas already had his helmet on and was trotting onto the field. It was October 21, 1956, and George Shaw had been injured a second straight year in Chicago. This time a tackle, big Fred Williams, caught him cleanly, and Shaw hadn't gotten up. His right knee had torn ligaments. Although he would play several more seasons, his career had been ruined.

J. C. Caroline intercepted Unitas's first career pass and returned it for a touchdown. And it got worse. The final was 58–27, Bears.

The next day, Don Kellett phoned Gary Kerkorian in Washington, where he was in law school at Georgetown. Kerkorian had played for the Colts in 1954 and 1955 and knew the plays, and so Kellett brought him back. Unitas figured he'd better win the next game, against Green Bay in Baltimore.

Ewbank designed a cautious approach, and it worked. Unitas threw only sixteen times. He completed eight, two for touchdowns, and the Colts won, 28–21. Lenny Moore made the difference with touchdown runs of seventy-nine yards and seventy-two yards.

The next week, the Colts upset the Browns in Cleveland, 21–7, as Ewbank beat his mentor and Unitas the team he thought he might end up with after being cut by the Steelers. He ran thirty-four yards to set up one touchdown. But, again, Moore broke open the game, with a seventy-three-yard scoring dash.

A few days later in Baltimore, equipment man Fred Schubach, going about his locker-room chores, wondered out loud when Shaw might return. Marchetti, the man who seldom spoke, piped up: "He's never going to be the quarterback again. Unitas is the quarterback."

◆

"An eighty-cent phone call . . . So many things that happen in life are so ironic."

Talking about Unitas turned Loudy Loudenslager wistful. It was Baltimore January, a granite-gray afternoon, and Loudy was down in his club cellar — in Baltimore they're not family rooms or club basements, they're club cellars. He was thinking back more than thirty years to 1956, when Unitas came to town.

"Little by little it started coming clear: Hey, maybe this Unitas guy is going to be something special."

In September 1957 Loudy formed Colt Corral No. 2. A man named Leo Novak formed the first of the corral fan clubs in May. No. 2 was made up of Loudy's fellow National Guardsmen, who would get together monthly at the Fifth Regiment Armory and plan trips to road games, other social gatherings, and volunteer work for charitable causes. The wives were included. Flo would bring black walnut cakes.

Loudy helped found several more Colt Corrals. At their peak there were thirty-three. Most nights Loudy would attend some corral meeting, at an armory, bar, or restaurant. Eventually he headed up a Council of Colt Corrals that still puts on an annual convention of corrals in Ocean City — "Downey Ayshin" is how they say it in Baltimore.

In 1960 Loudy began trekking to the airport to see the Colts off to away games and to welcome them back on Sunday nights. The only time Loudy ever missed going to the airport was in 1967, when he suffered a severe attack of angina — or, as he put it, "a little angeena." The setback also caused him to miss his only Colts home game in their entire history, from 1947 through 1983.

"Of all things to miss, the Packers and the Colts. The doctor put me upstairs in bed, wouldn't let me listen to it. Everybody was down in the cellar listening and all. And when it was over Flo came up and sat on the bed. The way she looked I thought they got beat. She said, 'Johnny threw a touchdown pass with 2:19 left, then Lou Michaels had an onside kick and the Colts recovered and Johnny threw another touchdown pass with 1:28 left, and we beat 'em, 13–10.' The way she sounded I felt like pushing her off the bed."

One week when the team's travel plans were changed — they were to take off on Friday instead of Saturday because of a bad-weather forecast for Detroit — an assistant coach, Dick Bielski, said to then head coach Don McCafferty, "This is one departure Loudy is going to miss."

"Nah, Loudy'll be there," McCafferty said.

"Ten bucks says he's not," Bielski said.

"You're on," McCafferty said.

Loudy was there.

He had this long extension cord that he'd hook up to his record player. He'd stretch the cord all the way out on the tarmac to the team plane so the players could hear the Colts' fight song he played as they boarded. And he'd hand out the cards with his poems, which he had stacks of in a box in his basement. Riffling the cards he said: "Lots of cards. I can't believe I wrote all that crap."

"Loudy never made demands on an athlete — he never wanted anything," Joe Ehrmann said. "He was considerate, caring, a very lovable person."

Loudy was a man in love in the truest sense. It could be four-thirty or five in the morning when the Colts would get in from a West Coast trip, and sometimes only Loudy and John Mackey's wife, Sylvia, would be waiting. One time the Colts came home and each of them got off the plane wearing a Loudy T-shirt. Loudy could hardly believe it. He cried a little that night as he walked to his car in the parking lot. And players could see in Loudy's look how much his heart ached the night the Colts landed after a rugged game in Chicago and Unitas still had blood caked on his face.

"It had to be one of the toughest ball games ever played," he said. "And when John got off that plane you'd have thought he'd been in a meat masher. Oh, his face. They beat him up somethin' terrible. But he come off with that crooked smile that he's got.

"Look here" — Loudy had a photo of a smiling Johnny U. "The left side of the smile points up. A different type smile. I don't like to say impish smile, but something like that. Not the type who would outwardly let you know his feelings. Friendly, but not overly. But that's not what he felt inside.

"Several years ago one of the corrals had a banquet in my honor and John and several of the players attended, and each one said a few words. And after John got done, he walked behind me, put his arm on my shoulder, and leaned over and said, 'Who loves ya, baby?'"

Of course Loudy loved Johnny, but it wouldn't be the truth to say that Loudy loved him any more than the others. "I love 'em all equally," he said, and that was easy enough to believe.

He turned on a lamp in the club cellar, and it wasn't just any lamp. He'd bought it, after the Colts won their first championship, at a store in Brooklyn and clamped it to his basement wall. The shade is a diorama of sorts, showing the winning touchdown in the "greatest game ever played." You can see it clearly when the light is on.

"I've always kept that," Loudy said, "because when it's lighted up it really puts Ameche right in the spotlight."

He gave me a letter to read. It was written in May 1968 by Sally Berry, Raymond Berry's wife: "One of the things I just have to do before I leave Baltimore is to tell you how much I appreciate all you have done for the Colts and us . . . I've worried in the past that people might not always appreciate you enough and that's why I just had to tell you how Raymond and I feel. It makes me very sad when I think of leaving Baltimore."

In his club cellar Loudy had hung nineteen Colts jerseys that the players had given him off their backs when they retired. He'd put up all the team photographs, back to 1947. The memorabilia was mounted and included linebacker Don Shinnick's knee brace and a Marchetti jockstrap — bronzed. He'd been given the jockstrap by several of the players.

The Baltimore Highlands row house, part museum really, had been Loudy's home since 1958, the championship season. Before then he and Flo had to manage in cramped quarters on Clement Street in south Baltimore with their two children, Bill and Janet, and Flo's parents. The kids didn't even have their own bedrooms — Bill slept on a sofa in the living room and Janet on a sofa in the dining room. Freight trains would unload on the next street; Bill told me how frightened he'd get from the sound of the grinding wheels of the locomotives when they'd start up.

Back then Loudy would drive around on weekends in his used '53 blue-and-white Buick Roadmaster, looking for a place to move to from the city. He felt bad about conditions on Clement Street, but he still was happy-go-lucky. He'd always be talking about such early Colts as Doc Mobley and George Taliaferro and Sisto Averno and Royce Womble, repeating the names, relishing the way they sounded. Bill, who didn't take an interest in the team until the sixties, would wonder, Who's Royce Womble?

It wasn't long after he'd moved into his new home in the Highlands that Loudy put up a flagpole. On the first day of training camp he'd run up a Colts' flag — GO COLTS, one of the early ones read. Sometimes when he'd get home from a loss at the stadium, someone would have lowered the flag to half staff. He never did find out who'd do it, but he'd always see it lowered just as he drove around the corner onto Norfen. "That sucker," he'd mumble. "Who's that sucker doin' that to me?"

"Now, Loudy, now, Loudy," Flo would say.

In the fifties it was nothing out of the ordinary for players to stop by Loudy's house. And they continued to as time went by.

After a Colts' upset victory in 1973 a big player paused at Loudy's seat at the stadium — the front-row seats Loudy and Flo sat in were near the dugout entrance to the Colts' locker room. The player asked Loudy to come to the locker room, but Loudy, sensing something was up, demurred. The Colt reached over the railing and lifted him.

The next thing Loudy knew he was behind a closed door with the Colt team. Joe Ehrmann began to award game balls: one to the coach, one to a rookie fullback, and one to . . . Loudy!

"This ball," said Ehrmann, "is for a man who was here long before any of us got here and who will be here long after all of us are gone."

The feeling between the players and the people helps explain the card Loudy got in the mail one Christmas. It was from Bert Jones, his playing days over, living back in Louisiana. "I know this may sound silly," Jones wrote, "but I miss you, Loudy."

◆

Pop was both a strict traditionalist and a quirky nonconformist. And he earned my lasting respect the night he came home from work to our Maine Avenue apartment and immediately went to bed with a 104-degree fever. My mother slipped a thermometer under his tongue; he was lying on his back with his head deep in the pillow. I'd never seen him sick. Approaching the bed, I asked him how he would be able to go to work the next morning. With certainty, he said he would go. I was surprised by the resolute response — amazed when he got up the next morning, assured my mother he was fine while refusing to have his temperature taken, and went, as though routinely, to his job. He never — not ever that I know of — missed a day of work.

But when he had a day off, or sometimes just an evening, Pop wanted to be going somewhere, doing something. Baltimoreans of the day — and now — like to sit and contemplate indeterminate times when they might do something. They meditate on marble stoops, on folding chairs on sidewalks in front of row houses, on street benches, on front porches, on back porches, on back-porch gliders if the porches are wide enough, on ends of piers while fishing, deep in beach chairs facing the waves in Ocean City. Pop, though, liked being on the move, getting to the stadium early, finding those certain places to sit in the stands that suited him — third-base side for baseball, first deck only for both baseball and football. On Fridays in summer he'd come home a little early when the Orioles were playing and ask me, "Want to go to the stadium?"

I came to anticipate those early arrivals, as did Mom. She'd have dinner ready, the food would be on the table and eaten quickly, Pop would kiss her on the lips — he'd pucker his lips exaggeratedly when he wanted her smile of approval despite his leaving her behind; he liked getting his way. Then

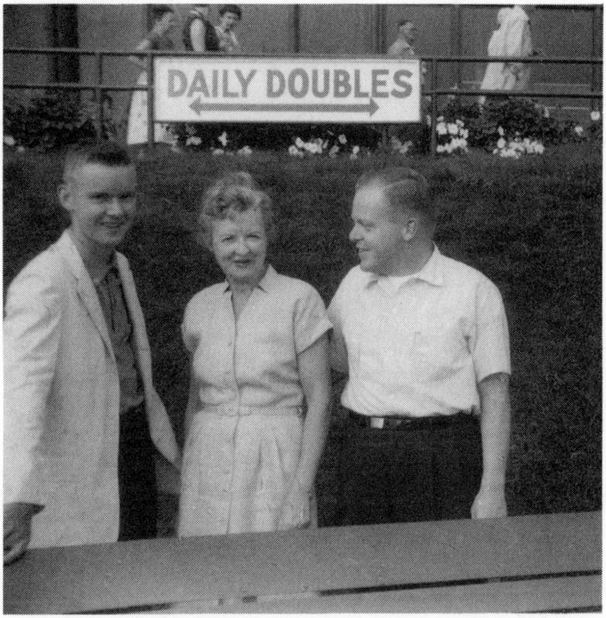

Pop took the photo of Mom, me (left), and Hugh McGovern, a cousin, at one of Pop's favorite places, Monmouth Park in New Jersey, 1957.

he'd hightail it out to the car, with me keeping up. Things were spontaneous with him. He did not put dates on calendars. He didn't have a calendar. If he wanted to know what date it was, he'd look for it on the front page of a newspaper.

He kept in mind certain upcoming games he wanted to see, but rarely mentioned them to me in advance, I'm sure because he wouldn't want to disappoint me if he had to work. One night I opened the *News-Post* on the kitchen floor while he was eating dinner. I was in about the fifth grade. "The Bullets are playing at Rochester tonight," I said. "If they were home, would you take me?"

"Sure," he said.

Pop and his granddaughter, Ann

"I fooled you," I sang out in a childish way. "They're playing Rochester *at home.* Are we going?"

"I guess we'll have to, don't you think, Mary?" he said. It was a school night, and the Bullets' games started unusually late, 9:15. "You promised," she said to him. He took us, insisting that I'd tricked him. Maybe I had, maybe I hadn't. I know he was happy to be at the Coliseum that night. We sat about midway up in the stands, and he told me about the slick Rochester guards whom we watched — Bob Davies (whose overheated red face alarmed Mom) and Bobby Wanzer. My mother told me once, "He always wanted a son to take to the games."

I don't know how many times I asked him why he didn't

just go ahead and buy Colts season tickets. No, no, he'd say, we might not go every Sunday. Sure.

Pop had a good general manager's ability to assess a player's worth and a good coach's or manager's strategic sense, but he never flaunted that knowledge or boasted. My Uncle Vincent, Pop's younger brother, asked me, "Did you know that your father stocked ships with medicine down at the port in Baltimore during the war?"

"I'm not sure, it sounds familiar," I said.

"Well, what did you two talk about when you were together all the time?" he asked.

I told him a lot of times we didn't say anything.

Pop was a fan who rarely raised his voice. His reactions to a play were more like a coach's: a grimace, a slight smile. His idea of a coach was Paul Brown because of his mind — Brown put the classroom into pro football. As a young man Brown had taught at Severn High in Annapolis, and Pop knew of his Maryland connection. In baseball, Pop liked Paul Richards, who managed the big-league Orioles in the fifties. Like Brown, Richards was cerebral. But both also could be intractable, sometimes cold, while Pop had a Jimmy Stewart-aw-shucks innocence. One night when we were driving home after a sandlot softball game Pop had played in (he was a short-center fielder, the odd position between infield and outfield in ten-to-a-side softball), he rubbed his ear and suggested romantically that a burly warehouse worker who'd hit a ball not only out of the field but also across a street and over a row house could play professional baseball. "I do believe," Pop said, "that he could play for the Orioles."

That home run into a Baltimore-sultry summer twilight, swarming with gnats and mosquitoes, instilled in me for a

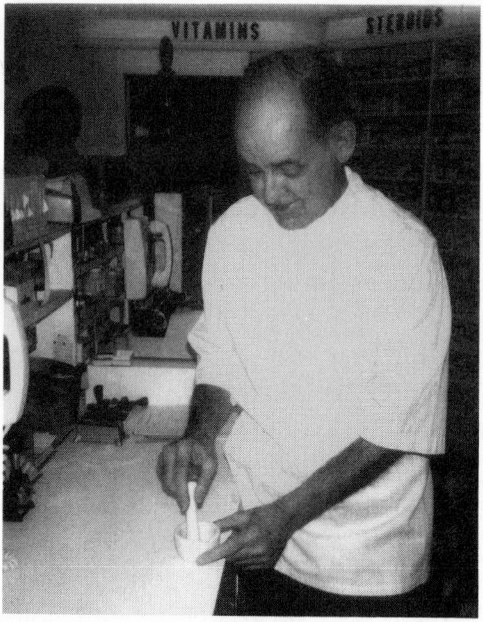

Pop, happily at work

lifetime the idea that almost anything is possible. But as for Pop's notion that our mighty Casey of softball could make the Orioles, even if only a minor-league team then? To me that was wholly unrealistic.

"He couldn't hit the pitching," I said as we drove home.

"You think so? . . . I guess so."

He was a father who could agree with a son's opinion. "He's got a good voice," Pop said of Elvis, surprising me one night when we were driving home from my grandparents' in Towson and listening to the radio. Those blips of conversation between us made me want to be with him. I look back on our time together, and I know: I was blessed.

Riding home together in an autumn sunset after a Colt

victory was a sweet quiet time to reflect on the day's highlights. There were no postgame talk programs on the radio. One of us might say something, or I'd just think about Unitas or Moore or Berry. I'm sure Pop was thinking about them, too. If my spirits were low from defeat, he would speak to my soul by the time we'd cross the Forty-first Street bridge and smell the vinegar from the works in the ravine below.

Mary Margaret Radomski told me that on hot summer evenings she and her sisters, Helen and Ceiley, after they'd gotten their warm baths and had powdered and dressed, would sit out on their front steps and watch the grain elevator that towers above the Locust Point neighborhood. They could hear songs from a radio through an open window on Towson Street. Could anything have been more magnificent than sitting there in the solitary dark listening to the Five Satins sing "In the Still of the Nite," Beethoven's Fifth of doo-wop?

The girls would listen to the music, and they would talk about the Colts and what was happening at training camp. They'd watch the lights on the lift that carried the night watchman to the top of the grain elevator, then follow his flashlight in the sky as he moved along an unseen ledge, making his rounds. Their dad, Joey, would come out and sit with them, following the night watchman's light, and join in the Colt conversation until their marble stoop became too hard for them to sit and talk any longer, and then they'd go inside.

◆

During training camp at Western Maryland College in Westminster, fans could engage the players easily on the campus pathways or as they trudged back from practice, carrying their helmets and shoulder pads. The field was set in a hollow, so the walk back to the locker room entailed climbing a slope where many of the fans had sat watching practice. Hot and sweaty as they were, the players almost uniformly paused to sign autographs, and some would collapse on the grass and talk at length with perfect strangers who'd come to see them.

I looked forward each summer to the easy mingling. At the camp you could stand next to a Colt and appraise his temperament, size, physical condition — barometers of the upcoming season. Pop and I would drive up to Westminster on the concrete state Route 140, which took its time weaving past vegetable and fruit stands, crossroads filling stations, weathered sheds, and a red barn with a Mail Pouch tobacco advertisement on the side. Inevitably the two-lane road left Pop and me poking along behind a produce truck. It was okay. We could talk.

We talked about desperately important matters. For instance, the football future of Billy Vessels. In 1956 I was thrilled that the former all-American running back at Oklahoma finally had joined the Colts after playing a season in the Canadian League for the Edmonton Eskimos and serving two years in the army. I was distressed about Lenny Moore, a number-one draft choice from Penn State; to me, he hadn't flashed any running brilliance in the Shriners' East-West college all-star game in San Francisco after his senior season. After watching that game on TV, I thought the Colts should trade him.

But Pop said the Kezar Stadium field in San Francisco was wet when Moore played on it and the game's outcome meant nothing; no, they shouldn't trade him. As for Vessels,

Pop said he had done himself little good not reporting to Baltimore instead of playing in Canada and now faced stiff competition from Moore — and Pop liked what he'd heard about Moore's speed and elusiveness. Pop believed — correctly — that Vessels would be relegated to the special teams. I couldn't believe that. We went back and forth on Vessels versus Moore, finally compromising — there was room for both — as Pop's Dodge eased over the hills.

Most of the Colts professed an affection for Westminster despite the searing heat of the days and the church-quiet nights, the tediousness of the routine and the bare-bulb accommodations, and, above all, the anguish of getting into shape. "I could never wait to get there," Gino Marchetti told me. "It meant getting together again with all the guys."

They'd roll into town in well-worn cars or trucks — Chevys and Fords filled the parking lot. Bill Pellington, a wild-man linebacker known for playing on in a game despite the pain of a broken arm, hitchhiked to camp for a tryout after being dropped by the Browns. "That guy was going to play," Paul Brown, who'd cut him, said years later. "You know what he'd have done if the Colts cut him? He'd have played for the Annapolis Sailors."

Westminster was summer camp for big boys, and often they behaved as campers do. On Sundays fried chicken was served, and one Sunday the servers had to rush plate after full plate from the kitchen as big Don Joyce and the massive Marchetti engaged in a chicken-eating contest. Joyce was known as "Champ" because he was a pro wrestler in the off-season. "Champ, you don't have to eat the peas and potatoes, too," Art Donovan cried out. Not that it mattered. Marchetti gave up at twenty-six pieces of chicken while Joyce devoured thirty-eight. He then washed them down with a pitcher of iced tea — after insisting on artificial sweetener because he was watching his weight.

But if Westminster was a town Norman Rockwell should have painted, it had a side I was unaware of growing up. Lenny Moore related that in the fifties and early sixties racial prejudice that he encountered in the town hurt him deeply; he and other black Colts had pizzas handed outside to them from a place that didn't welcome them inside. Romeo Valianti, a Westminster resident, told me that one night as he drove up Main Street he came upon Moore.

"'What are you doing?' I asked him.

"He said, 'I went to the movie, and they wouldn't let me through — racial policy.'

"He and I just sat in the damn car together."

Valianti's family and others welcomed all players who would amble down the hill to town. One day in the early fifties Buddy Young walked into the Deluxe Tailors at 185 East Main. The Deluxe was owned by the Valiantis; Vincent and Josephine, who'd settled there from Italy, lived upstairs with their children, Dino, Louis, Reno, Romeo, Clara, Mary, and Anna. Because he didn't feel comfortable wearing hip pads, Young wanted the insides of his football pants sewn shut where the pads usually went.

"I can't run with hip pads," Buddy told the man behind the counter.

"We'll fix 'em without 'em," obliged Dino Valianti, who ran the shop.

The Colts' team began to patronize the Deluxe. If practice jerseys or pants ripped, they'd send them to Dino to sew and clean. This was a time when things weren't summarily discarded if there was any chance they could be repaired.

After the team had run up a five-hundred-dollar bill one

summer, Don Kellett came in and asked Dino if he wanted some stock in the team or cash. Missing his chance at a small fortune, Dino took the cash.

With family pride, Dino's younger brother Romeo used to stand on the slope during team workouts knowing that the practice whites of any number of players had been stitched together at the Deluxe. Romeo happened onto the Colts in the summer of '49, when they first trained in town and he delivered ice. Happy to see him, the players would cool down by rubbing the chunks of ice on their necks.

One evening in the mid-fifties, Romeo was carrying a camera when he encountered Unitas reclined on a bench under a tree outside the dorm. "There was Johnny, all by himself," Romeo recalled. "He'd just come back from riding a bike. It was almost dark. I asked him, 'Mind if I take your picture?'

"'Hell, take it,' he said. That's how Johnny was. Sometimes he sounded gruff. He's hard to get to know. But he likes everybody. As far as I'm concerned, he's a pussycat.

"One time in Baltimore, after practice at the stadium, I had this football and I asked him to autograph it for a kid in the hospital. He said, 'Gimme that goddamned ball.' He took the football down to the hospital himself."

By then, Johnny and Romeo were friends. Romeo worked for the state of Maryland as head of its admissions and amusement tax division, and took his vacations in August so he could be home when the Colts came to town. Late one night, Unitas phoned him from the dorm.

"'Can you bring us up some shrimp?' He was rooming at the time with Earl Morrall. 'We're hungry for some shrimp.'"

Although it was long after 11:00 P.M. when lights in the dorm were supposed to be out, Romeo took the shrimp to

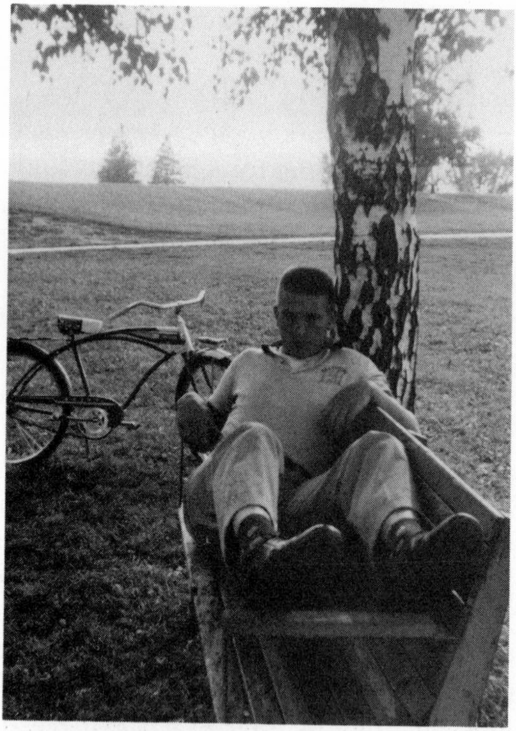

Johnny Unitas, as a rookie in training camp at Western Maryland College in Westminster, Maryland, 1956
Romeo Valianti

Unitas and Morrall. He also carried them a case of beer. Making a second trip into the dorm with the case balanced on his shoulder, Romeo stumbled in the dark and the case slid forward off his shoulder. Beer cans crashed one flight of stairs to the door of Don Shula, then coach. For some reason the racket failed to stir Shula, but an assistant coach, Don McCafferty opened his door. A tall, gray-haired, dignified man, McCafferty was known as "Easy Rider" for a reasonableness not normally associated with coaches.

"Romeo," Valianti recalled McCafferty asking, "what are you doing in here?"

"Geez, Johnny and Earl wanted some shrimp. They were hungry."

McCafferty looked at all the beer cans on the floor.

"Hey," Romeo said meekly, "they had to have something to drink with the shrimp."

Wise enough to know what to do if Unitas, the main man, wanted shrimp and beer at that hour, McCafferty said, "All right, Romeo, give 'em the stuff and get out of here."

"I scrambled around and picked up all the cans and hustled upstairs. We b.s.'d until two in the morning."

Romeo, married by then, had moved from above the Deluxe but only as far as 341 East Main, to a split-level brick home. Each summer, he hosted a crab feast for the players; Unitas regularly won the horseshoe-pitching contests in the backyard. Romeo owned a myna bird he named "Stoney" for linebacker Steve Stonebreaker. Bubba Smith would try to get Stoney to say "Bubba." George Plimpton, in *Mad Ducks and Bears,* recounts Bubba getting too close to Stoney and having his finger bitten.

"One time I came into the house," Romeo told me, "and there was Bubba with his face up near the cage. He was trying to teach the bird to say, 'Hey, Bubba.' He'd say, 'Hey, Bubba. Hey, Bubba.'

"Stoney wouldn't say anything, just whistle. Stoney frustrated Bubba.

"Bubba said to me, 'Why is this bird black?'

"I said, 'Bubba, that's how it is. I don't know of any myna birds any other color.'

"I guess Bubba was a lonely type of individual. He'd stop by a lot, and he'd always go right to the cage and look in at the bird and say, 'Hey, Bubba.' It took a long time, but

At training camp in 1957: linebacker Don Shinnick, Unitas, and receiver Raymond Berry
Marvin E. Newman

Bubba had success. The bird answered him back, 'Hey, Bubba. Hey, Bubba.'

"I said, 'Bubba, don't teach that bird any cuss words. I got a priest who visits here.'"

Romeo keeps a small photo he took of Bubba and Stoney and another snap of Unitas, a smiling, boyish, crew-cut Unitas sitting on the hood of a Ford, his legs dangling in front of its chrome grille. He has the look of uncomplicated innocence.

"Nobody was ever in a hurry," Romeo said.

That's my lasting impression of certain Colts in Westminster: Alan Ameche stopped on a sidewalk talking to fans or friends, his arm around a small girl; Bert Rechichar, walking along by himself with an orange — it was said he was the only Colt before Lou Michaels who could stand outside the dorm and throw an orange over a building on the other side of the quad; Weeb Ewbank taking time from practice to help seat a group of nuns in the small green bleachers; Unitas signing autographs for small boys surrounding him. Parents with blankets and picnic baskets and beach chairs patiently waited on their little ones, to whom Unitas was giving full attention. He was the athlete they all wanted to be someday, the one we wished we could have been.

Each time we'd drive home, Pop and I would stop at a roadside stand for ears of corn and ripe tomatoes. We'd load up the back seat, then continue the countryside dip and roll until the city's buildings came into sight. Pop would always say it was a city soon to be noticed because of its football team.

◆

Unitas would have fit well in Studs Terkel's book *Working*. Terkel writes that work "is, by its very nature, about violence — to the spirit as well as to the body . . . To survive the day is triumph enough for the walking wounded among the great many of us."

Unitas's mother, Helen, once recalled her son reassuring her after she'd express concern about the beatings he took as a player: "He always told me that as long as he could walk away from the stadium when the game was over, there was no reason to be upset."

After her husband's death, Helen Unitas hired men to

drive the coal truck until her son Len was old enough to take over. As youngsters, Len and Johnny did odd jobs that supplemented their mother's income. They shoveled coal that had been delivered to people's backyards into basement bins. The going rate for shoveling was seventy-five cents a ton.

When Johnny was seven, Len found a cartridge in the woods and the two boys threw rocks at it to make it explode; it exploded, and lead had to be scraped out of Johnny's leg at a hospital. When he was a high school junior he was cleaning a gun his mother kept in the house because there had been some robberies nearby. The revolver went off, and the bullet pierced the index finger of his right hand; the finger was saved after another rush to the hospital.

What was still on Unitas's mind when the Colts offered him a tryout was the money he'd "lost" not working construction while he tried out for the Steelers. "I would have been a lot better off working for those couple of months," he wrote in the sixties in a book called *Pro Quarterback*. "I would have been at least a thousand dollars ahead."

From a stark upbringing grew a strict pragmatist who didn't even celebrate his touchdown passes. Norm Van Brocklin, when he coached the Minnesota Vikings, said after a last-minute loss to the Colts: "We should've won, but Unitas is a guy who knows what it was to eat potato soup seven days a week as a kid. That's what beat us."

Unitas's hard-eyed view of things left him little room for romance or whimsy. Of those who might hold him in awe because of his football deeds, he once said: "Those kinds of things never fazed me. The notoriety and the celebrity and all that kind of stuff. I just go my way and do what I think is right and if people like it fine and if they don't it's not my problem."

Unitas was no buoyant interview at his locker after games, win or lose. He never offered one-liners, nor strove to say anything clever. Heroic and sentimental tales, even if he had prompted them with his play, were the business of newspaper writers. His matter-of-factness, a bluntness sometimes, was of no help.

Once after a big game in Cleveland, a *Sports Illustrated* writer called the locker room. "*SI* wants you," Romeo Valianti, who happened to be there, told Unitas. "It might be a good deal."

"Make out you're me," Valianti said Unitas told him.

Unitas never picked up the phone.

Garbo said: "Love is a romantic designation for a most ordinary biological — or, shall we say, chemical? — process. A lot of nonsense is talked and written about it."

"Sportswriters," Unitas once said, "always seemed to make some things more important than they should be."

Tom Callahan, who grew up in Baltimore, said that when he was writing for *Time*, Unitas began a response to a question of his with: "You bull crappers in the media . . ." He said it cordially, but it told his feelings.

What Unitas did offer after games were seminars in football tactics. He'd tell why he'd chosen a play and what went right or wrong and why. A disastrous play didn't affect his demeanor. He didn't cry, curse, kick things. He might say, "Well, that was a kick in the head."

Chuck Thompson, who broadcast the Colts' games, recalled: "The first time the Colts got close enough to win a championship they were defeated by the Rams in the Coliseum. After the game all of us were down in the locker room and it's not a happy place to be and I'm just leaning up against the wall staring at my feet. All of a sudden a finger came by and raised up underneath my nose and pulled my head up. It was John."

In a 1966 game against Green Bay in Baltimore, Packers linebacker Dave Robinson swept around from the side and hit Unitas's arm, causing a fumble. The Colts lost the ball, and the Packers ran out the clock to win, 14–10. Unitas accepted responsibility even though it wasn't his fault Robinson had gotten loose.

If ever there was a mythic defeat suffered by Unitas's Colts it was the final game of 1967 against the Rams at the Coliseum in Los Angeles. It was the Colts' only setback of the year. But in that era before layers of revenue-producing play-offs were added to the schedules, a single defeat abruptly ended the Colts' season. The record was 11–1–2 — improbably not good enough. After the game, I happened to be standing in the locker room next to team owner Carroll Rosenbloom when Unitas came out of the shower with a towel wrapped around his waist. He paused at Rosenbloom's side and said quietly, "I'm sorry, Carroll." That was it. Unitas moved on immediately — having left a heartfelt expression, but one so quick to the point as to preclude any chance for the owner to commiserate unless he trailed after the star, which he didn't.

Even his coach, Don Shula, whose jut jaw announces his toughness, felt Unitas's brusqueness. "One incident took place in a game against Green Bay where we felt we knew the defensive signals the Packers were sending in from the sidelines," Shula wrote in *The Winning Edge.* "If we got the blitz sign, I would signal to our offensive tackle who would say 'blitz' in the huddle and Unitas would call a play with one of our outside receivers, either Raymond Berry or Jimmy Orr. On one play I got the signal for a blitz and sent in the sign to the tackle who relayed it to Unitas. As it turned out, the Packers didn't blitz. I don't know whether they felt we had the signal and were doing something to counteract that or whether we didn't read the signal properly. At any rate, instead of having a one-on-one situation, we found that they were doubling up on the wide intended receiver and the pass was knocked down. After the play, Unitas glared at me on the sideline and kicked the dirt as he came off the field. I got upset.

"'Listen,' I said, 'it wasn't my fault. They crossed us up and I blew it by sending in the wrong sign.'

"'Unless you're sure of what you're doing,' Unitas snapped back, 'don't interrupt my play calling.'"

On rare occasions Unitas could be expansive. Tom Callahan, covering high schools at the time for *The Evening Sun,* was given an assignment one Sunday to write a locker-room sidebar after a Colts game. Standing timidly just inside the Colts' dressing room, he felt a tap on his shoulder. It was Raymond Berry. "You're the lostest looking guy in the room" is the way Berry put it. After Callahan concurred, Berry said, "Come here. What do you want to know?"

And after he'd answered Callahan's questions, Berry asked, "Is there anyone else you want to talk to?"

"Well, yes, I guess Unitas," Callahan said. "So Berry yells, 'Hey, John, come here a minute.' And Unitas leaves an interview in front of his locker and comes over and Berry says, 'John, say hello to my friend Tom Callahan of *The Evening Sun.*' Unitas pulls up a stool and starts calling me 'Tommy.' 'Well, Tommy, here's what we did. We wanted to do this so we worked such and such a play.' And he goes on at length. We just sat there and talked. I remember a TV guy after a while approaching sort of gingerly and Unitas giving him kind of a dirty look. Finally, I had everything and he says, 'Need anything else, Tommy?'"

Modern-day pro football bores Unitas. His belief is that while athletes are bigger, stronger, and faster, the game itself is not as good. To him, if his offensive linemen had been allowed to hold as blockers are in today's game, he could have been afforded even better protection. Although defenses have become more sophisticated, Unitas believes he would have been still more successful in the modern game in part because defensive backs can no longer rough up receivers as blatantly as they did in his day. In Unitas's heart is lodged the uncompromising belief that he was the best. He just never said it.

Not, that is, until my colleague Tony Kornheiser interviewed him for a television program. At the time Unitas was part owner of National Circuits, Inc., a circuit-board manufacturing company that would bankrupt him. Unitas's office and the plant were located in a flat building in an industrial park in northwest Baltimore, a mile from where I'd grown up. Unitas's lack of interest in pro football — his mentioning that more often than not he'll turn off a Monday-night game at the half and go to bed — prompted Kornheiser to press him as to his indifference toward many present-day players until Unitas finally blurted: "Yeah, but I did it better than anybody else. Why watch mediocrity?"

"You were the best?"

Unitas immediately looked sorry for his words.

"Well, that's what everybody says. So I guess I have to believe it." He backed and filled. But that's as genuine a self-appraisal as he's ever uttered publicly.

Even on his induction into the pro football Hall of Fame in Canton, Ohio, in the summer of 1979 Unitas, by one account, "was the only one of the four former standouts who didn't say it was his greatest thrill. He was sincere but not emotional, pleased but not ebullient."

Not long ago, a reporter asked Unitas if he'd ever given thought to his "place" in football history.

"Never concerned me," he replied. "Why would I worry about something like that? I have no reason to worry about that. Wherever anyone wants to put me, that's all right. My only concern is where does my family put me. How does my family feel about me as a father? How do I feel about myself as a father? Am I doing the right thing for them? The only thing that's valuable is your family. Football, everything else is nothing."

He paused and said: "I'll tell you one thing I would have done differently. I would have been a lot better student in high school than I was. But I had a very difficult time. My father died, and I had no one at home pushing me to open the books, or study, and that I regret to this day. I was able to get away with it then. Now you can't. It's even more important for kids now."

Unitas wrote in *Pro Quarterback* that he failed an entrance exam to the University of Pittsburgh and another at the University of Louisville.

But at Louisville he got a chance to appear before a college entrance board. The people on it must have been impressed with his earnestness because they let him in; it wasn't because he was a blue-chip football player.

He'd spent that summer in Louisville, taking courses and working to support himself. He swept up at a tobacco company after hours.

He worked at football, too. In his later years at Colt training camps he did calisthenics and ran laps that he didn't have to do. That was part of being a professional, part of the game.

"Practice, that's where you win or lose ball games," he said. "Practice. When you get in a ball game, it's easy. You have your timing down. You know what this receiver's doing, that receiver's doing. Because there were people who would get in my vision at the last second — and I always waited until the last second to throw the football. A guy would have a hand in your face, but you knew where you were going with the football anyway so you just hung it out there. A lot of times I didn't know whether somebody caught it or not until I'd hear the crowd."

He was, and still is, a worker: During his 1956 rookie season in Baltimore, he worked at Bethlehem Steel. In the mornings before he went to practice he was an ironworker. In 1957, when he was the league's most valuable player, he was a salesman for a corrugated box company. In 1958, the season he made the "greatest game ever" what it was, he worked as a paint salesman.

◆

We lived for Sunday afternoons, for 2:05, when the Colts took the field at Memorial Stadium. The crowd noise that greeted them poured down from the double-decked concrete horseshoe like water from a pitcher. The names . . . They were unique. Had anyone heard of a John Unitas — ever? Or a Gino Marchetti? There was only one Big Daddy Lipscomb. One Bert Rechichar. Bert Rechichar . . . Was that the perfect name for a football player? "Wretch-ih-char" sounds rough. Gino Marchetti . . . You can imagine him as a big kid in his leather jacket and boots, his hair pomade-slick. A particular boy growing up in Baltimore doted on

Buzz Nutter. He loved the name. He wanted to *be* Buzz Nutter. There was something onomatopoeic about the Colts' names.

There was magic in their numbers, too. To us they couldn't have worn other numbers. Nineteen *was* Unitas. Eighty-two *was* Berry. Twenty-four *was* Moore. Thirty-five *was* Ameche. Nutter had the perfect number for a center, fifty. Jim Mutscheller, the right end, could be identified without a number. You could tell him from the shape of his helmet, a snug, foam-rubber-lined helmet like the Chicago Bears used, not the suspension helmet worn by the other Colts. The suspension style slid around on Mutscheller's head and cut his ears, even gave him a cauliflower ear. Mutscheller wore a Bears-type helmet painted in Colt colors.

Memorial Stadium's playing field said everything about life: It was altogether imperfect. Part of the end zone in the stadium's cramped closed end stretched onto a cinder track. That end zone's right portion was called "Orrsville" for Jimmy Orr, who made acrobatic touchdown catches there. The early games each season were played on the dirt of the baseball infield. After baseball season, sod was put down, but it was squishy soft for a couple of weeks, and after that daily practices ate away just about all the grass so that by late November and December the field was shorn to bare earth.

It looks especially like a neighborhood field in a certain color photograph of Roger Carr catching a pass in stride behind a Buffalo Bills' defender because they're running toward the stadium's open end and none of the permanent seats are shown. Fans in the small end zone stands, wearing orange parkas and yellow slickers and Colts' blue-and-white wool caps, are standing, and, beyond them and beyond the game, are two trees tall and stark, and, further yet, high up on Thirty-sixth Street, a white-faced house to the left and a stone house to the right, set against a gray-darkened sky.

It was the homely girl of stadiums. I'd watched it being built; games went on even as the second deck went up. During a Friday-night high school football game, Calvert Hall versus Patterson, I walked up the steps of the first deck and stood in dim light under a freshly poured section. To me a second deck meant that we at last had a big-league stadium, so that when I stopped beneath a light bulb and noticed the huge concrete pillars that would obscure hundreds of lower-deck views I thought they were sensational.

Women behind the concession stands called everyone "hon"; vendors sold little cans of hot chocolate and opened them with church keys. And then there were the Colts' cheerleaders, clad almost as chastely as modern nuns. Five on each side of the field, they carried signboards, each with a letter: "C," "O," "L," "T," "S." Each would leap up with her letter, and everyone in the section of stands in front of her would give a great shout, "C," and so forth, concluding with one give-it-everything cry of "COLTS!" Then the opposite stands would respond. Then both sides would repeat the cheer. The place echoed like a canyon.

A white horse, Dixie, with its girl rider, would thunder around the sidelines, half scaring some of the visiting players as she steered it close to their bench, and the Colts' volunteer band would step out playing the fight song, and thousands, as if the Colts were a college or high school team, would sing along.

Bud Coward played tuba in the band from 1947 to 1959, when he became leader for several seasons. His wife, Betts, made the tuba covers with the Colts' letters on them, and

The Baltimore Colts Marching Band majorettes
were part of Memorial Stadium Sundays.
Harold C. Decker, Jr.

took care of the sheet music, and packed picnics, which the musicians feasted on in the stadium's east parking lot after the games. Players, after they'd showered and dressed, would stop by and join in the conversation and sometimes eat something.

Betts still lives in a red-brick row house on Pleasant Plains Road, off Loch Raven Boulevard. Bud, who worked for the Bank of Baltimore, died in 1977. Betts keeps Bud's two Colt band uniforms hung in her club cellar. The older one is the original green and gray with the gray riding cap and green bill, gray cape with a green collar, green pants. It's gabardine. It was prickly, and on hot September Sundays it could be stifling, and it was heavier yet when it rained.

"The royal-blue-and-white ones were really striking," said Betts, serving me coffee and a hot sticky bun one morning, then bringing out a more modern, lightweight uniform with the white cowboy hat, blue shirt with white fringe, white trousers. She told me that her Uncle Willie Wise was in the band, too — he played the cymbals. I told her the truth, that Bud and Uncle Willie and the others sent shivers down our backs each Sunday.

Betts said that old Colt Steve Myhra used to live around the corner on Thetford and kicked "field goals" over the telephone wires. The receiver Art DeCarlo would stop over to see Betts and sit in the living room and talk because she painted signs for his miniature golf course on Loch Raven.

When the Colts began staying at the Holiday Inn on Loch Raven the evenings before home games, Mutscheller and Marchetti and sometimes Unitas and Shula, then coach, would attend eight o'clock Mass on Sundays at the Cowards' parish, Immaculate Heart of Mary. After Mass they would linger and sign autographs and chat with parishioners.

Bud wasn't as high-stepping a band director as his predecessor Bob Cissin, who'd suffered a heart attack. Though just as passionate, Bud simply was quiet and a model father. He and Betts raised two daughters, Donna Marie and Patricia, who became nuns. Bud and Betts, after he'd retired from the band, used to visit Donna Marie in the novitiate on Sunday afternoons — one Sunday afternoon a month was the only time parents were allowed in. Bud would take his transistor radio, with its wire and earpiece, so he could listen to the Colts. One Sunday an elderly sister whispered to Donna Marie, "It's a shame your father's hard of hearing."

What made Sundays complete for me was the voice of Nelson Baker, for many years the Colts' public address announcer. "Ameche carried the ball. Stopped by . . ." The voice reverberated in the closed end of the stadium and rolled away to the open end. You could always hear Nelson Baker above the din.

GIs in the Pacific who had shortwave radios listened to Baker broadcasting the news from his wartime assignment in . . . San Francisco. An admiral who found Baker kicked back one evening in a Nob Hill bar advised him, "Don't trade your job with Halsey."

In Baltimore Baker worked for WFBR radio. His sports show featured a "Beat Baker" contest in which he picked ten college games and listeners tried to do better. You marked your choices down on a postcard and mailed them in. One week he went seven for ten; I picked all ten. I'd "beaten Baker." About a week later a tie clasp arrived in the mail.

After the games on Sundays, the Colts had their routines. They'd eat dinner at Artie Donovan's place, the Valley Country Club, or at Andy's Restaurant & Lounge on York Road, or at Unitas's Golden Arm, or at Pellington's Iron Horse.

Pop and I usually went straight home. But one Sunday we picked up Mom at the Boulevard Theatre on Greenmount Avenue, where she had gone to the movies while we had gone to the game. Then, Pop took us downtown to the Park Plaza restaurant on Charles Street. After we'd gotten settled, Pop nudged me. Almost elbow to elbow with me at the next table — and I hadn't even noticed — was Ray Krouse, a defensive tackle. Carving that prime rib, he looked bigger to me than anyone I'd ever seen, ever.

◆

What I'll always remember about Lenny Moore's seventy-three-yard run across the frozen ground of Memorial Stadium on November 30, 1958, is how fast he was going when he passed the Colts' bench. The players who weren't in the game were on their feet, as if expecting something, when Moore got the ball on a pitchout from Unitas and cut wide to his left, heading upfield toward the open end of the stadium. From the stands behind the Colts' bench I could see him only as he passed in the spaces between the players on the sideline. He raced along in what looked to me like a rapid-fire sequence of snapshots. Then he cut to the center of the field, swerving directly away from two defenders but head-on toward two others. I finally could see his every move. Would-be tacklers aimed at his long legs, but he suddenly stopped and started up in a new direction, slicing back toward the sideline and away from everyone. He crossed the goal line without a single person touching him.

It was the most important touchdown the Colts had ever scored. It happened with eleven and a half minutes left in a game against San Francisco and enabled the Colts to go ahead, 28–27, after having trailed, 27–7, at halftime. When the Colts won, 35–27, they'd captured their first divisional championship. To this day the Colts who played in that game consider it their greatest half of football, their "greatest game ever."

Unitas brushed tears from his eyes as he left the field. He admitted to reporters, "I guess emotion got the best of all of us."

Delirious spectators who'd swarmed out of the stands carried Moore from the field.

"I just ran," Moore told the writers. "I just ran."

To me it was his finest run of a dozen seasons of fine runs.

Moore gave great joy, but often he didn't get joy. "The color line" of the fifties, dividing black and white communities, gnawed at him. Whites, for the most part, didn't cross that line, didn't even think to cross it, and didn't know the pain being experienced on the other side.

On our side of the line life was almost idyllic. One evening, in the Baltimore in which I grew up, the Roman Catholic Baltimore, I happened to be standing in line for confession at the Immaculate Conception Church, on the hill in Towson. Unitas, Shula, Donovan, Mutscheller — they all went to church there. As I waited my turn in the dim light I couldn't help sensing a restlessness next to me. It was a large man scraping his feet, snorting even like a horse. I looked up into his face and it was Gino Marchetti. Towering, menacing-looking — but a reassuring presence, too. Life was good and the Colts were a real part of it.

Actually, the city was divided by race, by religion, by ethnic group. And the divisions were strong. While I didn't think of it then, Sundays at the stadium brought everyone together, if only for a short time.

I regret that Pop and I never went to Bugle Field or Westport Stadium, where we could have seen Baltimore's black baseball team, the Elite Giants. Roy Campanella and Junior Gilliam played for the Elite Giants before they played for the Brooklyn Dodgers. I wondered about the Elite Giants from reading small articles about them in the *News-Post*. But I never thought to ask Pop to take me. And he never brought up the possibility of going to what was a very different Baltimore. "We were locked into one area, Pennsylvania Avenue," Moore said. "You couldn't go to the movies downtown. You're supposed to be relaxing, thinking about a game, getting ready, and you're carrying this thing."

In 1968, after retiring from football, Moore was hired by CBS — he became the first black analyst on pro football telecasts. But he wasn't prepared to do TV. "No training at all," he said. "That mike opened up, boom, I froze."

As much as he hoped for a second season on the air, he was never called back.

He called CBS.

No return call.

He called again.

Nothing.

He went to New York and stayed two days at a hotel across from CBS. He'd go over to the offices but could never get past the receptionist.

"That's the way that ended," he said.

In 1969 he spent six months back in New York looking for work. He thought New York was the place for him. "That little taste of CBS . . ." That had done it.

He went to ad agencies.

"'Oh, yeah, we remember number twenty-four'" — that was the sort of vague response he received. "I came home, funds depleted. We'd made no money playing football. We lived off what we made. We were just like the average working folks. Now I said to myself, You've got to get a job, get yourself together. You've got to eat. Keep the roof on. The kids. So I started banging around here looking for work and didn't do too well." Moore sighed. He was sitting at the dining room table of his modest brick home in the Baltimore suburb of Randallstown.

Of some players in later life it's said they still look good enough to put on their uniforms. And then there's Lenny Moore. He's six feet one, 190 pounds — just what he was when he played. He's big in the chest, slim-waisted, taller and stronger-looking than I'd thought of him. He was a lithe runner but a load to bring down.

Lenny Moore
The Hearst Corporation

In 1970, three years after he'd played his last game, Moore walked into Snelling & Snelling Employment Service in Baltimore.

"Aren't you Lenny Moore?" asked a man, looking up from his desk.

"Yes."

"Played with the Colts."

"Yes."

"What are you doing in here?"

"What does one come in here for?"

"You mean to tell me you can't find a job?"

"I need work now."

Moore was desperate. He was almost broke.

Snelling & Snelling referred him to an ad agency that included the army among its accounts. Moore spent from 1970 to 1974 making appearances on behalf of army recruiters. He owned the Club 24 on Gwynn Oak Avenue — but didn't have much enthusiasm for it and made next to nothing from it. Then, in late 1974, general manager Joe Thomas called and hired him to do community relations work. Lenny Moore was back in football.

He was written up in the newspapers again, and people remembered how feared a figure he'd been on the field.

He was probably the first pro running back who was an equal threat as a runner and a receiver. He could take a handoff or catch a ball and, with a high, elusive step, leave opponents grasping only air. Other teams rearranged defenses to stop him.

When Moore ran, his legs pumped conspicuously because of all the tape he had wrapped around his shoes. He learned to tape his shoes from another running back at Penn State. The late coach Rip Engle didn't want his runners wearing low-cuts and, Moore recalled, "I don't like that leather up around my ankle."

But he saw this other player winding tape around his high-tops. "I said, 'Hey, man, why are you taping down over your shoes like that?' He said he'd injured his ankle and that it provided support. I said, 'Let me try that.'"

Lenny Moore would become known in the NFL as "Spats."

He was durable, too. But in his eighth season, 1963, Moore was plagued by illness and injuries. He had appendicitis, but still only missed one game. Once when he was tackled his helmet was ripped off and he was kicked in the head; he couldn't shake the dizzy spells that followed. Yet even people connected with the team doubted him. He believed, after all he'd done, some considered him a slacker. At the end of the season owner Carroll Rosenbloom called him in for a meeting — the two of them and Coach Don Shula.

"He asked me one question: 'Lenny, do you want to play for the Baltimore Colts in 1964?'

"I said, 'Yes, Carroll, I do.'

"He said, 'Meeting's over.'"

And so in his ninth season, Moore scored twenty touchdowns.

"It was most gratifying, most gratifying," he said.

Yet for all his success Moore seems haunted by what might have been. "People say we were one family. Well, we weren't. Because society would not allow that we be one, that we be together socially. When the game was over, the white players would go out to the Towson area and we were in the inner city. So we had very little social contact. We knew each other as ballplayers. But we didn't know each other as men. We didn't know the real person.

"So people would say, 'You guys were really something during those days. What kind of a guy was Johnny Unitas?'

"I'd say, 'John Unitas the football player was something else. Johnny Unitas the man I couldn't tell you anything about' . . .

"Gee, I wish I had known him. I mean, really known him . . .

"Oh, yeah, we slept in dormitories, we went on trips together, but that's not knowing the person. If you've been to a person's home and mingled with the family, then you know the person. So I'd say, 'I can tell you nothing about Unitas, Donovan, Marchetti, none of them.'

"We respected each other as players. But it was a respect that went only to that level."

Moore said that only one white Colt ever spoke to him about the unspoken, the obvious second-class status of black athletes in the fifties and later. It happened before the opening exhibition game of 1959 between the Colts and Giants, billed as a "replay" of the '58 title game. The game was played in Dallas, and the black players from both teams, angered over being shunted to all-black motels, met and talked about the possibility of striking the game, although eventually they decided not to.

"Raymond Berry came around," said Moore, "and apologized for the situation we were being put through. He wanted us to know that he was sorry. He was the only one.

"Years later, Alan Ameche came to me at one of the team's alumni functions — this was in the late seventies out at Donovan's club. I really appreciated what he had to say. It was indicative of the man that I really never knew, that I would have loved to know.

"He said, 'Lenny, I've been meaning to say this for years. I know that the black guys on the team were treated very unfairly during the heavy years. That really bothered me. Probably it was one of the biggest things that bothered me in my career. And I never did anything about it.'"

A double standard, racial slurs — these were the sad facts that nagged at Moore.

"'Put a towel around your neck,' they'd say if you had a cold. But they'd send the white players home.

"It wasn't subtle. You would get the old watermelon thing, those old minstrel jokes."

Moore rarely let his feelings be known. For instance: "When I turned pro I was very apprehensive whether or not I could make it. After the All-Star Game [in 1956] I went right to Hershey, Pennsylvania, where the Colts were playing the Eagles in an exhibition game. And they put me in on the kickoff-return team and I was scared to death. That was my first experience because I didn't know the system and basically was sitting out, observing, listening to the sound of those blows. Wow, I don't know whether I can handle this or not. I'll never forget it. There was this table where they kept tape and equipment between the two benches, the offensive and defensive benches. And the Eagles knocked this Colt out of bounds and about two or three Eagles jumped on him and they splintered that table. I said, Man, is this what this game is all about? Can I take those blows?"

He kept the more important feelings to himself as well while yearning for a genuine brotherhood among the Colts' half-dozen black players and their white teammates. He knew: Had the white players known him the way he wanted, they would have realized Lenny Moore wasn't nearly the happy guy he was thought to be by white teammates and fans. Especially teammates. As Donovan wrote in *Fatso,* Moore was "one wild man."

Moore admitted it. He wasn't prepared for city life and its temptations after rural Penn State — "You're like a hermit on a mountain with no social life. Then you come down here. Woom! You're looking for 'life,' and next thing you know you've got no family. You get caught up in all the things out there." His first marriage lasted only a year after he arrived in Baltimore.

Even as he matured he still "liked to laugh and joke," and his image remained that of "carefree." In fact, "There were things I felt I couldn't say in the fifties that I could say in the sixties. It was very, very frustrating."

Ameche's sentiments finally prompted Moore to unburden himself. A group of old Colts had gathered at Bill

Pellington's Iron Horse. He didn't plan a speech, he just happened to be called on.

"I said, 'I have to say this, guys. We've been playing the game too long, playing around it.' I said, 'I'm sorry that I never got to know you. I'm really sorry.'" His voice dropped as he reenacted his talk. "'I wish that I had the opportunity to have really known you. It's not your fault. It's not my fault. It was society's fault.' I said, 'We don't know each other. I wish that weren't so. It's sad.' You could hear a pin drop. I was looking for reaction. Because I've lived this all my life."

But none of the white players that day mentioned anything about what he'd said. Why they didn't is still a mystery to him. Were they embarrassed? They *must* have cared. Maybe it was the wrong timing — a party too long gone to allow for a few serious words.

Moore stayed a while and then left. "You know when it's time to leave," he said. "You can sense when the drinks start rolling. I always knew exactly when to get ready to split." He spoke with resignation in his voice and leaned back on his dining room chair.

He and the late Willie Galimore of the Bears had concluded during their playing days that the black-white chasm was about the same on all teams. But that was no solace for Moore.

"The situation probably affected what I could have been," he said. "With both groups giving out and reaching out, maybe I could have been even a better ballplayer than what I was. Because it affected you to the point that sometimes you ended up getting moody, and that hurt you . . . Like if I could just play football without this pressure and tension and constant thing on me, what a joy it would be." His voice rose. "What a joy it would have been if all I had to do was just play football, which is all they had to do."

It wasn't until his second time around with the Colts, after Thomas had offered him the job of community relations director, that Moore could relax and be himself. He felt wanted. Free to make what he would of the job, he worked for the Colts from 1975 to late 1982. He worked almost daily in the community, making appearances, shaking hands, doing everything he could for the Colts. He thought up an ad campaign, posing old players with current ones who played similar positions: Unitas and Bert Jones, himself and Lydell Mitchell, Marchetti and Ehrmann. The photos appeared on billboards, on buses.

But Colt fortunes began to fall in 1977. Owner Robert Irsay sided with coach Ted Marchibroda in his power struggle with Thomas and fired Thomas. Thomas's most valuable asset had been his ability to keep Irsay occupied with his business interests in Chicago and safely out of the football team's day-to-day operations. Not anymore. With Thomas gone Irsay took charge in Baltimore. And Irsay was unpredictable. "You got into chaos," Moore said. "And up until the time the team left it got worse." Irsay began cutting jobs in the front office. During the 1982 players' strike he lopped off Moore. "No, no, no, you're not released, you're only laid off," Moore said Irsay told him. "As soon as the strike is over you'll be back."

After the strike ended, Moore called a friend in the Colts' office who tried to intercede. But Moore said that Irsay never got back to him. Finally he cornered Irsay at Memorial Stadium before a late-season game.

"No, no, no, you're not fired, you're just laid off."

"Well, how long will I be laid off? I've got to start making other plans."

Irsay told him to keep in touch with the staffer. Moore pointed out that he already was, adding, "What better for me to do than to talk to you. Tell me what's my role, if I have a role."

"Everything's all right. You're just laid off."

One day in March 1983, Moore said to Edith, "Sweetheart, I think we better forget it."

Edith was the person who'd made Lenny's life a whole lot better — who changed it.

In 1975 Moore's second wife, Erma, was stricken with cancer. It was just a year after they'd been married. That was also the year he was elected to the pro football Hall of Fame. He took Erma to Canton, Ohio, for his induction ceremony on August 2; she'd wanted to be there, but it was all she could do to make it through the day. She needed nurses and a cot. She lingered another two months, then died.

"That was the year I asked the Lord to take my life," Moore said. "I meant that literally. I had nothing to live for. My first marriage had ended in divorce and now . . ."

But shortly he met Edith, and they were married in 1976. In 1981, "led by my wife's prayers," he became a born-again Christian. After Irsay dumped him Edith and Lenny prayed together.

"I started going around, job hunting again. I was really nervous. It was like I was doing this for the first time."

It took him a year, but he caught on with the Maryland Department of Health and Mental Hygiene's juvenile services division — in substance-abuse prevention. "It was hands-on with the kids, kids who've run afoul of the law. It's satisfying working with young people because they've got so much life ahead of them if you can intervene and point them in another direction.

"The whole process that I've learned in my later years is

to give, man. That's bottom line, that's the whole thing, regardless of whatever venture I may be in. That's fulfilling, that's what life's about. What can I do that can help you?"

Moore mentioned that often he's called on Donovan and Mutscheller to join him in his work with troubled young people — meet them, talk with them — and that his two former teammates have always helped. The reliable Mutscheller does the driving, makes sure Donovan gets there.

"I've been able to find a peace I never knew," Moore said. "Touching one of these kids is the most important thing I could ever do. The majority of these kids have never had anyone tell them they're loved. It sounds like a minor thing, but it's very major in their lives, very major. Just putting your arm around them is a major thing because in a lot of cases no one has done it."

◆

About 9:00 A.M. on Saturday, December 27, 1958, John Steadman entered the tiny lobby of the *News-Post,* turned right, and took the elevator to the fifth floor. No one was there. The place was a sea of desktop clutter. Steadman had come in early to write his column for the *Sunday American* — to forecast what he thought would happen the next afternoon in New York when the Colts played the Giants for the NFL championship. No one in Baltimore knew more about the Colts than Steadman. Nor does anyone now. Still a popular Baltimore sportswriter, Steadman is a ruddy-faced, wavy-haired, bushy-browed writer with strong opinions, one of which is that the city was "plundered" — to use one of his gentler characterizations — of its football team.

In the late forties and early fifties Steadman covered the team as a reporter for the *News-Post.* After a stint as the

Colts' publicist, he succeeded Rodger Pippen as the *News-Post* and *Sunday American* sports editor on January 6, 1958. Pippen had been sports editor for fifty-two years. My father rightly judged Pippen a "blowhard." He was — and more. Steadman told me that Pippen, because he'd taken twenty-four boxing lessons, fancied himself a fighter; Pippen covered boxing well but many a time had duked it out with dissenting readers. But Pippen offered Steadman some sound advice when handing over his desk: "Don't get bogged down in entangled sentences. The best sentence ever written contained only two words: 'Jesus wept.'"

Steadman wrote up to six columns a week until the paper folded in 1986 (the name was changed to *The News American* in 1964). He wrote about such characters as Balls Maggio (who found old tennis balls and sold them), Good Luck Slim (a former circus thin man), and Mr. Diz (a racetrack regular who had a horse named for him).

Unlike his imperious predecessor, Steadman was a pleasure to work for. He gave me my first newspaper assignments — on busy Saturdays when events such as semipro soccer had to be covered — after an introduction from my friend, Steve Gavin, who was a year ahead of me in high school and, being very facile, already worked on the paper. I typed my accounts tentatively, cowed by the hubbub of the *News-Post* newsroom. Then I'd watch Gavin run my copy through his typewriter — rewrite! As humbling as the experience was, I thrilled to the appearance of my much-altered work when it came out in the *Sunday American,* even though it had no byline and was buried deep in the sports pages. I was hooked by the newspaper business.

Steadman himself had had a more difficult time breaking in. In 1945 he'd gone directly from City College High School to minor-league baseball. Signed by the Pittsburgh Pirates, he'd played briefly until he suffered a career-ending arm injury. His dream dashed, he came home to Baltimore and, at the age of seventeen, presented himself without newspaper experience to Pippen — in front of the desk that someday would be his.

"No, son, there're no jobs," Pippen sneered.

Steadman recalled asking, "'Sir, could you send me to a lower paper?' I thought newspapers were like baseball. You could be sent to the minors to learn."

Pippen looked up again and said to the nervous youngster, drawing out each word, "Mister Hearst has all *big* papers."

Steadman bore the news as he'd been taught, hiding the anguish and humiliation; he'd grown up in a strict Irish Catholic family not unlike my own. And like myself, he was further disciplined by nuns. One of the Sisters of Notre Dame at Blessed Sacrament School on York Road had slapped Steadman's palms repeatedly with a ruler in the cloakroom after a Hochschild, Kohn department-store delivery man reported two boys throwing snowballs at his panel truck. In my case, Sister Miriam Irene, third grade, and Sister Rita, eighth grade, were the terrors of my early life at All Saints School; both were heavyset time bombs who could explode literally at the drop of a pencil. When we weren't writing or turning a page in a book, we sat with hands clasped on the edge of our desks.

"The two words I learned as a kid were 'suspended' and 'dismissed,'" said Steadman, the oldest of three children. He heard these around the house, a duplex on Forty-first Street near York Road, when his father might be talking about what had happened to a colleague. John Steadman, Sr., was a deputy fire chief who always made himself available to counsel coworkers; firefighters who'd been disciplined or had other problems regularly came by the Steadman house seeking advice or consolation, and John Sr., after clearing the living room of family members, would hear out each individual and give his best opinion. He was known for his love of sports and loyalty to colleagues.

So was Pop, as a store manager for Read's, and starting in the late fifties as a Read's supervisor who would make daily rounds to a dozen stores. Charles Pang, a pharmacist now in Takoma Park, Maryland, told me that Pop, as supervisor, put him to work behind the liquor counter in Read's at North and Maryland. "When he'd come into the store, he'd always come over to me and ask how I was doing. Being from Korea, I didn't know much about American business. In the beginning he told me, 'Don't try to learn everything at once. Don't worry.' Later, he moved me behind the prescription counter, as drug clerk. He knew my interest in pharmacy because he would talk with me."

Just as "Doc" Spang in Aberdeen had been for him, Pop was mentor to any number of Read's workers. Charles Tregoe, director of drug control for the state of Maryland, was a young pharmacist at Read's in the Woodmoor shopping center when Pop was supervisor. "We talked sports every chance we got," Tregoe said. "Sometimes we'd go to the delicatessen next door for a sandwich. Your father was not a typical executive. He was more of a worker. He lugged merchandise in his station wagon; if we needed a particular item, he'd bring it from another store. He was a truthful, caring man. He said if you make a mistake on a prescription, admit it. He said, 'Always show people you care about the medicine they're taking.' And he never worked off the clock."

I remember Pop hanging up the phone at home one night and saying, "Number four's on fire." That was the smallest Read's store, which was the reason I liked it so. It was across the street from a side entrance to the Lexington Market. I watched that fire and was saddened by the black smoke spiraling from the roof. Firemen barreled through the front door. Courage of that sort was one reason John Steadman, Sr., was his son's hero.

But Steadman Sr. could be strict with the son. As an eighth-grader, young John spoke up one evening, while playing marbles on the living room rug with his brother: He would not wear knickers to high school. "If I tell you to wear them, you will," replied his father, seated in his chair.

"I won't," John Jr. persisted.

"It's time for you to go to bed," said his father with a suddenly stern tone. It was an order.

Steadman remembered: "I left the room and went to bed in a huff. The next morning he came into our room to say good-bye. He'd get up at six o'clock. At the time he was making the St. Francis Xavier novena at St. Ignatius at seven o'clock, and he'd be at work at eight. I told him, 'Dad, I could never be mad at you.' I kissed him good-bye." It was March 7, 1940. That afternoon at work Steadman Sr. died instantly of a heart attack. He was forty-nine.

Steadman's benefactor on the *News-Post* was Frank Cashen, later to be president of the New York Mets. Cashen, a *News-Post* staffer, got Steadman a job on the paper keeping track of the baseball scores and race results. Steadman was paid fourteen dollars a week. He worked his way up.

During the first weekend of January 1958, my father told me that a new sports editor was taking over at the *News-Post.* Pop reasoned that Steadman would know his subject matter, probably because he was coming from the Colts. Pop and I anticipated Steadman's first column, which appeared on a Monday evening. Pop read it in his living room chair, nodded approval, and passed the sports section down to me. I was sitting on the rug and spread out the paper.

The column was the opposite of Pippen's usual bombast. Steadman wrote humbly about the difficulties in succeeding a legend. I told John how Pop and I had waited for his first column. As sincere as he was the day he gave me my first assignment, he voiced amazement that we could have cared so much about his first piece as sports editor. I assured him it was so.

On Saturday morning, December 27, 1958, Steadman — "Steady," some fellow workers call him — tapped out his column about the next day's title game. He left it behind with his prediction of the score, to be placed under a big block heading EXPERT OPINIONS. He picked the Colts, of course. He said it would be 23–17. With that, he departed the building.

Just before the bulldog edition's 2:00 P.M. deadline, the copy cutter in the composing room, a man named Vaughan Anders, called the sports department. Where was John?

He was gone, Anders was told. Steadman had taken the train. He was on his way to New York.

Anders knew sports, and he wanted to save Steadman embarrassment. Twenty-three was a strange number to have in a football score, the man realized. What could Steadman have been thinking of?

"We can't print this," Anders said on the phone.

The fellow in sports, by Steadman's account, replied, "John's gone. We have to run it. We don't have any choice."

And so on the morning of the championship game, the

first pick listed under EXPERT OPINIONS read: JOHN F. STEADMAN, SPORTS EDITOR — COLTS 23, GIANTS 17.

◆

That Sunday, a cold wind blew across the Baltimore waterfront. Breakfast finished, Joey Radomski pulled on his wool jacket and, heading out of his row house in Locust Point, turned up his collar. He'd already been to Mass, at Our Lady of Good Counsel at the end of the block. Most days on a green park bench across the street from the church, retired longshoremen with peculiar names — Hambone, Koby, Slim — would retell stories of their days on the piers even as their grown children loaded and unloaded cargo nearby. But on Sunday morning the streets were empty and practically the only sound was church bells.

Joey headed the other way from church, past the red-brick fronts of Towson Street, left onto Clement, right onto Hull, to the one-story cinder-block headquarters of the International Longshoremen's Association No. 32. The harbor was filled with ships to be loaded or unloaded, and if Joey Radomski had orders posted that morning, Sunday or not, he would be obliged to work. But Joey did not want to work that day. He wished he'd put in for a vacation day. He wanted the day off to watch the Colts and Giants on television. He hadn't wanted anything so much since eloping with Agnes twenty years before.

Joey had intended to take Mary Margaret to New York to the big game. He'd asked around and gotten tickets. This was considered remarkable for Joey because ordinarily he would have been too shy to ask. On Saturdays, for instance, Joey would stand outside the window of Altman's meat market, sometimes for up to an hour, waiting for the man inside to carve just the slices of lean corned beef he wanted. When he saw what he liked being cut, he'd hurry inside and order — when all he had to do in the first place was go in and speak up. On these tedious occasions, one or more of his girls usually were waiting in the car, restless for Joey to return and reward their patience with a bag of chocolate-topped cookies from Stone's bakery.

But Joey never got to go to the game. Mary Margaret, who was eighteen then, hemorrhaged from having a tooth pulled two weeks earlier; she'd even been ordered to bed for a few days. Afraid that she would hemorrhage again, Joey decided against the trip. He wouldn't go without her. With a heavy heart he gave away the tickets.

But on the morning of the game Joey's mood brightened. No orders had been posted for him; he was free to watch the game on television. As soon as he walked back into their living room Mary Margaret knew from his smile that they'd be watching the game together. Agnes planned a late dinner, even though on Sundays she usually had an early one. Either way, it didn't matter to Mary Margaret. She'd get so worked up for a Colts game she could never eat before or after.

Two hours before kickoff Joey positioned himself in his chair in front of the television. Typical of the houses down the Point, the Radomskis' was so narrow the rooms were laid out in single file. On the first floor, from front to rear, were the living room with its stained-glass transom, a sitting room with the RCA floor-model TV, the dining room with a picture of *The Last Supper* on the wall, and the kitchen with a beauty of a Philco refrigerator that had only recently spelled the end of the iceman.

The tight quarters of the second floor always caused trouble for Joey when he went to the bathroom in the middle of the night. He'd have to go through Ceiley and Helen's bedroom, between their beds. Because Helen slept with brush rollers in her hair, she'd strategically let her head hang over the side of the bed. Invariably Joey would scratch his bare leg against the curlers as he passed. "Aaah, those damn rollers," he'd say, waking the girls.

With the game about to begin, Mary Margaret sat down in a recliner next to Joey's chair. She was her usual wreck. At the kickoff she squeezed her rosary beads. If the Colts were granted victory she'd vowed to make an eight-day novena.

◆

Pop and I watched from the middle deck at Yankee Stadium. I never thought to keep the ticket stub, but I did make a scrapbook. It's filled with quaint headlines: COLTS WIN FOR GINO, FALLEN HERO and LUNATICS, 30,000 OF 'EM, JAM AIRPORT. "Unitas was the greatest pitcher I've seen since Hubbell," Bob Considine wrote.

We had taken the subway from Aunt Bea's. There were some Colt rooters in the subway station waiting. "Gimme a 'C,'" one shouted. "'C,'" roared the group. "They ought to throw them on the tracks," harrumphed a New Yorker, dapperly attired with hat and scarf.

The Colts were three-and-a-half-point favorites. The day was gray but the temperature at game time was a mild forty-nine. Most of the players were relaxed before the game, according to Steadman, who stayed at their hotel in the Bronx. In the Yankee Stadium locker room Alan Ameche delivered a few lines from the Gettysburg Address to no one in particular. Ewbank made a pregame speech that Knute Rockne would have admired. In a recitation that current coaches wouldn't dare resort to and players wouldn't sit still for, Ewbank cited a great number of his Colts and told how each had been rejected by other teams. No one in the room heard anything unfamiliar, but still the schmaltz had its effect.

Ready to play, the Colts scored two touchdowns following fumbles by Frank Gifford. Leading 14–3 in the third period, they tried to put away the game, disdaining a field goal on fourth down at the Giants one. Just below my seat, Unitas pitched out to Ameche. It looked like a slow-developing play; Ameche was thrown for a loss. It could have been 21–3, Colts. Instead, events changed dramatically. The Giants stormed back and helped make the game great.

Of course Unitas remembered the play when I asked him about it. Ewbank hadn't sent out the field-goal team, so Unitas knew it was up to him to beat a tough Giants defense with the likes of Sam Huff, Rosey Grier, Andy Robustelli, and Emlen Tunnell. But that's what made Unitas the quarterback he was: the way he thought. What he thought that time was a pass by the fullback.

"Who would have expected Ameche to throw the football?" said Unitas. The play he called was 428. "It was designed for Ameche to catch the pitchout, take two, three steps, just raise up, and throw. Jim Mutscheller was wide open, standing in the end zone." Ameche never threw.

"He just thought it was a run all the way," said Unitas. "He never heard the '4.'

"If you look at the film, you'll see Mutscheller standing right there in the end zone. All Ameche had to do was shot-put it. He didn't even have to throw it."

You can imagine Unitas's surprise at the time, but he gave no hint of how he felt. He loped off the field, head bent.

The Giants struck for two touchdowns and a 17–14 lead. It grew colder, and darker. The stadium lights shone. The

Giants were trying to run out the clock when Marchetti smacked down Gifford. In the pileup Big Daddy Lipscomb fell on Marchetti and broke his teammate's ankle. The referee spotted the ball, and Pop and I, from the distant end zone, squinted to see where he placed it. The Giants have always claimed that the official's placement of the ball cost them a first down and the game. They say he moved the ball back from where Gifford was downed. It was fourth and inches, and the Giants punted. With about two minutes and twenty seconds remaining, the Colts were eighty-six yards from the Giants' goal line.

And then . . .

Three Unitas-to-Berry passes totaled sixty-two yards as the Colts drove to the Giants' thirteen-yard line. The second hand on the Longines clock moved up toward zero. The Colts needed three points to tie.

With time almost out, the Baltimore field-goal team rushed on. The players tumbled into place with the clock moving, only seconds remaining. Steve Myhra was no automatic three even if he only had to kick the ball twenty yards; he'd made only four of ten field-goal attempts during the season.

George Shaw knelt to hold the ball for Myhra. Shaw's hands were cold. As he'd left the sideline Dick Szymanski had said to him, "For crissakes, George, don't fumble the ball." Shaw wished Szymanski hadn't said that.

I buried my face against Pop's shoulder. I still remember the feel of his wool overcoat against my nose.

"What happened?" I asked.

"He made it!"

I looked up to see Myhra whirling and leaping. Shaw, relieved, clapped. On the sideline, players shouted and jumped. They'd play overtime, an unprecedented "fifth" period.

Unitas stood with his hands on his hips, filling in as cap-

Johnny Unitas
The Hearst Corporation

tain for Marchetti for the coin flip at midfield. The Giants won the toss and received. But they just missed a first down and punted. With that, Unitas directed an eighty-yard march. He salvaged two third-and-long situations with dart-like passes, including a twenty-one-yarder to Berry on third-and-fifteen.

To me, that pass to Berry was the equivalent of a Rembrandt stroke. With mincing steps, Unitas drifted out of the pocket to his left and calmly directed Berry. Robustelli and company were after him, but Unitas gave a little wave as if he were parking a car and in no particular hurry.

"The guy who was covering him had fallen down and Raymond didn't notice it," Unitas told me, "and I moved outside and motioned to go on downfield. And I just threw him the football."

On the next play Unitas saw that the middle linebacker, Huff, who had been a bulwark, was edging over to help against the slant-in passes to Berry. "When I noticed that Sam had started to get a little bit deeper," said Unitas, "I checked off at the line of scrimmage to a trap play. [Dick] Modzelewski was coming hard so [Jim] Parker trapped him and [Buzz] Nutter blocked back. George Preas made the block on Sam. Sam was usually up tight where the tackle can't get to him, but he got out of the hole in the linebacker position and the tackle was able to cut across and hit him. Ameche went right up the seam." He went twenty-three yards to the Giants' twenty.

Then, another unorthodox call by Unitas: He passed into heavy traffic to Berry to the Giants' eight-yard line.

Still more Unitas audacity: He threw to Mutscheller at the right sideline, to the one. Ewbank said he "almost fainted."

Ameche plunged over right tackle, and Baltimore rooters from the other end zone seats spilled onto the field. They tore down the goal post, which barely missed one fan, who stepped clear at the last instant. The ball got loose from Ameche, but Nutter, surrounded by fans, saw it at his feet and picked it up. In the locker room he gave it to Marchetti.

A clipping of a locker-room photograph I've saved shows Ameche with his arm around Unitas's neck, kissing him on the cheek. In the photo Ameche's nose is bent against Unitas's face. Unitas is smiling. It was about as happy as he got.

◆

Listening on his car radio when Myhra kicked the field goal, a Colt fan drove into a telephone pole. Another leaped and cut his hand on a ceiling light bulb and had to be treated at an emergency room.

Thirty thousand greeted the team at the airport. People

ran onto the tarmac, surrounded the team bus, danced on its roof, and rocked it so hard the players feared the bus was going to be toppled. Police moved in and rescued the team, clearing a path so that the bus could drive away. After the celebration had subsided, a man looked back on the blacktop where the mob had surged and noticed the litter of women's shoes that had been lost in the crush.

My friend George Clayton watched the game on TV at the Christian Brothers' scholasticate in Elkins Park, Pennsylvania. The brothers owned a set, but the scholastics could watch it only on certain occasions. "It had to be an educational experience," George said. "'The Game' was declared an educational experience."

The novitiate in Baltimore where Donna Marie Coward was preparing to be a nun also had a TV. Why it was there was a mystery; nobody was allowed to watch it. There was no rule, however, about *listening* to it. The mother superior, a Colts fan, turned on the TV and covered the picture with a blanket. She and Donna Marie sat in front of the blanket and rooted. After hearing that story, Betts Coward said to her daughter, "I can't believe you didn't have a temptation to lift the blanket when they said Unitas faded back to throw a long pass."

Joey Radomski thought for sure that Mary Margaret was going to start hemorrhaging again she was so nervous during the game. She'd stand up and sit down. She'd climb the stairs and come right back down. On crucial plays she'd pull her rosary-draped hands to her face and gasp. When the game went into overtime a frazzled Joey yelled at Mary Margaret: Jesus, girl, sit down, relax, it's just a game. Words to that effect. Mary Margaret kept praying "Hail Marys." But then the TV screen went blank. For two and a half minutes of overtime there was no picture because a spectator at Yankee Stadium had jostled loose a power cable. Joey thought the problem was in his set. He smacked the top of the console and ran off a litany of stevedore's oaths. Just a game, eh?

In the bucolic Baltimore suburb of Riderwood, there was a mad scramble for a radio. Ogden Nash, who had moved to New York in the fifties to write Broadway plays, and his wife, Frances, were visiting their daughter Linell and her husband. "We almost went mad," Linell said. "I never felt such panic in my life. All of us — my grandmother and grandfather, my mother and father, my husband and I, our children, four generations! — sitting, watching that game. Then, looking for the radio, our behavior was something absolutely appalling. And then we didn't know which station had it."

Then the picture came back on. Cheering erupted in Riderwood. In the Radomski household, Joey shouted, "How'd we get to the eight-yard line?"

Mary Margaret didn't stop praying to answer. When Ameche scored, Joey cheered and Mary Margaret wept with joy.

In the evening he drove her uptown to see the celebrating. The intersection of Baltimore and Charles streets was solid humanity. Cars were backed up for blocks, horns blaring. Firecrackers went off. People on the sidewalks carried hand-lettered placards and pennants, cameras, babies. From the back of the crowd Joey and Mary Margaret stood and watched.

◆

That night Pop and I took the Pennsy home, returning as if from enemy soil, tired but triumphant. Getting aboard wasn't easy. People crowded the platform. Pop motioned me forward until we reached the dining car, and there we went inside. One table was free at the front of the car. Pop slipped our one small overnight bag out of sight at his feet beneath the bright white tablecloth.

Facing one another, we sank our forearms into the deep padding. The room was warm and relaxing. I had on a heavy brown wool suit that stuck to my legs in the steamy heat coming from the kitchen next to us. I didn't mind, I'd gotten cold late in the day when the temperature fell. In this windowed capsule we sped through industrial New Jersey, the blackness outside the long window broken periodically by the half glimmer of street lamps in empty business districts. We ate prime rib.

After Philadelphia, we found seats a few cars back. An hour or so later we were racing a hundred miles an hour south through the Maryland countryside, past Aberdeen. I glimpsed familiar surroundings: the lowered gates at the crossing, the line of waiting cars, the red neon of the New Theatre on the far side of the main intersection.

I thought about my grandfather, who used to take me on walks from his house to that crossing. He and the gate man were friends. They would talk next to the southbound tracks until one of six little white bulbs affixed to the front of the gatekeeper's unpainted wooden shack would come on, signaling an approaching train. Promptly, the man would crank down the black-and-white-striped gates and my grandfather would grip my hand and we'd wait. In seconds we'd hear a whistle in the distance. If the train was coming from the north, the engine's light would come into sight, like a shiny dime, on the curve at Osborn's cornfield. Standing just a few feet behind the gates, I'd shudder at the size of the approaching black engine, growing immense as it roared up to us so close you could see on the facing of the engine a gold striping of "cat's whiskers." Then I'd recoil at the awful slam-whine as the train hit the air in front of us.

The shack is gone, the gates have been replaced by an overpass. But each time I go through Aberdeen on the Amtrak I look out and think of the tall old man and the small boy at his side as they must have been seen so many blurred times from train windows.

The night Pop and I came home from the game it was quiet on the cobblestone platform in Baltimore. Upstairs in the station a handful of revelers chanted "Colts" and waved blue pennants. I looked for a morning paper but didn't see one. I felt I needed to verify what had happened. We walked past the lines of waiting Yellow and Sun cabs with their engines running and up to St. Paul Street, where we'd parked our car the afternoon before, and then Pop and I drove home.

Part Three

ONE DAY IN MAY 1963 I was walking along Charles Street and stopped to cross at the corner of Redwood. I felt as if more years had passed than actually had because I had been off at college and in the army. Now I had gotten a job on the copy desk of *The Sun.* It was midafternoon, and I was due at work at 4:00 P.M. Waiting for the light to change, I looked down at a stack of papers on the sidewalk. *The Evening Sun*'s page-one headline blared: BIG DADDY LIPSCOMB DIES. I stood still and read the first paragraphs of the story. He'd been killed by a heroin overdose. Big Daddy, thirty-two, had been dead on arrival at Lutheran Hospital. He had been playing for the Pittsburgh Steelers but had continued to live in Baltimore. The medical examiner who did the autopsy ruled out speculation that someone else injected Lipscomb. Teammates, though, never have believed that. Lenny Moore told me: "We were leaving for New York to catch a jazz session that morning he was pronounced dead. We saw each other every day. We were like brothers. Because Daddy didn't have what you'd call a family. He and Sherman Plunkett lived together.

"His death is still a mystery to me. You see, the needle was in Daddy's right arm. Daddy's right-handed. You're not going to mainline with your left hand. Daddy was scared of needles. Everybody knew that about him.

"We know that he'd been drinking. That was his bag. His Seagram's V.O. was it. But how did this needle shot happen? Maybe he drank to the point to get himself some nerve and he said, I'll try that. But I would doubt it."

What is certain is that Big Daddy suffered a loneliness larger than anyone realized.

We had taken for granted that Big Daddy was happy. He took up professional wrestling in the late fifties under the tutelage of a promoter named "Waffle Ear," then broke the "death grip" of "Mr. Moto" and threw him out of the ring. Years before Neil Armstrong's moon landing, Daddy envisioned the scene almost precisely, only with him in the role: "I'd look around, wave the American flag, declare the territory for America, and pick up a little glory for Big Daddy, too."

Who didn't enjoy the sight of Lipscomb helping up a guy he'd tackled, reaching down to assist him — his trademark glad-handing that drew attention to linemen? I remember smiling at those Sunday-afternoon player introductions at the stadium: "From the University of San Francisco, number eighty-nine, Gino Marchetti . . ." They included the player's college. But since Big Daddy never went to college it was always, "From Miller High School . . ." To me the contrast seemed amusing. But it wasn't to Big Daddy. A few years later he revealed that a lack of education made him feel different from the other players in the NFL.

Daddy never knew his father — he died while working for the Civilian Conservation Corps. Growing up in Detroit, Lipscomb lived with his mother for eleven years in a single room. One night a policeman came to the room and told him his mother was dead. She'd been standing at a bus stop. A man stabbed her forty-seven times.

In a 1960 *Saturday Evening Post* article Lipscomb was

quoted: "I've been scared most of my life. You wouldn't think so to look at me. I'm six feet, six inches, I weigh 283 pounds, and I'm an All-Pro tackle . . . but I still get feeling scared sometimes. Every once in a while it gets so bad I cry myself to sleep. I don't know exactly why this is. I think part of my fear comes from being self-conscious about my size and part of it from being alone so much. And part of it comes from being a Negro."

Big Daddy's death struck me as a demarcation, evidence that, as we'd learned growing up, anything is possible and not all pleasant. It shook me. And there was something else about it, kind of a finger snap into real life. Dejectedly, I walked up town toward *The Sun* building, seeing the headline on almost every corner. It was one of the last times I learned from a newspaper something that stunned me so. After that television almost always brought the news first.

◆

One of my first assignments after joining *The Washington Post* in 1965 was to cover the major NFL game each Sunday. It meant dividing most of my time between Baltimore and Green Bay. Covering the Colts meant not letting my heart get in the way of the words. I did what I could.

It was the year that both Johnny Unitas and his backup Gary Cuozzo were injured and late in the season running back Tom Matte had to play quarterback with the plays written on his wristband. In a play-off game at Green Bay, Matte and the Colts almost prevailed, but a missed Packer field goal was called good. Even some Packer fans will admit it was so. The Packers won the game in overtime and went on to win the title — and the league raised the goal-post uprights to help officials make their calls.

Three years later Ogden Nash wrote in *Life:*

Is there a Baltimore fan alive
Who's forgotten Tom Matte in '65?
The Colts by crippling injuries vexed,
Unitas first and Cuozzo next —
What would become of the pass attack?
Then Matte stepped in at quarterback.
He beat the Rams in a great display,
He did, and he damn near beat Green Bay.
Ask him today to plunge or block,
Tom's the man who can roll or rock.
In Tokyo, they say karate
In Baltimore, they call it Matte.

Nineteen sixty-five was the year Nash returned to Baltimore. "New York just got too depressing," he told a reporter. "Everything was getting so expensive . . . $9.90 for theater tickets a year from now . . . $12 for a bunch of lilies of the valley . . ." He settled into an apartment at Cross Keys Village, where, at sixty-three, he tended dogwood trees and mint bushes. He was just a short drive in his Dodge Dart both to the stadium and the Pimlico racetrack.

Nash resumed Sundays at the stadium with gusto, and then in that December 7, 1968, issue of *Life,* he celebrated several of his favorite players during a championship season:

When hearing tales of Bubba Smith
You wonder is he man or myth.
He's like a hoodoo, like a hex,
He's like Tyrannosaurus Rex.
Few manage to topple in a tussle
Three hundred pounds of hustle and muscle.

He won't complain if double-teamed;
It isn't Bubba who gets creamed.
What gained this pair of underminers?
Only four Forty-niner shiners.

He wrote this tribute to Earl Morrall, the quarterback who substituted for an injured Unitas most of 1968 and who in January 1969 would lead the Colts into Super Bowl III:

Once a grim second-stringer, a sad Giant castoff,
Earl today is the spark of a thundering blast-off.
Though the fables of Aesop still wear a green laurel,
They end where the Colts now begin, with a Morrall.
For it's Morrall to Mackey, yes, Morrall to Mackey,
A refrain that is driving the corner men wacky.
They lock up against Richardson, Perkins and Orr,
Then it's Morrall to Mackey, right through the front
door.
Perhaps it is hindsight, perhaps it's a sophistry,
But the Colts owe a lot to Giant front-offistry.

Alas, just a few weeks later the Colts were stunned in the Super Bowl by Joe Namath and the New York Jets, 16–7. The Colts had been seventeen-point favorites. In Baltimore a bookie gave *forty* points. "Some of the players had even spent their winnings before the game," recalled Steve Rosenbloom, son of Colts owner Carroll Rosenbloom.

What poetry could explain it? On the game-turning play, what should have been a touchdown pass just before the half, Morrall failed to see a wide-open Orr, who was obvious to everyone else in the Orange Bowl except his quarterback and the Jets. Orr waved frantically — to no avail.

A devastated Carroll Rosenbloom became the first NFL

owner to lose a title game to a team from the upstart American Football League. Ordinary defeats were bad enough. "We couldn't talk to him until Wednesday," said Steve Rosenbloom. "That was the M.O."

The "victory" party the elder Rosenbloom had scheduled at his Golden Beach, Florida, home the evening after the game proved to be an awkward affair, with uneasy guests wanting to get in and get out. "Everybody felt like hell," said Steve Rosenbloom. "It was a morgue. Ted Kennedy came. He said, 'Well, Carroll, look at it this way, nobody died.'"

But Carroll Rosenbloom's ego was such that he turned vindictively on the coach he had praised lavishly up to the kickoff that day. After one more season, Shula relocated to friendlier climes in Miami. The Colts he left behind went on to win Super Bowl V over Dallas in January 1971. But no one I've known in Baltimore got over Super Bowl III.

A month or so after Super Bowl V Ogden Nash went to the Bowie races. Knowing he was going into the hospital for abdominal surgery, he bet a gray horse named "Get Going Doc." It won.

A few weeks later he visited his daughter Linell's horse farm in Sparks to see a foal and name her. Linell recalled: "She was a Restless Native filly. Restless Native was Native Dancer's son, and Daddy was always fond of Native Dancer. He named her May Margret. She was out of an elderly English mare — May Margret was very ugly. But he said she'd turn out to be beautiful. He took the name from an English fairy tale, the story of a worm May Margret who became an ugly dragon and was turned back into a beautiful May Margret again."

Nash would not recover following surgery, although his

spirits were raised by a visit from Tom Matte, who also was a patient at Union Memorial, in for football repairs.

By then, early 1971, a romance that should still have been blooming was fast fading. Rosenbloom fell out with fans, who balked at buying exhibition-game tickets with their season books, with city officials, who wouldn't make the old stadium right for him, with John Steadman of the *News-Post,* who criticized an owner he saw as increasingly greedy and threatening the pleasures and rights of the fans. Rosenbloom devised an ingenious plan.

Steve Rosenbloom, who'd risen from ball boy to team president, remembered a conversation his father had had with an ill Dan Reeves, the Los Angeles Rams' owner, on the Colt bench before a Colts-Rams game. Reeves said, "Carroll, if something happens to me it'd be great if you could take over this team." Reeves's death on April 15, 1971, opened the way for Rosenbloom. His scheme was to find someone to buy the Rams and then trade the Colts for them in what amounted to a tax-free deal for him. Robert Irsay, of Skokie, Illinois, an industrial-air-conditioning-and-heating magnate, was served up to Rosenbloom by Joe Thomas, who had quit as the Miami Dolphins' personnel director and wanted to be Irsay's general manager. "Irsay bought the Rams," said Steve Rosenbloom, "knowing full well that they were going to pass through his fingers. That was the only way he was going to get in on the deal." On July 26, 1972, the Colts — a juggernaut that had won more games and played in more postseason games than any NFL team the previous fourteen years — belonged to Irsay.

A bulky man with white hair and a flushed face, Irsay once took over the headphones and called game plays himself. He had a temper and castigated players and coaches.

His impatience hurt. In 1983 he traded quarterback John Elway to Denver just days after the Colts had drafted him. Irsay's heavy-handed ways turned off Colt fans like a bulb. The longer he owned the Colts, the more he looked for a place to relocate them. And the more disgruntled the fans became.

"Did your father know about Irsay?" I said to Steve Rosenbloom, now out of football and living near New Orleans.

"The kind of guy he was? Yeah, oh yeah. I think that was a legacy my father left Baltimore on purpose. I don't think he could have been more delighted that the guy was like he was because at that time in his life my dad was not very happy with Baltimore."

A "*legacy*"!

Thomas decided to tear the Colts apart and rebuild them, bulldozing a legendary quarterback near the end of his career but not yet willing to retire. After the Colts had lost four of their first five games in 1972, Thomas ordered that Unitas be benched. Colt fans were aghast; some of Unitas's last heroics were fresh in their minds. There was the 1970 game in Houston when he beat the Oilers, 24–20, with time running out. He passed deep to Roy Jefferson for the winning touchdown. Having thrown the ball, Unitas turned his back to the play and headed for the sideline — *while the ball was still in the air.*

"Did I see that right?" Colts publicist Ernie Accorsi asked him.

"I'd done everything I could do," Unitas replied.

In 1971 at Oakland, Unitas had another excellent game. Beforehand, a group of Colts went to Sunday Mass near the Oakland–Alameda County Coliseum. On the other side of the aisle were several Raiders. "They were looking over at

Unitas," Accorsi said. "It's one reason the Raiders had trouble beating Unitas, they were in awe of him. And that day he was everything he'd ever been. God, I wish I had a film of that game. When he walked off the field I think the score was 30–0 and Morrall finished up; the final was 37–14. On the plane home that night, Unitas was almost giddy. I've never seen him that way before or since."

And in the second game of 1972, Unitas passed for 376 yards in a duel with Joe Namath, a 44–34 Jets victory in Baltimore.

Years later, Unitas's voice wavered as he recalled Thomas's treatment. "He told [Coach John] Sandusky that I would never play another down in the Baltimore Colts' uniform."

The message was clear, but as if grappling with the significance, Unitas asked Sandusky, "What does that mean?"

"He said, 'He does not want you playing.' Marty Domres was the backup quarterback. I said, 'I'm not going to run the clock out for you. Don't get ahead and expect me to go in there and play second fiddle to Domres because that's not going to happen.'

"He said, 'I would never do that to you.'

"So we played Buffalo and Domres gets hurt. I'm just sitting there on the bench. Sandusky looks at me and I'm looking at him. They don't have anybody else to put in. So I took my stuff off and put my helmet on." He spoke the words evenly, an edge in his voice.

When he trotted onto the field that day — it was December 3, 1972, at Memorial Stadium — the people went wild. And just then, in what would become part of Colt lore, a small plane circled the stadium pulling a banner that said UNITAS WE STAND. Even Unitas had to admit, "It was a very climactic type of event, or whatever."

The second play he called was a pass to Eddie Hinton.

With hate in his heart for Joe Thomas, Unitas sailed a love note to the fans: He let fly to Hinton, who caught the ball in stride. The play went sixty-three yards for a touchdown. For Unitas, that was good-bye.

The photo of him after the pass to Hinton is blown up big and hangs above the mantel of Unitas's home in Baldwin, Maryland. He keeps other mementos, mostly in boxes, "only because my wife doesn't permit me to get rid of them." But in that one picture, Unitas is walking off after the touchdown pass and lineman Dan Sullivan, laughing, is congratulating him, and Unitas is smiling, too.

Soon after, Thomas shipped Unitas to San Diego. Unitas's version of Thomas's phone call to him: "'You've just been traded to San Diego,' and bang, he hung up. That was it, after seventeen years with the ball club." Unitas had wanted the Baltimore Colts to be his life.

He didn't look right in a Chargers uniform; the gold pants made his legs seem even skinnier than they were.

I took my two sons, Billy and David, to see him play when the Chargers opened the 1973 season in Washington against the Redskins. The Washington fans gave Unitas a prolonged ovation when he was introduced. I felt a chill. They didn't shout, they stood and clapped. It was the sort of acknowledgment given artists at the Kennedy Center. The boys were too young to remember that game, but I guess it's just as well. The Redskins won 33–0. Unitas had no protection and eventually was removed from a contest that was typical of his last season.

"That was a very poor football team," Unitas said. "Poor organization. Terrible. Some of 'em were smoking dope or taking pills. They had all the malcontents, and that's what I walked into. I mean, it was really spooky.

"I had never been involved or confronted or had seen anyone take pills or smoke grass — and those guys used to do it going to the dressing room. There were a lot of good guys there, but some people were completely obliterated all the time.

"Some of the wives called my wife one time and said they were going to have a party, a team party, and they were going to invite me. 'But we know how John feels about pills and smoking and all that kind of stuff.' They just wanted us to know that we were invited but that stuff probably would be going on, 'so that if you're interested in coming, park your car in this parking lot and give us a call and we'll come down and get you.' Needless to say . . ."

Mr. High-Tops had met the New Age.

Happily, he went back to Baltimore the next year and found a job.

◆

On May 1, 1975, Loudy retired from the National Guard. That day he got a call from Eddie Rosenbloom, the Colts' business manager and nephew of the team's former owner.

"Loudy, I want to talk with you for a minute," Rosenbloom said. "You retired today, didn't you?"

"Yes, I did."

"Well, how would you like to come to work with the Colts?"

"Right now?"

"No, Loudy, not right now. Whenever you feel like you're ready to come."

"I'll be there tomorrow."

For three years, 1975–77, Loudy officially belonged to the Colts. He did odd jobs: helping with equipment, driving players to doctors' appointments. Loudy was part of Baltimore's last winning seasons, division-winning ones. Of course, it was hard to differentiate his official tenure from his perpetual presence before and after.

One day in 1973 Loudy happened to be in the Colts' locker room when Joe Ehrmann, then a rookie defensive tackle, stormed off the practice field in frustration. Ehrmann walked into the locker room and burst into tears. Loudy, though dwarfed, held the bigger man close.

"I was so fed up with football," recalled Ehrmann, still a 260-pounder, only now with a gray-white beard. "I had a lot of personal problems, a lot of personal confusion that I had brought to the NFL, a lot of emptiness in my life. I had anticipated finding the answers in the NFL. But the NFL only added to my personal confusion. I'll never forget walking into Loudy that time because it took me out of the very nonreal world of the NFL and put me into the arms of someone very real."

Growing up in Buffalo, Ehrmann had frequented bars and hung out on street corners in tough parts of town. Newly arrived in Baltimore as a first-round draft choice from Syracuse University, he gravitated to hard-drinking, east-side saloons. But in 1978 Ehrmann did a personality flip. "He changed from outgoing, always joking, having fun, to very quiet," said Loudy. "He'd come to practice, sit at his locker, usually reading, until it was time to work. A remarkable change."

It was because that July Ehrmann's brother Billy, just eighteen years old, contracted cancer.

"We had grown up without a father — we had an absent father," Joe said. "I was ten years older than Billy and basically raised him. He was probably the person I loved the most in the whole world. I'd gotten him a job with the

Colts the summer before he was going to go to college — he helped the trainers and equipment men. Then one day he was diagnosed with cancer, the kind of cancer that is almost always terminal. That devastated me.

"We found out in the summer, and he died a couple days before the last game. One of the real blessings was that Ted Marchibroda, who was coaching then, allowed me to put my brother ahead of the team, which I'm not sure a lot of coaches would have done. He gave me a great deal of freedom — practice time and all that."

Loudy was there when Joe took Billy to the Colts' camp the last time. Billy had on a hospital mask, and he was weak. He'd been bigger even than Joe, but now he sat on one of the tables in the training room, looking frail. Loudy talked with him, hugged him. Joe took Billy out of Johns Hopkins Hospital in his final days, and Billy died at Joe's home in Cockeysville. "It tore Joe up something terrible," Loudy said.

Ehrmann recalled: "With the death of my brother I got an opportunity to examine my life and saw tremendous holes in it, which football always left. We think that in becoming a professional athlete somehow you'll find great purpose in your life and heal many of the wounds that you accumulate. For me football only compounded those wounds. With the death of my brother I had a radical change in my life, and at the core of that was the religious change. You're led to believe in this culture that if you can make it economically, if you can make it athletically, if you can make it sexually, if you can achieve those things there's some sense that you're going to find significance, you're going to find security. I found that you'll never find any of that stuff in sports. There's a deeper, inward journey that you have to make."

On June 28, 1982, the Ronald McDonald House, a hospice for families of seriously ill children, opened in Baltimore. Ehrmann's work made it possible. Ehrmann also began study for the ministry while finishing up his football career with the Detroit Lions and Arizona and Orlando in the defunct United States Football League. In 1985 he completed his training at Westminster Theological Seminary in Philadelphia, specializing in urban ministry. The following year he returned to Baltimore.

A nondenominational minister, Ehrmann opened what he called The Door — "a means of entrance to people locked outside of mainstream society." It operates out of an old German Lutheran church at 219 North Chester Street. Its aim is to work with schools, recreation centers, and churches in fighting inner-city ills faced by youngsters and adults. A white man working in a predominantly black east Baltimore neighborhood, Ehrmann said, "'The Door' battles against such problems as illiteracy, substance abuse, and teenage pregnancy." The day I visited, he had on a dress shirt with sleeves rolled up, a tie loosened at the neck, jeans. He wears glasses. With the beard he looks like a large Moses.

Once committed to football mayhem, Ehrmann now gently described a sixteen-year-old boy known as "Spoon," who came to The Door as "an emotionally depressed, insecure, and very lonely thirteen-year-old." No more. "He is a productive young man with a great big heart for helping children who are in need of love and an understanding ear. The Door employs him part-time to help in the after-school program. He is also the director of the children's computer center. Spoon learned computer from his years at The Door and now uses his skill, passing his knowledge to the younger children."

Ehrmann and his wife, Paula, have three children. He also has an older daughter from a marriage in college that ended in divorce. "There used to be a radio personality here, Commander Jim, a legend back in the middle seventies," Ehrmann said. "He had a radio-dating kind of show, and I was a 'celebrity' date. My wife and I actually met over the radio.

"The agreement was, I was to get a couple of dinners from the sponsor and a few tickets to a football game, which I would give to her and then meet her after the game. I met her after the game, and we've been together ever since. That's a Baltimore story."

◆

No one in Baltimore ever imagined that someday the Colts would leave. The night of March 28, 1984, when the unimaginable happened and Irsay ordered a fleet of Mayflower vans to be loaded with all the Colts' belongings and roll to Indianapolis, the weather was appropriately miserable—half rain, half snow.

Loudy had fallen asleep in a soft living room chair in his row house in the Baltimore Highlands, south of the city. The phone woke him. His friend Mike Gregor on the line was sputtering, "Loudy, you're not going to believe this, but I just heard on the radio that the Colts are leaving. Moving vans are there tonight."

Loudy hurried out to his car and headed for the beltway, bound for the Colts' offices. The windshield wipers flapped on Loudy's old blue-and-white Monte Carlo. He could hardly see the road, not so much because of the slanting storm but because of the tears in his eyes.

Ken Ryland worked for Mayflower Moving and Storage. By about two o'clock in the afternoon of March 28, 1984, he had put in a full day's work, visiting prospective customers.

On his way home, Ryland stopped by his office in Alexandria, Virginia.

"My general manager says to me, 'We want you to go supervise an office move.'"

"I says, 'Well, where's it at? What's the office move?'

"'We can't tell you where the office move is.'

"I'd been working there over twenty-five years at the time. I think, this must be a heck of a move if they want me to come supervise because usually I'm out making bids instead of supervising.

"My boss says, 'The people don't even know they're moving.'

"I think, God, it must be the CIA. I says, 'Okay, let me call the wife.' This is a true story — I call her and say, 'Honey, I'm supervising a move, but I can't tell you where, who, or what time I'll be home.'

"I hang up, and I get these instructions: 'Go halfway to Baltimore and dial this phone number, and the woman on the other end will tell you where to come to.'

"I didn't know what was going on, didn't have any idea. Then I thought, Heck, if I'm going to go halfway I might as well go to my house in Beltsville, which is halfway between Alexandria and Baltimore.

"So when I get home I call and she answers: 'The Baltimore Colts.' The Colts!"

That morning Irsay had read in the paper that a bill to give the city of Baltimore the power to seize the Colts through eminent domain appeared headed for approval in the state senate. With that, he'd given the order to move.

"I don't think I want to go over and do this," Ryland recalled.

"The lady on the phone says to me, 'When you get here

there's a phone behind a tree next to the side door. Call me and I'll let you in. When you get in here, don't tell a soul what you're here for — none of the coaches or anybody else. Just tell 'em you're taking inventory.'"

She gave Ryland directions to the Colts' building in Owings Mills, west of Baltimore. Then he hung up and thought. He'd heard talk that the Colts might move. Now the team *was* moving. And *he* was going to be in the thick of it.

"You're torn. You live here in this area. But you have to show respect to the company you're with. It'd be tough to say, I'm not going to do it, because then they could have gotten somebody else to do it and they would have looked down on me. I don't think they would have appreciated a 'no.' Being with the company as long as I have, I got too much at stake to lose on retirement and everything else . . . It was not in my power. I could never have stopped it."

Ryland, still employed by Mayflower, recalled telling his wife that it was the Colts' move he would be supervising. His job was to tell his office how many trucks were needed, how many men, how much packing material.

"I was worried, honestly worried about going over there. At that time Mayflower had given me use of a car from Indianapolis — Indianapolis is Mayflower's home office. I think, I ain't going over to Baltimore in my car from Indianapolis. I might not get out of there. My son had a '69 Dodge, and I says if that has problems I can worry about it.

"So I got over there — I guess it was about ten minutes after five — and I went to the phone behind the tree, called the lady, and she came to the side door and let me in. She took me into Mr. Irsay's office, and there was a man there, not Mr. Irsay.

"'Look,' he says, 'we want to try to get some trucks in

here tonight. All you have to do is go make an estimate, how many trucks and how many men and how much help.' He says, 'But do not tell *anybody* why you're here. Just don't tell 'em.

"'And if anything happens I want these three or four file cabinets to get out of here first. Get 'em on a truck and get 'em out of here.'

"So I went through, made my estimate, and everybody kept asking me, 'What are you doing here?' I says, 'I'm just making a list for, I guess, this year's inventory.' I was writing everything down. When I was done I called my boss and ordered eleven trucks to come in there."

So it was, the infamous *eleven* vans . . . the yellow-and-green eighteen-wheelers, each to hold twelve to fifteen thousand pounds of Baltimore Colts' belongings.

"They did not get any vans from Baltimore," Ryland said. "We have a Baltimore agent, but they didn't want him involved. I think you would have had an argument from the Baltimore people. And rather than get into that situation, our company got the vans from Pennsylvania and Virginia and wherever. They got a bunch of guys from a local fraternity to come over there to help with the move, and then they put these guards on the gate.

"After I got the bid in I just looked around the building. Everything was neat. All the team pictures from over the years were up on the walls. Unitas's pictures, all these pictures. It was something to go through this place, mind boggling . . .

"Sure enough, at nine-fifteen the first truck shows up. I wanted to make sure the move was done properly. The way we normally do it, we inventory everything, we put it on the trucks, we pad everything. So we started out doing that with the one truck that pulled up. Then it started raining a

A moving van leaves the Baltimore Colts' complex with equipment and furnishings in the early hours of March 29, 1984, bound for Indianapolis.
UPI/Bettmann

little bit. Then about nine-thirty a helicopter flies over, shining a light down, and everybody says, 'Oh my God, what's happening?'

"I said, 'Pull a truck up to every door and to heck with this inventory. Just start loading the vans.'

"We started throwing things in boxes. The secretaries' desks, everything, the weight room downstairs — all that had to be loaded on the vans. As fast as we got 'em loaded, they'd pull out. We had two or three loading at the front door, and we had 'em on the opposite side of the building.

"About eleven-fifteen I called my wife. There was a television on inside the building and the move was on the news. I says to my wife, 'I guess you know everything.'

"About that time some of the secretaries started to show up, five or six women trying to get their stuff out of there, which we let 'em — anybody who wanted to take anything that was theirs was welcome to it.

"Later I guess it started snowing. I always remember that picture of the truck pulling out of there in the snow — if I've seen that picture once I've seen it a dozen times. The last van pulled out between five and six in the morning. I don't even remember driving home, I was so tired."

Loudy had felt silly, standing helplessly by a fence with a dozen others as the vans full of everything that was the Colts roared past, splattering his pants with mud. He also felt the sadness that presses like a weight when something good is lost.

At home that night, Unitas turned to his wife, Sandy. "It's a shame Irsay has to treat the fans this way," he said softly. "Baltimore's always loved this team."

When dawn broke, Steve LaPlanche was still there, standing by the side of the road, next to the sign BALTIMORE COLTS. When he could see his clothes he realized how wet and cold he was from his all-night vigil in the rain and snow. He was alone. It was absolutely still. The night before he'd been sitting in the Sunset lounge in Glen Burnie and someone had burst in saying he'd heard it on the radio that the Colts were moving.

The Colts moving? His father had taken him to his first game when he was three. He tore out of the Sunset so fast he forgot to pay his bill. He cried that night as he stood there, and in the morning, too, as he called his office. A captain with the Anne Arundel County sheriff's department, he was a tough man in tears.

"Hey, I can't come to work."

"I understand," his boss said.

LaPlanche drove back to the Sunset and paid his bill, then returned to the Colts' building. Several radio stations had preempted regular programming, and all day there was talk about the move and tapes of old games: Chuck Thompson screaming, "Mackey scores . . ." and Bob Wolff doing his radio play-by-play of the '58 game from Yankee Stadium. Disc jockeys played the Colts' fight song. *The Sun* carried a photograph of LaPlanche from the night before, watching a Mayflower van pull away, his foot on the rear bumper of his VW Rabbit with the license plate COLTS 1.

And that's where he was the next morning when a friend came by. It was Chris Hinton, offensive tackle. Hinton invited LaPlanche to his house, and the two sat around all afternoon and drank beer, and Hinton said how he didn't want to leave Baltimore and LaPlanche over and over said what a miserable thing this was to happen. "The Colts," he said not long ago, "were my friends."

The Colts' leaving moved *The Sun*'s Michael Olesker to quote from *The Great Gatsby:*

"'What'll we do with ourselves this afternoon?' cried Daisy, 'and the day after that, and the next thirty years?'

"'Don't be morbid,' Jordan said. 'Life starts all over again when it gets crisp in the fall.'"

To which Olesker appended: "Not anymore."

The departure prompted the novelist Robert Ward, a Baltimorean, to reminisce in *GQ:*

"One hot summer afternoon, my best pal Johnny Brandau and I went around to the red brick row houses on Cold Spring. We had heard that the Colts' starting quarterback, George Shaw, lived there, and we had our autograph books and pens ready. But when we shyly knocked on a door, a grizzled man in his underwear answered it. I recognized him immediately as Carl Taseff, the Colts' defensive halfback and expert punt returner. He looked exhausted and grouchy, and I stammered, 'Uh . . . You're Mr. Taseff, aren't you?' He looked at us hard for a second, and then said, 'Sure, kids. Come on in.'

"Johnny and I wandered into his furnished room. He offered us both Cokes, which we accepted, smiling and winking at each other over our extraordinary good fortune. Soon we were talking to him about an interception he had made in last week's game. He smiled, said it was luck. Our courage bolstered by his good mood, we asked if any other Colts lived in the neighborhood.

"'Sure,' he said, yawning. 'We got a quarterback right next door.'

"We were both positive it was George Shaw, and both of us felt our hearts racing. Taseff threw on some shorts with the words PROPERTY OF THE BALTIMORE COLTS on them (and what crime would I not have committed to have those shorts?) and took us next door to introduce us to the quarterback.

"But when we got outside, the quarterback was already there. He was throwing passes to another player we didn't know. The passer sure as hell wasn't George Shaw. He was a funny-looking guy with a crew cut and a kind of twisted grin.

"'Think fast, kid,' he said to me, and that was how I caught a pass thrown by Johnny Unitas.

"I threw it back to him, and he sent a soft floater to Johnny Brandau, who was much the better athlete of the two of us. Johnny threw him a bullet back, and the three Colts laughed and said, 'Hey! Good arm!' We were then introduced to this strange, skinny-looking guy, and even his name sounded funny. He signed our autograph books, and after a little more awkward chat, Johnny and I went back across the sunbaked Little League field to Winston Road.

"'What was that guy's name?' I asked.

"'Johnny Un-a-tiss — or something,' Johnny Brandau said.

"'Well, he sure isn't George Shaw.'

"'Yeah, but at least he was a quarterback.'

"'Right,' I said. 'And at least we got to meet Carl Taseff!'"

To me the Colts had been the best reminder since the Brooklyn Dodgers of how something so simple as a team could arouse emotional attachments.

Then, like the Dodgers from Brooklyn, the Colts were gone.

"India-naaa-polis, you gotta be kiddin'!" cried Rosie the waitress at Chiapparelli's in Little Italy.

More than outraged, though, Baltimore was left overwhelmingly empty. If the Colts could be taken away, Baltimoreans realized absolutely nothing was forever. Irsay's night flight had to signal the same clear message to anyone in America who ever loved a team.

Even now in Baltimore a melancholy endures, heightened by the presence of so many of the old Colts who live there. On any day a person might bump into a Baltimore Colt as did a friend of mine who stopped at an out-of-the-way eatery on a Sunday morning not long ago. Paying the bill at the cashier's and heading out the door alone was — could it be? — of course, Johnny Unitas. He smiled — a crooked, engaging smile — and nodded.

◆

"I says, you're nuts, they're never gonna leave. First thing I know, I was watchin' TV, the eleven o'clock news, and they have the Orioles packin' up in Miami and comin' north, and the next thing I know I see a Mayflower van and it's snowin'. Well, I said, it don't snow in Miami. I think, Hey, maybe I better change the brand I'm drinkin' here.

"No, they were talkin' about the Colts, movin' out. In the dead of the night. They rode off into the dark, into the dead of night."

Art Donovan, number seventy, was talking about his Colts as he drove his Chevy truck past Sam and Elmer's barbershop — vacant; past what had been the trolley barn but now was Johnny's Auto Body and Fender, less than a mile from where the Hilltop Diner used to be. Art Donovan — adopted Baltimorean and now the city's resident morale chief.

"Little Arthur" of the Bronx was son of the boxing referee Art Donovan, "Big Arthur," the third man in the ring for eighteen of Joe Louis's fights. "Little Arthur" grew up to be a Colts colossus. And in what he calls his "twilight years," he's a modern media figure who has spawned a cult with his appearances on David Letterman, telling football stories. Squealy teenage girls saw him as "a big cutie" — a 325-pound crew-cut dumpling — when he dove into a goal-line pileup of hot dogs on a TV commercial for the Maryland State Lottery. He was an improbable sight in another lottery commercial, sitting in a Chesapeake Bay dinghy, completely filling the little boat as he fished for lottery success. Except that the producers made so many takes on that one that when somebody said, "That's it," Artie had sat so long he couldn't move. Couldn't get up out of the dinghy until a heavyset man held the boat while several others pried him to his feet as water splashed on them all.

Donovan owns a tennis and swim club, into the empty

pool of which he once slipped and dropped twenty-three feet. He didn't crack the pool bottom, as some say, but lay in agony for an hour until someone found him in a broken heap. For a time he also was a beer salesman. Schlitz, his favorite beer. (Twelve to eighteen cans a night, twenty to thirty hot dogs a sitting before his heart attack in 1991.) When I called Artie some time ago, he just happened to be doing the first of a few gigs for Schlitz. Visiting liquor stores, pushing his brand. "Come on over," he said. "You can ride around with me."

He didn't need the money. He just likes the beer. For twenty-one years he owned a liquor store; that's where he made his big money. Until, near the end, he was stuck up five times. Once, a man aimed a shotgun at him. "It felt like I was lookin' through the Lincoln Tunnel."

As a beer salesman, Artie could get a proprietor's attention even when he was only semiserious.

"Where's the Schlitz?"

"Where's the Schlitz? It's in the back."

"You told me you were gonna put it up front. Well, do you want me personally to put it up front?"

"I'll put it up front . . ."

This is how much he likes Schlitz: "I went to California with my wife and we drove eleven hours up to Reno and I couldn't find Schlitz in Reno. You know what I did? I drove all the way around Lake Tahoe to California, and they had Schlitz. I bought myself a case. Then I come out and a kid wants to start a fight with me. I said, 'I think I'm a little too big for you.' 'Nobody's too big for me.' He said I had him blocked in, and I didn't. I got out of the car. I said, 'Let's think this over.' I called him a name and then I left."

Donovan has been famous in some way most of his life.

Every Bronx kid knew him because of his old man. Then he became the Colts' giant fun guy with a knack for knowing which direction a play was heading, then trundling laterally from his defensive tackle slot in plenty of time to stuff it. He made it to the pro football Hall of Fame. And now . . . Now . . .

"Now, my picture's all over the place with this lottery. We go to all these liquor stores and my picture's on the door — they got glasses drawn on 'em, they got cigars in my mouth . . .

"Is this going to be my claim to fame? Eating hot dogs? Seventy-two times I had to bite into the hot dog to do that commercial. Yeah, they made seventy-two takes. I kept biting. Cold hot dogs. Seventy-two bites."

How did fame strike again? First, by luck, NFL Films included him in a show on the golden age of pro football. Somebody from "Late Night with David Letterman" saw it. Then an agent in Atlanta saw Donovan and put him on a lecture circuit. Then somebody else called about the lottery commercial. Then Schlitz called. "I can't say no," he said.

He was happy the way it was. "I have no ax to grind. I was lucky. I played. How many guys play high school, college football never play pro football? I wouldn't want to go back over my life. I've done it all. I wouldn't have wanted to miss the Marine Corps. I wouldn't have wanted to miss the war. I wouldn't have missed college. Or playin' for the Colts. I got all the money I need. Five children. I got a truck. I have no regrets whatsoever."

Donovan's voice echoed through the big, 120-year-old, empty house of the Valley Country Club that he has owned since 1955. He was talking on the phone, in the kitchen. A serious-looking man who spoke softly was with him, holding a football and getting Donovan to sign it. It was Mutscheller, the right end of the championship teams, who caught the pass from Unitas that took the ball to the Giants one-yard line in overtime of the 1958 title game.

Mutscheller gathered in the unconsciously daring Unitas pass into the flat that caused coach Weeb Ewbank's heart to quake. Now, Mutscheller said he was going up the road to get Tom Matte's autograph on the ball, and Donovan said that Ordell Braase was coming by. They've never drifted apart; it's just that someone's taken their team away.

In the bar, three generations of Donovans are on the walls. His grandfather, Mike Donovan, fought in the Civil War at age fifteen — his medals are up there — before he became the middleweight boxing champion. ("Ahhh, he must have been some tough guy," said the grandson.) Mike Donovan taught prizefighting at the New York Athletic Club, where he worked for forty years. He was succeeded by Big Arthur, boxing instructor there for fifty-five years. There's Big Arthur, pictured with Little Arthur at the Colts' training camp. Big Arthur ("the toughest man I ever met in my life") lived to be ninety, well after he had seen his son play on the 1958 and 1959 title teams. Big Arthur is just out of that picture of Little Arthur and Richard Nixon in the locker room after the 1959 championship game in Baltimore, this time an easier (31–16) victory over the Giants.

"I wanted to get my father in the picture with the vice president, but he was too busy talkin' to the mayor of New York. The mayor, Wagner, he's askin' my father what's he doin' here, and my father's tellin' him I play with the Colts."

And Nixon?

"He asked me what I was gonna do with the money."

He got almost five thousand dollars that day. That was a

windfall. He had grown up in the Bronx with few material goods but fourteen cousins within a two-block radius. He had been born in his grandmother's house and raised for several years, with his sister, in a small apartment on 202nd Street. "When I was seven, my father started makin' a little money, and we got high-class and moved two streets up to the Grand Concourse." He went to church and school at St. Philip Neri, and when he started getting big his mother sent him to the brothers' school, Mount St. Michael. When Donovan came onto the Yankee Stadium field for the big game of 1958 he heard a guy in the stands yell, "Ya better be better than ya were at Mount St. Michael."

He was just Big Arthur's kid then, Big Arthur, who was never so presumptuous on the day of a fight to take his bag with his ref's stuff (the pants, shirt, boxing shoes, bow tie) when he went to work at the New York Athletic Club. The way it would work was, the afternoon of the fight somebody from the boxing commission would phone him over at the NYAC and tell him he'd be working that night, and then Big Arthur would call home. "Mary, would you get the bag ready?" Every time. Little Arthur would take the bag to Fiftieth Street and meet his father outside the Garden, or to Yankee Stadium or the Polo Grounds.

Big Arthur and Little Arthur met by accident, during the war, on Guam. Big Arthur had volunteered, even though he was in his fifties, and worked in USO sports tours. There, one day on Guam, this big troop came walking down the road. By God, it was — could it have been anyone else? For then he was big — Little Arthur!

"So then," said Donovan, "they dropped the bomb and we all went home." It was the beginning of his second epoch, highlights of which hang on the bar walls: a plaque certifying that Art Donovan has crossed the Arctic Circle, a picture of his wife, Dottie, with Pope John, a football from Colt Corral No. 5, a Boston College Hall of Fame plaque, a plaque on the retirement of number seventy on September 16, 1962, a yellowed newspaper story titled DONOVAN GOES ON FOREVER.

Jim Wertz, a short man, came into Donovan's club. A Schlitz employee, he would go around with Donovan this day to six liquor stores. This was only Donovan's ninth day on the job. "Gotta get the product moving," Donovan liked to say. "I drink more than they sell."

He drove, hunched forward, his stubby arms jutting from the big sleeve openings of his raincoat, meaty hands gripping the top of the steering wheel. "I just got that script about that movie down in Beaumont. I'm going to be in a movie. The big stars of it, evidently, are Bubba Smith, Dick Butkus, and Alex Karras. But the script doesn't say what I'm supposed to do. I guess drink . . ."

He pulled into a shopping-center parking lot, and he was talking about Marchetti. "Ooooh," Donovan went. "He never said anything. Played alongside him for ten years, and he never said anything. The only thing he ever asked me was, What was the defense. I said, 'For cripes sakes.' We were in the same formation, a four-three, ninety-nine percent of the time. We never blitzed. They figured we should put pressure on the passer without the blitz, and we didn't want to blitz because we figured we were all doin' our job. Gino, he never said boo.

"The only guy who used to scream and holler all the time was [Bill] Pellington. Crazy. But tough. You know he played five plays with a broken arm?"

Into Padonia Liquors. A customer did a double take.

"Hittin' anybody recently?" Donovan said to the man behind the counter. The man behind the counter was Jim Wertz's brother Charlie. Artie Donovan's Baltimore is a metro village, where everybody knows everybody and a good portion seem to be related.

Outside, he pointed to a restaurant. "Up there is where I used to have my radio show. They must have had five hundred people in this place, listening to this goofy radio show. [Ordell] Braase and I were on it.

"On my radio show, Miller was the sponsor. And I'd say, 'Give me another Miller.' And I'd open a can of Schlitz. The liquor store here, they used to send me up twelve cans of Schlitz on the house so I could drink the Schlitz."

He drove along, remembering things. "Fifty-eight. They say it was the greatest game ever played. I don't think it was. But if they say it was, who am I to say no? The greatest game was the '58 game here in Baltimore against the 49ers. They were beatin' us, 27–7, at halftime, and we come out in the second half and we absolutely annihilated them. I mean, annihilated them. Unitas and Berry and Moore and Ameche, our offensive line, they just killed 'em. In fact, I'd only get on the field to block for the extra points. I'd say to Leo Nomellini, 'You comin', Leo?' That's how I knew if he was going to rush. And he'd say, 'Hell no, it's all over now.' So you knew, he was just going to lean on you. But if he was to say, 'Yeah, I'm comin', watch out, here they come . . ."

"Everybody in the stadium screaming . . ." Jim Wertz interjected. "Greatest fans in the world."

"They were," Donovan said. "They were wild. I'm tellin' you, they were wild. This town, in 1955 till when I got through, this town was so wild that ladies used to knit us sweaters for our kids, hats . . ."

We arrived at Fink's Discount Liquors. Big Donovan. Small Wertz. Bernie Fink said, "Now I know what they mean by the odd couple." Commotion. A customer talking to Donovan, Wertz talking to Fink — Baltimore talk (the old guys, whom they married, how they're still there). Like in *Diner.*

Next stop: Pinehurst Gourmet & Spirit Shoppe. The proprietor with the handlebar mustache, who's the brother of a guy at Eddie's Super Market, one of the next stops, remembered Donovan from the days he was starting out with a distributor. "He came in one day, when he was playing for the Colts, and I think we needed a case of Dewar's scotch. It came packed in a wooden case, with metal bands around it. He came in with it in one hand, like this. 'Here's your case of scotch.' Carried it like a little parcel."

Over to Anthony and Sal's, Donovan's old store. On the way: "Right down here, we lived together. Shula, I, and Pellington. You know, in the years when you got hurt and there was a time-out charged against you, we had three guys on the sidelines walk up and down with Weeb — it was Shula, Taseff, and Rechichar. And if somebody got hurt they'd run out on the field and drag 'im off so we wouldn't get charged a time-out. God's honest truth. 'Go get 'im.' Guy have a broken leg, they'd pull him off the field . . .

"There's Anthony." He was wearing an Orioles cap.

"Hey, Anthony, got my picture hangin' up here?"

In back is a deli with meats and salads and slaw and cakes. Everybody got a sandwich to go, everybody but Donovan. Wertz: "The one meal he eats is unbelievable. Twenty-five, thirty hot dogs. He'll take two hot dogs, two rolls. He'll take one hot dog out of the other roll and put the two hot dogs in one roll."

Next was Eddie's, on Roland Avenue. It's Donovan's town

he was driving through, but it could have been otherwise. "In '54, I went up to New York to take the exam to go on the New York Police Department. They were going to let me come down here and play football for six months and go back and be a cop. Two of my uncles were inspectors and detectives, and three other men who lived in my neighborhood were all big shots in the department.

"I would only have stayed a uniformed policeman for about six months, and then I would have got into the detective bureau. But in the meantime, I got a job working here with Schenley. So I said, 'Well, this is it.' I got married. We bought the club. I'm not blowin' my own horn or anything, but I'm a big fish in a small pond. Everybody knows me. Where in New York, all my next-door neighbors didn't know I played for the Colts. They don't give a damn in New York."

After the Colts beat the Giants in 1958, Donovan went home to the Bronx. "The next day I'm out in front of Mr. Goldberg's candy store and Mr. Sherman looks at me standing there and says, 'You out of work again, you bum?'"

Outside a drug store next to Eddie's, a man called over his shoulder, "Who's that guy blocking the doorway? Looks like an old football player."

The cashier greeted Donovan with word that she'd been out to his club for a wedding reception and that he knows her father's cousin, no less. Her husband used to be the radio engineer for the Colts games, way back, "when the guys sat out there and froze to death. Now they sit in a booth."

"Hey, Artie, tell us about the time . . ."

Artie retired during training camp in 1962 and was honored at the opening game that season. Asked to put on his uniform, he said he no longer felt worthy of dressing with the team in the locker room. So he went into a closet. And when it was over, when he had been given more stuff than a game-show winner, he just managed to get to the tunnel, where he put his head against the concrete-block wall and cried like a baby. The team doctor, Dr. Mayer, a short man, was alongside. He reached up and gently patted Artie's broad back.

"Thirty years of my life I put into this team, as a player and as a fan," Donovan explained. "When I first came here in 1950 we were undoubtedly the worst professional football team ever assembled. A lot of guys on that team went into their 'life's work' in a hurry. But in eight or nine years we became what I consider the best NFL team ever. That's why it means so much to me, why it still hurts real bad."

In Eddie's, at the meat department, Donovan ordered liverwurst to take home. On the sidewalk, he said, "So I'm walkin' out without payin' for the meat. Way to be a salesman."

Past Pimlico racetrack and on to Jim Parker's liquor store — Parker, another Hall of Famer, number seventy-seven. Donovan parked his truck and walked down the sidewalk. From behind, his form filled the horizon, shoulders sloping like mountains under a tan raincoat. Like that bent-edged, black-and-white photo of him, taken from behind, leaving the stadium in the twilight, the shoulders then covered by a cape with a Colt on the back.

As I followed him, I thought of the day when I looked into the store window on Howard Street and saw the "Gladiator" photo of Artie. I had been walking from my high school toward Pop's drug store at Howard and Lexington streets. And there was the blown-up black-and-white glossy of a young Artie caught in the gladiator's pose, helmet under arm, a jacket across his massive shoulders, as he watched the action from the sideline, a full stadium behind him. Caught by a crouched photographer with the camera aimed up, Artie stood like Apollo at the entrance to the harbor of Rhodes. Afterward, I'd go out of my way to walk down that block and just stand starry-eyed, gazing at that picture. Imagine, I'd think, Artie Donovan playing football right here in Baltimore.

Halfway down the block toward Parker's corner store, youths gaped. He was walking right at them.

"Hey, you're . . ."

"It is. It is!"

"ARTIE!"

"Hiya, fellas." Said in a faint New York rasp, a big man with a little wave, reaching a new generation.

Donovan and Parker. Behemoths. Parker embraced the visitor he calls "Fatso Fogarty." Parker's hair is gray, and he smoked a pipe. He pushed his glasses back up the bridge of his nose after every guffaw. Standing in the center of the floor, next to the Billy Dee Williams Colt 45 poster, Parker told the story of an old awards banquet: "We were up on the stage. The man was introducing us. He said, 'Art Donovan.' He stood right like this. He said, 'Jim Parker.' We stood like this. 'Big Daddy Lipscomb.' He stood up. BAMMMM! The damn stage fell. Everybody went into the basement."

They laughed so hard their bellies almost bumped. What more can a man ask? They have their memories, and they still have each other.

Above Parker's door is a picture captioned the "Magnificent Seven," for the first seven Colts inducted into the Hall of Fame. Above the counter are Parker's high-top cleats

Two Hall of Famers, Jim Parker and Art Donovan,
at Parker's liquor store in Baltimore, 1986.
Gary A. Cameron, The Washington Post

and Colt helmet, white with the blue horseshoes on the sides, everything dusty. Since 1967 they've hung there.

"Hey, I don't have that picture," Donovan said. "Is that us with the Giants?"

"This is the only man I know," said Parker, pointing his pipe toward Donovan, "who's got a million dollars and is too poor to have somebody to paint his pool. He got into the pool, fell off the ladder, buried down there. Couldn't get up and couldn't get out. They had to call the fire truck to pull 'im out."

"I'm serious," said Donovan. "The guy says, 'You think you can go up the ladder?' I says, 'I just came down on it.'

"They took my kneecap out. I broke all my ribs. I broke

my wrist and my elbow. They got me to the hospital and they put me on the table and the table's too small. I fell off the table."

A man wanted Donovan's autograph, and he wanted Donovan to draw a little star next to his signature. "Aren't you a Hall of Famer?" "Yeah." "Can I shake your hand?" "Yes, sir . . . Hey, don't break it." Big Parker shooed the man with, "You got everything. First time in your life you ever saw two Hall of Famers in one store."

"I'm on the plane with Lenny [Moore]," Donovan said to Parker, "and he's readin' the Bible. Lenny Moore on the plane readin' the Bible! Says he's a born-again Christian."

"He learned it from me," said Parker. "He said, 'Why're you so happy all the time?' I said, 'I'm a born-again Christian.' He said, 'But you're still sellin' this.' I said, 'Makes no difference.'"

"You don't drink?" Donovan asked.

"No."

"You still lie, though."

They laughed again.

Driving home, Donovan said, "So many great players . . . And the guys you didn't hear about, they were great, too. Like Alex Sandusky. Alex Karras called me, first time I ever talked to him. I said, 'We often talk about you, Alex,' Alex Sandusky and me. He said, 'You know, you were on your way out when I started, but Shula told me to watch all your movies, the way you played.' He said, 'As far as I'm concerned, you were the best.' Now he didn't have to say that because he was a good football player himself."

Pulling into the long driveway, where his big brick home sits next to the even bigger clubhouse, Donovan remembered. He was late for his ten-year-old's car pool. But then he knew his wife, Dottie, his long love and partner in the

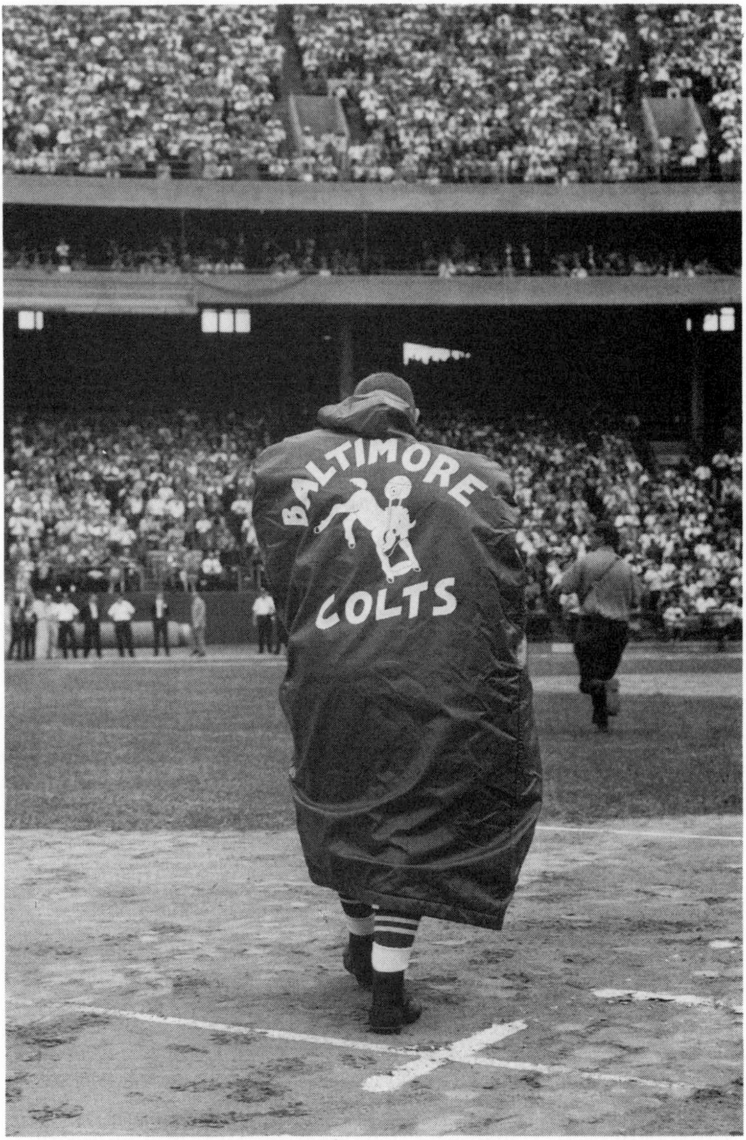

Art Donovan, saying good-bye at Memorial Stadium, 1962,
photographed by Lawrence McNally of the *News-Post*
The Hearst Corporation

club, without whom he'd made no decision and without whom life could not be this way — he knew Dottie had picked up the kids. He knew this because when he rounded the bend, her new creamy Mercedes 420 SEL — "Forty-six thousand dollars!" — was in the driveway. She liked the Mercedes; he preferred the truck.

"I'll be around," he said. With a limp not from football but his fall into the empty pool, he headed inside, walking away as he had in his cape at dusk on Sunday afternoons in the stadium when the games were over.

◆

Typical of parents, mine were proud when I got to cover the Colts. I hadn't thought anything of it until I received my first road assignment, a Colts-Packers game at Milwaukee, and Mom said, excitement in her voice on the phone, "Congratulations."

When I covered Colts games I thought how much fun it had been sitting with Pop. A lot of Sundays in the sixties when I had a seat in Memorial Stadium's football press box I knew he was somewhere down below, usually alone. I'd find out where when we'd talk that night. We called each other most days around dinnertime or after.

One Saturday afternoon in 1981 he called. Mom had had a heart attack. He told me not to worry, the doctor at the hospital had sounded hopeful, and she seemed in good spirits when we visited her. The next day she fell into a coma and the next day died. She was seventy-three. She and Pop were married forty-eight years. My daughter Maria, then ten, stood by him at the funeral home the next two nights. Tom Bodie, my cousin, said it was the sweetest thing he'd ever seen.

We realized how much Pop loved Mom one Sunday afternoon at our house in Bethesda when Mary Fran served dinner for the four children and me and Pop. In the middle of the meal Ann, then four, said, "Wouldn't it be nice if Nanny was here?" Pop left the table in tears, and Mary Fran held Annie close.

But Pop did well enough after Mom's death. He didn't go to the Colts anymore. Irsay, not Pop's increasingly delicate health, was the reason. Long retired, he took to the races — Laurel, Pimlico, Timonium. He continued living in an apartment near York Road, the area he and Mom had lived in after selling our Gwynn Oak Avenue home. I don't know that Pop ever knew the Maine Avenue apartment house had been torn down; I didn't find out myself until years later. I took my friend Arthur to the old neighborhood, and he told me that when we drove past 4412 Maine and I saw instead of the home place a one-story brick building, the Bibleway Freewill Baptist Church, my whole body tightened.

Every morning in his later years Pop bought *The Post* at a small shop a few doors from Unitas's Golden Arm and took many of his meals at the Horn & Horn cafeteria at Taylor and Loch Raven. He went to two or three places on York Road because the crab cakes had back-fin lump meat.

He took up the collection basket at Sunday Mass at the Basilica of the Assumption downtown, which surprised me because it seemed almost too public an act for him. But going to the Basilica in a way was like the outings he'd taken years before to favorite movie houses: It involved a drive and in the end some inner satisfaction. His last ten years he drove an increasingly faded red Olds, "the red bomber."

In 1987, he underwent back-to-back operations, the second for a precancerous growth in his stomach. Seventy-eight, frail, he could not recover his strength. He lay in Union Memorial for several weeks. Al Aaronson would visit and read him the sports pages. Sometimes I'd stand just outside the door to his room and through the window at the end of the hall I'd see the concrete rim of the stadium.

I told him I wished he could see the view. But I knew he never would the day Al came by with the newspaper and Pop motioned for him not to read.

◆

When I heard that Alan Ameche died, I felt as if someone were squeezing all the air out of my body. It was August 1988. I sat down in my living room chair, sat for maybe a half hour. Then I had to go to work. That day I was assigned to write a story of hockey's Wayne Gretzky being traded from Edmonton to Los Angeles. I could hardly think.

The next morning I was back in the chair. That's when Mary Fran said, "What's the matter?" I said, knowing that it was going to sound strange, "Alan Ameche died."

"But you didn't even know him."

Maybe, I said, it's a reminder of Pop. I said something about Ameche having been a good player at what had been a special time for me, that it was a shame he had to die at just fifty-five years, that I was sure he'd been an awfully good man. "I'm sure he was," she said. "But you shouldn't let it affect you." She got me going again. And off I went again to *The Post.*

Yet I still felt something deep for Ameche when I visited his wife, Yvonne, almost five years later.

She lived in a large stone house in the Philadelphia suburb of Paoli. We talked about the first Ameche's Drive-In Restaurant which opened in July 1957 on Reisterstown Road. Weekend nights you had to wait for a space to pull in. Cars with big chrome grilles lined up side by side, radios roaring rock 'n' roll. I used to drive there with a car full of friends in Pop's Dodge. Carhops would carry out orders on trays to the cars. Yvonne Ameche and Nan Campanella — the players' wives — were carhops.

Had Yvonne Ameche served me a Powerhouse, I wondered. I told her I'd been a regular among the hordes at the first Ameche's, and she told me how she and Nan had an advantage over Lou Fischer's wife. The drive-ins had been Fischer's idea, and his wife worked inside, wearing a headset and taking orders. "Nan and I got the tips, and we'd use the money to pay the baby sitters," Yvonne said.

When her husband and his partners decided to expand they had no trouble getting Colts owner Carroll Rosenbloom to cosign notes for whatever money they needed. Soon there were six Ameche's. Gino Marchetti joined the group, and Ameche-Gino Foods, Inc., was formed. You went to one or the other, Gino's or Ameche's. Neither player dreamed of making the kind of money they did.

Ameche grew up with few material goods but in a closely knit family in Kenosha, Wisconsin, three houses from the railroad tracks. August and Betty Ameche, both born in Italy, christened their son Leno Dante Ameche; he legally changed Leno to Alan at the age of sixteen. August and Betty never owned a home or a car; he worked in a Simmons mattress factory. When Alan was three, they returned to Italy to live for a few years. On their return, Alan could speak no English and had a difficult time in school because of that. Yvonne recalled him always being a slow reader.

Alan Ameche and Yvonne Molinaro met in junior high school when they were both thirteen years old. Yvonne's father had enrolled her in various lessons: dancing, singing, elocution. Speaking was her favorite. Alan first saw her dancing onstage in a ballet recital. "Afterward he told me how 'brave' I'd been." The remark impressed her, a tender word from a big boy.

Both went to Kenosha's Mary Bradford High, where Alan wanted to try out for football. But August Ameche disliked American football, informed his son that he should be working, and refused to sign a slip giving him permission to play. Alan got his older brother Lynn to forge the signature.

In time the father forgave — and a few years later offered good advice when his son began to feel pressure from big-time college recruiters. Notre Dame, for one, had a distant relative of Ameche's, the actor Don Ameche, phone on its behalf. Even Yvonne favored Notre Dame for Alan because it had no girls. But Alan liked the home-state school, and August told him, "Son, if you want to go to Wisconsin, go to Wisconsin. The hell with all the big offers."

On Thanksgiving Day of his sophomore year at Madison, Alan married Yvonne, and by graduation they had two children. She was pregnant again when they arrived in Baltimore in 1955. The Horse signed with the Colts for a record $15,000 salary. He was six feet, 217 pounds, and his dark hair always seemed to be combed, even during games when he'd take off his helmet on the sideline.

Where he'd gotten the nickname was debated. One Wisconsin assistant coach claimed he'd called Ameche "The Horse" "because he worked like a horse at practice." Another assistant reportedly had blurted: "That boy is a horse!" A Kenosha sports reporter had likened Ameche to Citation. Tom Braatz, a high school teammate, said: "He got the nickname from the players because he was kind of built like a racehorse, very strong physically but with very skinny, long legs."

A young blind boy once asked Ameche, "Can I ride 'The Horse'?" And: "Does 'The Horse' neigh?" Ameche obliged both requests.

The two tickets Pop and I bought for the Colts' 1955 opener against the Bears put us on about the forty-yard line, Colts' side of the field, positioned well by luck to see Ameche's seventy-nine-yard touchdown run the first time he carried the ball in his pro career. He ran from our right to left, toward the open end of Memorial Stadium. I see it still. He broke over right guard/right tackle and found an opening. Then he swerved toward the left sideline — he was the first fullback I'd seen wearing low-cut shoes — and he rumbled close to the chalked sideline, past the Colt bench, and then away into a brilliant sunlight, alone. Right then, I fell in love with Ameche, and I guess a lot of other people did, too, judging from the sound.

He won the NFL rushing title that season with 961 yards, although he never won it again — he wasn't Jimmy Brown. He wasn't all that fast. A college coach likened him to Bronko Nagurski, but Ameche said: "I was a blocker, not a runner." And he was somebody special. Ernie Accorsi, former Colts publicist and later general manager, said, "He probably was the most *beloved* Colt."

After he'd scored the winning touchdown in the "greatest game ever," Ameche was introduced in the audience by Ed Sullivan. Back in Baltimore the next day, Ameche's phone rang constantly. There were invitations, offers. But he'd promised Romeo Valianti he would go to a Knights of Columbus meeting that night in Westminster, and this he did. Valianti was amazed. "Of all the opportunities he had," Valianti said, "he came up here to my house and went with me."

Ameche retired following the 1960 season, a difficult one for him. He'd suffered a separated shoulder, a concussion, and, finally, a torn Achilles' tendon. Yet he could have played again. Instead, he chose to retire. He was only twenty-eight.

After Don Shula took over as coach in 1963, he phoned Ameche, hoping to persuade him to make a comeback. "I need a fullback," Shula pleaded. But Ameche had other interests. His family was growing — he would have six children. He had his business; he had moved to the Philadelphia suburbs, setting up an office of A-G Foods in Wayne, Pennsylvania. He would become a successful land developer. He enjoyed classical music — his collection of classical records would grow to more than twelve hundred. Often he played his music near full volume on forty-eight speakers in his home in Devon, Pennsylvania.

In later years Ameche was sought out because of his wealth, and he joined various boards, but they always were ones he cared earnestly about: the United Negro College Fund, the Fellowship of Christian Athletes, Multiple Sclerosis, the Philadelphia Orchestra, and Malvern Prep, where his four sons went. He contributed to a tuition fund for Philadelphia inner-city youths.

Ameche *did* things. Most concerned young people. He bought several downtown Philadelphia city blocks that were going to waste and had playgrounds built on them — eight in all, a dozen more renovated. He took a leave of absence from A-G Foods and worked for several months with inner-city youth. He'd been inspired during a church retreat by a priest who spoke about achieving fulfillment by working for others.

"I had given lip service and offered compassion," Ameche said at the time, "but I had not become involved. Now I'm involved."

Ameche didn't want any of his children to think they had to duplicate his athletic accomplishments. In his home he never displayed his Heisman Trophy or any football memorabilia — there was, in fact, no sign that he had played.

Yet football had brought them such fine times, Yvonne said. She recalled when they lived across the street in Baltimore from Shaw and Szymanski and played cards with them on quiet evenings.

"At Donovan's one night we made this home movie," she said. "Alan was the bad guy who'd gotten me pregnant. Art was my father."

She remembered pieces of mail, packages usually, that would come to the house with messages written on them, put there by employees in the post office: "Good luck Sunday" or "Great Game!" — little phrases that she found to be part of a city's poetry.

Yvonne mentioned to me how so many of the Colts and their wives have remained close and that several players had come up from Baltimore to her husband's funeral. Donovan was one — she called him "Dunny." Donovan had told me that he and several other Colts had been to the Ameches the week before Alan died to attend the wedding of their daughter Beth. "'The Horse' mentioned he was going to Houston for his heart, but he didn't indicate it was a big deal," Donovan said. "Then he dies. We're back on the road again. First the wedding, then the funeral. Coming home from the funeral I felt awful. I was thirsty, I think I was dehydrated." Donovan had been overcome by the heat of the day, the impact of Ameche's death, and the tribute to her husband that Yvonne delivered at the funeral Mass in St. Patrick's, a small stone church in Malvern. She knew how to speak; it had begun with those elocution lessons.

"I couldn't have done it," Donovan said. "And it was all true. Jesus, 'The Horse' was some guy."

Before Yvonne and I talked any more about Alan, she offered lunch — a smoked turkey, tomato, and lettuce sandwich on whole-grain bread and iced tea. She suggested that while she fixed things, she start a videotape for me that Alan and she had done following the death of their son Paul in an automobile accident in 1981. She warned, "It's pretty heavy. But I think this will give you some idea about Alan." A junior at Ithaca College, Paul had been home for the Christmas holiday. He'd been out partying one night. Legally drunk, he drove his car into a tree. He was twenty-two.

In the video Alan and Yvonne and their other children discuss coping with the sudden loss of a loved one. She said they'd sold the video rights for a dollar, making it available to counselors, groups, and individuals dealing with similar tragedy. She turned on the TV, put the tape in, and went to the kitchen to make lunch, leaving me to watch the beginning of *A Family in Grief: The Ameche Story.*

Alan, wearing a long-sleeved brown shirt, his black hair combed perfectly as I always remembered it: "It was completely devastating both physically and mentally. I don't think I'll ever forget the moment that I heard the words that Yvonne spoke of Paul's death . . . Grief is such a powerful emotion that you literally have physical reactions to it. It feels as if you have a shock put in your belly. You double over as Michael did, you sob hysterically, literally out of control. Your body reacts so violently to the power and force of the emotion that you can't control it. You're swept away by it."

Yvonne put the sandwich and tea on the table in front of me. But I had to wait to eat until the tape was over. I was wrought up from the tension, from the heartbreak, from the sad faces of Alan, Yvonne, Brian, Alan Jr., Patricia, Michael, and Beth.

Alan: "Part of that grieving is the problem of seeing your children also grieving, which sort of adds to your own grief. It's just another dimension, deeper dimension, and it's helped me to talk about it with them. It's helped also for us as a family to get together and share those things with one another . . .

"Wherever I would walk in the house or out on the property or anywhere I would have this view of Paul having been there. You know, just the memories are everywhere . . . I talk to Paul just about every day. And there are many times when I really feel his presence. And I really don't feel as though I've said good-bye to Paul . . .

"I do believe that there is a life hereafter and that I'm going to be united again with Paul . . . And that really makes it all bearable."

Yvonne played two other tapes for me. One was of Ameche's induction into the GTE Academic All-America Hall of Fame, with Don Shula introducing her at a ceremony in Raleigh, North Carolina, the other a tribute to Ameche with footage of Alan in college and with the Colts. Ameche looked young and buoyant — how he always seemed to Yvonne until one day in the late seventies when he came home from playing golf and said to her, "There's something the matter with my heart." She said, "What are you talking about?" He said, "My heart isn't right." And it wasn't: He underwent bypass surgery in Houston.

In the summer of 1988 Ameche planned to return to Houston for another bypass after Beth's wedding.

"The night of the wedding," Yvonne said, "he left the party early. He said he was tired. I noticed he had trouble going up the stairs; he had to stop."

The following Friday he underwent surgery and received a valve replacement. But before, during, or just after the surgery — the doctors were not sure — Ameche had a heart attack.

"By Sunday afternoon he became a candidate for a heart transplant," Yvonne said. "The doctors called me into the room and said, 'If we can prove that he is neurologically sound he will qualify for a heart transplant. What we want you to do is get him to hold two fingers up and have him squeeze your hand.' He held two fingers up. He squeezed my hand. The nurses began to cry. The doctors cheered. But you know, nobody told him what we were doing. Why didn't I tell him?

"Waiting for someone to die in order for my husband to live was a terrible feeling. A priest said, 'It's a Sunday night, and we get a lot of hearts on Sunday night.' But a heart never came."

On Monday Ameche died.

◆

As I drove onto an entrance ramp of the Baltimore Beltway, Loudy groaned. He was sitting next to me. "What is it?" I asked, looking over. He pointed, straight ahead. A Mayflower moving van with its full-masted ship on the side was heading along the beltway.

"Every time I see one of them vans, one of them yellow-and-green vans, I get to feeling awful."

Loudy wasn't in good health. He had heart trouble, and every few steps he took he wheezed and had to stop. But he'd wanted to show me the training site the Colts had used in Owings Mills, their last Baltimore home. When we reached the western suburbs, he directed me onto a two-lane road, Bonita Avenue. We crossed railroad tracks and climbed a ridge. There on the right, across the desolate landscape, was a plain concrete building. No one was in sight. Never did a place seem more quiet.

We turned onto an approach road. As he saw two crooked goal posts with peeling yellow paint — "Look at that, oh, my" — Loudy rubbed his eyes. "It tears the heart right out of your body," he said.

Pointing to the side of the road where security guards had stopped him the night the Colts left, he said: "I stood right there. In the rain and snow. You couldn't believe what you were seeing. These damn vans pulling in here and you knew what they were here for. What a dirty trick to do to somebody. Oh, geez, it's so unfair, so unfair. To see them leave was heart-rending, like a death in the family."

Loudy had me drive around to the back, to the dock where the vans had been loaded. On a brown door was the lone hint that the Baltimore Colts had ever been there. White block lettering said: COLT PERSONNEL ONLY. The players used to come out the back door on their way to practice, Loudy said. Looking out toward a field of weeds: "I can picture in my mind all the guys out there. There were an awful lot of thundering hooves." He liked that, smiled, and repeated: "A lot of thundering hooves."

Loudy and trainer Eddie Block used to sit in beach chairs by the edge of the field and watch practice. This was after Eddie had had his first heart attack. Every afternoon, the two men sat side by side.

"If one of the guys had something wrong, Eddie would see him limping and say, 'All right, into the trainer's room.' Eddie would work on him and tell him some story, some corny joke, make him laugh. Eddie cared for each guy like a son. There aren't a lot of people in the world like that."

We parked in front, and a guard let us in. Loudy took

one look inside: "Oh, geez, the Super Bowl trophy sat right there, in the middle on the top shelf." A trophy case just inside the door was empty. Everything was empty. "Buddy Young's shirt used to hang in there, and Weeb Ewbank's hat. All these walls were covered with portraits of the players."

Loudy sighed and walked down a hallway. His legs were stiff; arthritis pained him. His voice echoed.

"Marge Blatt sat in here. She was a great lady, God rest her. She had a real deep voice, a gruff voice. First time I ever spoke to her on the phone I thought it was a man. She'd do anything in the world for you, anything in the world. Marge didn't know the Colts had left until the next morning. When she got here to clean out her desk, her desk was gone . . .

"Lenny Moore's office was here . . . And through that window there you could buy your tickets . . . In here they used to store stuff."

Downstairs was eerie: two handball courts, meeting rooms, a whirlpool and sauna, a weight room without weights, showers with Colt-blue tiles. I was happy to get back upstairs. Loudy told me of the day fans were invited to see the building. The Colts held an open house, and to him it had felt like a country fair. It had been a fresh spring day — May, he believed — and more than fourteen thousand people had come. The Colt band played, and he helped with refreshments.

In the lobby we said good-bye to the guard and walked to the car. "I just want to sit here a minute," he said. We sat silently, Loudy looking at the building. Finally he said, "The fans brought this team here, not Carroll Rosenbloom. The fans came through by buying season tickets, and that brought the team back in '53. If the fans hadn't bought the tickets, there wouldn't have been any Baltimore Colts. It's that simple. Rosenbloom made millions off this ball club.

Then Irsay. It's so unfair. I know I'll go off this earth not being anything like these people with their millions and everything they want. But they're missing some things, I guarantee you, that are more important . . ."

I turned on the ignition and inched the car away. Loudy glanced back from the ridge. "Oh, to see this place fixed up again, the way it was."

As we drove ahead, there was no one on the road.

◆

About three months later Loudy called me. He wanted to know how I was, that was all. He told me he was going to Ocean City to help arrange for that summer's convention of Colt Corrals.

Loudy died the next week. He'd had a heart attack. It hit him at Ocean City. He was seventy-four. On a late April Thursday he was buried by his wife, Flo, his son and daughter and others in his family, and by friends, many being Colts: Unitas, Moore, Donovan, Nutter, Mutscheller, Mike Curtis, Fred Miller, Rick Volk, and Stan White. And Sean Landeta, the punter whom Loudy had befriended when he played for the Baltimore Stars of the short-lived United States Football League before moving on to the New York Giants.

The remarkable thing about Loudy had been that the Colt players loved him as much as he loved them. It's hard to explain love between a man and a team, except to say as Joe Ehrmann did in his eulogy at a funeral home in Brooklyn that the players knew Loudy always was doing something for them. Said Ehrmann: "The love he displayed for those around him must now be expressed by all of us toward other people."

As he'd requested, Loudy was laid out in the Colts' colors,

a white T-shirt with the club logo and blue short pants. His coffin was bedecked with floral designs in the shape of footballs and horseshoes, most with blue-and-white carnations from such players as Raymond Berry, Bert Jones, Ordell Braase, and Bruce Laird. One, too, with a card that read: "From Robert and Jimmy Irsay and the Indianapolis Colts."

Unitas, Donovan, Curtis, Nutter, Volk, and Landeta carried the casket down the brick steps of the funeral home for the trip to Glen Haven Cemetery on Ritchie Highway in Glen Burnie. The Anne Arundel County Police Department provided an escort for the caravan of cars.

At graveside, against a blue sky, an army bugler sounded taps. As the sound faded, four members of the Baltimore Colts' band, which still exists, played a muted version of a familiar tune. It may sound silly to some that Loudy was buried in Glen Burnie to the soft, slow strains of the Colts' fight song, but that was Loudy's song, and when they played it some wept and some smiled through their tears.

◆

Andy's Restaurant & Lounge is a two-story brick-front on York Road near Cold Spring Lane between the Hair Above Salon and the York Road Animal Hospital. The Colts used to hang out in Andy's — in the lounge afternoons after practice, in the restaurant for dinner after games on Sundays. Andy Lambros assured me, "They came in regular."

Art Donovan was one of the first Colts to find Andy's. He arranged to meet Dottie Schaech there on their first date. She was a pharmacist who'd started out working for Read's and owned her own drug store on Harford Road. Her parents had owned a truck stop on Pulaski Highway —

that's where she learned to run a business. She also played piano for a band called the Queens of Rhythm. Within the year Artie and Dottie were married downtown at the old cathedral.

Johnny U. had one of his first Baltimore dinners in Andy's. Andy likes to say it was Unitas's *first* dinner in Baltimore. "He had chicken," said Andy, a short, baldish man with glasses in his late seventies. "He drank milk. The first time in here he had milk!" Andy laughed and slapped his thigh.

Gino Marchetti used to be the dark, brooding presence on the right-end barstool closest to the door. People came in, passed him by, left him alone. Bill Pellington. Rechichar. Don Shula — when he played, not when he coached. Ordell Braase. They all went to Andy's and drank beer. Donovan drank Schlitz.

Andy's was strategically situated for many Colts, on their way home from the stadium toward Towson. It was quiet in there. Still is.

"I treated each of 'em as just a customer," Andy said of the old Colts. "I'd let 'em sit there, have a beer. Of course I'd say, 'Leave 'em alone,' if I had to. This one time, this guy Mike, he was saying things like, 'You bums, you played lousy.' Hey, they felt bad enough after they lost a game. I said, 'Mike, don't say this. These guys'll kill you.' I threw his ass out."

Andy walks with a limp from arthritis. He hangs a cane on a hook near the front door when he comes to work.

"Been here forty-four years," he said, sitting down stiffly in a swivel chair in a small back room. He'd been around long enough to have seen the Colts leave Baltimore twice.

Andy's was one of several places the Colts went: Sweeney's, the Bear's Den, the Stadium Tavern, the Swallow at the Hollow, Casey's Pub. Buzz Nutter, George Preas, Braase, and Ken Jackson used to go to Al Flora's club on Gwynn Oak Avenue. All these places throbbed with Coltdom: the posed, glossy photographs — of high-stepping running backs and angry-looking linemen in crouches, Colts mugs and plates, framed cartoons on the walls, blue-and-white streamers. Outside Manny and Dino Spanomanolis's basement bar in Brooklyn, the Club 4100, is Unitas's right hand print in cement.

Andy became an original season-ticket holder when the Colts returned to Baltimore in 1953. He had his choice of seats in the stadium. "I was third or fourth in line," he said. "The guy said, 'How many tickets ya want?' I said, 'Gimme twenty-five.'" All the seats were on the fifty-yard line, in section ten behind the Colts' bench. He kept three seats for himself and tried to sell the rest to his patrons. "But in the beginning I had to *give* the tickets to some people, *give* 'em to 'em, believe me. I ran two buses from here every game. It ended up I could have had four buses, a hundred tickets — that's how popular the Colts became."

One of Andy's favorite Colts was Art Spinney. "Came from up in New England. Boston College. Good family man. Worked hard. Beautiful guy, Art. You could never say anything about him. Very quiet. What was he? Yep, a guard.

"Most times he'd come in by himself and sit at the middle of the bar. I always used to sit next to him, keep him company. One day he was talking about his wife and saying she was Greek. I says, 'Hey, my wife's Greek.' My parents are from Greece, too. Anyway, I says to Art, 'Jesus Christ, Mary always makes Greek food for us. C'mon, I'll take you up my house.' I called home. 'Mary, cook up some food.'

"We both ate, supped the Greek food. Great. The next thing, we were sittin' there in front of the TV, both of us, sound asleep."

Some Sunday nights after Spinney had had dinner at Andy's restaurant, Andy would go downtown with him to a Turkish bath. It was in a basement at Fayette and Eutaw streets. The steam took out the soreness of the game for Spinney. Andy was happy to go along.

One night in 1960 Spinney was sitting at the bar. Andy came around to his side, and the two sat there. Neither said anything. Spinney was hurting from a long season, especially two brutal games with the Bears.

"Andy," Spinney said finally, "I think I've had it."

That was Art Spinney's retirement announcement.

By the late sixties the Sunday-night crowds in Andy's began to thin.

"Lemme show you," said Andy, leading the way with a hobble out of the back room. He pushed open a side door near the jukebox and flipped on the lights in the next room. We walked into a dining room that hinted of elegance. "It's a duplicate of the Governor's Club," he said. "Good paneling, no crap." All the tables were set, and with the wall lights dimmed it seemed as if guests were expected.

But no one comes to dinner anymore. He opens the room on weekdays for lunch only. When the Colts played on Sundays, Andy would get back to the restaurant after the games in one of the two chartered buses and prepare for the players' arrival. He'd put on his white chef's garb and broil charcoal steaks and prime rib at the back of the dining room. He knew how each player liked his meat cooked.

"Ordell and the guys used to sit over there," he said, pointing to a round table near the front door. "Johnny used to sit here." He put his hand on a little two-seat table next to the barbecue pit.

When Unitas had the Golden Arm, Andy used to sit at the bar in there and Johnny would come over to him and put his arm around him. "'You fat, bald-headed Greek,' he'd say. Good guy, Johnny. Johnny never got what he deserved. He always got the shit end of things. Business-wise. They used Johnny's money, that's what they did. Everybody took advantage of Johnny, that's how I feel.

"Johnny should have gotten much more out of life. You see all these millionaire, multimillionaire athletes today. Like Cal Ripken. I like Cal Ripken. But what's he, one of the highest paid players in baseball history? Why couldn't Johnny get something like that?" Suddenly I was feeling badly myself for Unitas because I was beginning to understand how widely shared that sentiment was. I wondered if Unitas knew the extent to which people wished better for him.

Andy almost exhausted himself with emotion, but he wanted to take me upstairs. We climbed a steep back stairway, he stiff-legging it from step to step. A darkened room at the top had been used as another dining room. Half gasping: "This place on a Sunday used to be full, down and up."

We passed through a bedroom with an unmade bed and around a corner into a walk-in closet. On two hangers were clumped dozens of old neckties, mostly browns. He reached up to a shelf and began taking down framed charcoal sketches of the old Colts, ghostly beneath dust.

"Miss Jo Anna did them."

She had a studio across the street, and she'd draw them from photos and from seeing the players in the bar. Her works once adorned Andy's. He thought himself remiss in not having taken them home, cleaned them up, hung them in his club cellar.

There was a Marchetti, an Alex Sandusky, a crew-cut Unitas, Rechichar, and Bill Pellington. "He's got Alzheimer's.

God bless 'im." The disease led to Pellington's death in 1994.

Downstairs, as we walked through the main dining room, Andy shook his head and said, "I could kick myself, all the money I put into this." Then he took another look around and, cocking his head, added, "Ah, shit, it served its purpose. I have no complaints."

He turned out the lights.

◆

Baby, we belong together.

Unitas and Berry . . . People mention them in the same breath. But they always went their separate ways.

When they were young, when Unitas was married and Berry still single, Berry used to stop by for an occasional meal. Unitas's first wife, Dorothy, cooked. In later years Berry and his wife, Sally, had Unitas over. But only rarely. "John has always been a private person, not one who readily talks about what he thinks," said Berry. "I remember I'd known him twelve years — it was my thirteenth and last year in Baltimore — and he was over my house and he'd had a couple of beers and he said, 'Guys I grew up with, they're in jail or on drugs or they're dead. The only reason I got here was football.'" It was the only time Berry could recall a wistful Unitas.

Unitas was a fierce loner, and Berry was, too. Berry devoted himself in fanatical detail to offsetting his minimal physical assets so that he could play the game as he aspired to. He wasn't fast, he wasn't muscular, he had poor eyesight. As he compensated he acquired a reputation as an eccentric. Berry used to begin daily practice early, alone. He'd run pass patterns against phantom defenders, catch nonexistent footballs at the sidelines. Often the team would come out for practice, and Don Shula, impatient to begin, might shout sarcastically, "Let us know, Raymond, when you'll join us for practice."

A typical response: "Just six more patterns."

Berry invented the "net drill." He took part of the netting from the baseball Orioles' batting cage and rigged a backstop of his own so that after practice he'd get Unitas to throw to him in front of the net, fifty to seventy passes, high ones, low ones, behind him, every pass delivered at a difficult angle. Berry would dive or leap or stretch out beautifully in the air. If he missed, the ball would hit the net and drop and he wouldn't have to chase it. It was a time-saver.

Berry lived on West Coast time a week before he went there to play games. He took a scale on road trips to keep his weight exact. He hung on to footballs even in hotel lobbies. He knew when the sun would set, and the angle of its rays, at the Los Angeles Coliseum in case the team happened to be moving in that direction at that time of day. He washed his own football pants to make sure they wouldn't shrink.

Teammates figured that after his playing days the quirky Berry, having mastered pass receiving, would want to move on to something new. They envisioned him in some kind of ivory tower, involved in esoteric matters, because although he was one of them he also was one apart. Maybe he'd be a minister. They all knew he was religious, but most didn't know how he got to be that way.

One night while driving away from the Ameche's at Loch Raven Boulevard and Taylor Avenue with born-again teammate Don Shinnick, Berry pulled his '57 Chevy to the curb and, in his words, "accepted Jesus Christ as my savior."

Berry told me he had no idea what made him do it, but that he did, and he was glad of it.

The stolid Unitas seemed easier to understand. In his case teammates figured he would always be part of football, the front-office trophy . . . Mr. Colt. But Irsay fixed that. And later Unitas went bankrupt.

Few icons of American sport have been able to play the after-game as elegantly as they played the game itself. DiMaggio has; he's kept us at a distance, a shy boy grown to an ever-private man. Arnold Palmer has; he keeps drawing us to him because the game he plays enables him to keep on being Arnie — he's just on the seniors tour.

Unitas the football player reminds me of a certain American World War II pilot who said: "There's no way to tell you how it was, in an airplane, alone at thirty-five thousand feet. No noise. No clutter of the earth." Consider Lindbergh in the cockpit, too, and how it was with him in later life. When Unitas came back to earth it was different from when he was the monkey man on the pile-driving outfit, 125 feet up, and he never could blend with the awaiting ironies and ambiguities.

"John is the product of bad advice and strong loyalties to those he shouldn't have been loyal to," said Steve Rosenbloom. "It's tough out there in the world, and players aren't businessmen."

"Poor guy" — Unitas was on my Uncle Eddie's lips a few days before he died.

"The banks are trying to get everything they can out of me," Unitas said matter-of-factly at his Timonium office. From his account, he seemed to have groped from business to business:

"There was always the intent of trying to get some kind

of a business involvement for yourself. That was the way that [former NFL commissioner] Bert Bell used to preach the thing, try to get involved somewhere and work within the community and get some kind of a position, a job, something for yourself going. I got into the bowling business; I've always had some kind of business going."

Bowling — Johnny Unitas's Colt Lanes, with the Colt blue-and-white decor — was a harbinger. Unitas's business dreams and failures included a fiasco of a deal involving Florida real estate. Finally, National Circuits, Inc., sank Unitas and his partners so deep that their debts outstripped their assets.

People wanted Unitas to enjoy business success. "I prayed for him to do well," said Doc Levin, the doc who knew the boxers and the football players. "I really did. I always have."

Levin explained, "Johnny and I were down at the Holiday Inn, downtown, and we were parked in this small parking lot. He had a station wagon, I had my car. When we came out, only two cars on that lot were banged up. That told me about him. Jinxed."

There were other embarrassments. Once Unitas associated himself with a gambling sheet called *The Huddle,* which quoted him as saying: "I will knock down the Las Vegas point spread for you every weekend from now on up to the Super Bowl. And by that time I'm sure — as you're driving around in your new Cadillac — you'll know what real handicapping is all about . . ."

SAY IT AIN'T SO, JOHNNY U headlined the *New York Daily News.*

"The thing that frustrates me," said Ernie Accorsi, "is that Unitas ought to have had a postplaying career like DiMaggio's. In the context of making the game what it is, Unitas did for pro football what Babe Ruth did for baseball.

From 1950 to 1955, just before John came along, pro football was a level above sandlot ball. College football was king. Pro football was a game played in baseball parks. He was the one most responsible for changing that. I think the game owes him a tremendous amount. It hasn't done nearly enough for him."

Berry, it turned out, stuck with what he knew. His father had been a high school coach in Paris, Texas, strict, too — the son had to earn his way to first-string, and it took him until senior year. Berry kept to his expertise, coaching receivers for various NFL teams. For a time in the eighties he was head coach of the New England Patriots. That appointment simply puzzled many of his former teammates. "Geez, Raymond is an awfully nice guy," said Gino Marchetti, "but I can't imagine him as a head coach."

In fact, when he got the Patriots' job, Berry realized he needed a broader perspective, and quick. From New England, from the blue, he phoned Unitas: "If I fly down, would you come out to the airport? I'd like to talk to you about the two-minute drill."

"What do you mean?" Unitas asked. "Without you I couldn't have done it."

"But I only know what *I* was supposed to do," Berry said. "I don't know what *you* were doing."

Unitas met Berry in the Red Carpet Inn near Baltimore-Washington International Airport and gave the new coach a tutorial in the two-minute drill.

Not until 1993 did Berry take a sabbatical year — and he wouldn't have done that had he not been part of a Denver Broncos' staff that was fired. Berry finally had some time. He spent a month back home in Texas with his father, then eighty-nine. He visited with his three children and their families. He accepted an invitation to be inducted into the GTE Academic All-America Hall of Fame and again called Unitas, this time to ask if he would give an introduction speech for him. Unitas gladly accepted.

A few weeks later Unitas suffered a near-fatal heart attack. He had been in Baltimore's Kernan Hospital for a knee-replacement operation and was doing rehab there when he suffered shortness of breath and chest pains. He was rushed to the University of Maryland Hospital Center in downtown Baltimore and immediately underwent triple-bypass surgery. The first trip Unitas took after getting out of the hospital was to Indianapolis to take part in the ceremony for Berry. "I was surprised he made it," Berry said. "I didn't expect that he would be that strong. But we had a wonderful time. Sandy was with him and Sally was there, so we really got some time to spend together. He seemed to enjoy doing it, like he was glad to get out. I said, 'You really don't look any different.' He said, 'I've lost a lot of weight.' His suit fit looser. We talked about the heart attack. The consensus was the hospital was the only place to have had it. Otherwise he wouldn't be here."

In June 1993 Berry went back to Baltimore at Ehrmann's request to speak at a fund-raiser for The Door. And that's when I caught up with him. He stayed four days, his longest visit since he'd left after the 1967 season. It made him feel good that much of what he found remained unchanged. In Westminster he walked the tidy campus of Western Maryland College, where he'd spent those thirteen training camps. A pale, thin man of fifty-nine, he went unrecognized. He looked up toward the attic of a dorm where he'd roomed as a rookie in 1955. It had been like a monastery cell. "We always had a buzz fan because we needed it." He looked into a basement room, simple as ever, where the team used to meet and where it had a laugh at his expense when Weeb Ewbank showed a piece of game film a few days after Berry's debut as a Colt: He'd lined up against Philadelphia's fearsome linebacker Chuck Bednarik. Berry was positioned at left tight end; a running play to the right was called. Berry came off the line and Bednarik's hand came up and caught in Berry's facemask. When Bednarik saw where the play was going, he ran across the field but couldn't get his hand loose from Berry's mask. "He dragged Raymond along," said the other end, Jim Mutscheller. "Raymond's feet were flopping out behind him like a sack of wheat. Weeb ran it over and over. He said, 'Raymond, you're going to have to get a hatpin if those guys won't let go of your helmet.'"

In Pikesville, Berry drove past the armory where the practice field had been. Up the street the movie theater he'd gone to on off days, Monday afternoons, still stood. One day he and Sally took Unitas's first wife, Dorothy, to lunch. Another day he and Sally drove downtown to have lunch with Dr. Joshua Breschkin, an optometrist. "My career never would have gone past my second year if it hadn't been for him because my eyes were deteriorating," Berry said. "I was very nearsighted and it was getting worse, and it got to the point I was having trouble seeing the ball. I couldn't see it at night at all. He had the ability, in those early days, to fit me with contact lenses, which were absolutely critical for me to be able to play. He spent a lot of time working on them for me, getting them to fit properly so I could play football." Berry had no trouble finding Dr. Breschkin's office at 107 West Saratoga Street. "He has the same phone number, same address — a spot that has never changed."

Again, Berry got together with Unitas.

"You know, I think our memories, all the experiences we had in Baltimore, those have become more precious through the years. Now we appreciate how fortunate we were, and we enjoy each other's company."

Around the country Berry had traveled, from team to team, from Dallas to Detroit to Cleveland to New England to Detroit to Denver, until he'd come at last to the beginning . . .

◆

It seems like a long time, it has been a long time, since Unitas threw touchdown passes to Berry and Pop worked at Read's filling prescriptions by hand, meticulously scraping healing powders into each single capsule. Yet their images remain as indelible as I could hope them to be.

Like Eddie in *Diner,* I'm not embarrassed that the Colts still mean a lot to me. Little Buddy Young streaks through my imagination, dodging tacklers with high-strutting steps, and big Artie Donovan rumbles across an old stadium's scuffed field chalked freshly in my mind.

When I think of the Colts I think mostly of Pop. The Colts were the generational glue that bound us and fixed him in my memory. When I still sometimes imagine him with me I know it's because that's where he was on so many Sundays.

From the high ground above where Pop lies buried in the New Cathedral Cemetery in west Baltimore, I can see much of the city. I look one way and there's Memorial Stadium in the distance. I remember what it was like going there the first time after Pop died. The Orioles were playing the Red Sox, and I took my daughter Maria, then a teenager. It was a sunny Saturday in August, and I thought about the pleasures, some of which I had never even understood, that had bound my father and me so close. I sat there in the stadium's first deck as I had so many times before, and with Maria at my side I wondered how he'd felt all those times he'd taken me.

And yet, these days when I visit the cemetery I feel better looking forward than back. I can look over the top of the Gildea headstone and see another half of the city: the harbor and the new buildings, although I can't see the new downtown ball park because it's tucked artfully among the streets. Pop found the piece of ground next to a bend in a lane near a tree that still seems young. He found it for my grandparents, for my Aunt Catherine, for Mom and himself. I was with him when he chose the spot, carefully, as if he were picking a seat at the park.

My Uncle Len and cousin Francis bring flowers on holidays, when they make the rounds to all the cemeteries where family members rest. They may be the last of the resolute group that Pop himself was part of. I stop when I can. The best times, I've found, are certain autumn days close to five o'clock when the gates are locked. The sun sets behind the stone crosses atop St. Joseph's Monastery, softens the harshness, lights my way.